A morally deep world

A morally deep world

An essay on moral significance and environmental ethics

LAWRENCE E. JOHNSON

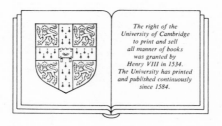

The right of the
University of Cambridge
to print and sell
all manner of books
was granted by
Henry VIII in 1534.
The University has printed
and published continuously
since 1584.

CAMBRIDGE UNIVERSITY PRESS

CAMBRIDGE

NEW YORK   PORT CHESTER   MELBOURNE   SYDNEY

Published by the Press Syndicate of the University of Cambridge
The Pitt Building, Trumpington Street, Cambridge CB2 1RP
40 West 20th Street, New York, NY 10011, USA
10 Stamford Road, Oakleigh, Melbourne 3166, Australia

© Cambridge University Press 1991

First published 1991

Printed in the United States of America

Library of Congress Cataloging-in-Publication Data
Johnson, Lawrence E.
A morally deep world : an essay on moral significance and
environmental ethics / Lawrence E. Johnson.
p.   cm.
Includes bibliographical references and index.
ISBN 0-521-39310-8
1. Ecology – Moral and ethical aspects. 2. Human ecology – Moral
and ethical aspects. 3. Animal rights. I. Title.
GF80.J64   1991
179'.1 – dc20   90-43042
                                                                        CIP

British Library Cataloguing in Publication Data
Johnson, Lawrence E.
A morally deep world : an essay on moral significance and
environmental ethics.
1. Environment. Ethical aspects
I. Title
179.1

ISBN 0 521 39310 8 (hardback)

For my children
Freja K. Johnson
Nicholas A. Johnson
in the hope that they may live deeply
valuable lives
in a morally deep world

Contents

Acknowledgments

I wish to express my thanks for helpful advice and criticism to Richard Sylvan, John Passmore, Rodney Allen, many students, and various anonymous readers. Thanks to Sally Fraser for patience and typing, and to Carolyn Viola-John for invaluable help in preparing the manuscript for publication. Thanks to family and friends for putting up with me. Responsibility for shortcomings is, of course, entirely mine.

As well, my very special thanks to the natural world – not merely for making my existence possible, but just for being there, and for inspiring my love and respect.

Lawrence E. Johnson
Flinders University,
South Australia

Introduction

Toward the horizons of the moral universe

Ethical criteria have been extended to many fields of conduct, with corresponding shrinkages in those judged by expediency only.

The land ethic simply enlarges the boundaries of the community to include soils, waters, plants, and animals, or collectively: the land.

A land ethic changes the role of *Homo sapiens* from conqueror of the land-community to plain member and citizen of it.

A thing is right when it tends to preserve the integrity, stability, and beauty of the biotic community.
It is wrong when it tends otherwise.
            Aldo Leopold, *A Sand County Almanac*

Galileo disturbed a great many people with his opinion that our earth was one of several planets revolving around the sun. The official view at the time was that the earth, man's home, was the center of God's creation. The difficulty was more than a conflict between competing astronomical theories. Partly, it was a matter of the authority of scripture as revealed truth. A few scriptural passages suggest that the sun moves around the earth, and the book of Joshua (10:12–13) records the sun's standing still on one occasion that was evidently quite singular. That problem could have been re-

1

solved in ways consistent with biblical authority. There was a deeper reason, a moral reason, why Galileo's theory was so shocking. Man, made in God's image, was the completion and moral center of the created world. It did not seem *fitting* that the moral center of creation should hold such an insignificant position in the physical universe. Physical centrality was understood to signify moral centrality, and Galileo appeared to be denigrating the dignity of man and denying God's scheme of values.

Astronomical fact eventually prevailed, and it was accepted that God had chosen to place his favorites on a moving planet in a less conspicuous location. The belief that humanity is the moral center of the universe has had more endurance. There have been dissenting voices, but the predominant opinion has been that humans are, rightly, of overriding or exclusive moral significance. In our actions regarding the nonhuman world we have usually been concerned only with human values. Our practical questions concerned how best to utilize the natural world to benefit humans, while our moral questions concerned the implications for other humans. When we have been concerned with nonhuman values, this has normally been on a vertical rather than a horizontal axis. We have generally been concerned for supernatural values, rather than for values in the natural world. It is not out of concern for pigs that Jews abstain from pork. Various reasons, religious and secular, have been given for our preeminent moral standing. Humans, unlike the lower animals, are said to have souls, or to be morally superior by virtue of their rationality. Or we are said to deserve our privileged position because we are seemingly the victors in the evolutionary struggle. Or perhaps the reason is just that we make up the rules.

In recent years there has been a revival of interest in the question of whether there are values in the nonhuman natural world. This interest has not been entirely lacking in the past. Plutarch, for one, advocated a vegetarian diet out of compassion for animals. Others between then and now have been concerned with such issues. Many non-Western sys-

2

tems of thought have also recognized some moral significance in the natural world. On the whole, however, the Western tradition has been almost exclusively human-centered in its value schemes. These days, more and more thinkers are coming to suggest that we need a Galileo-like change in our conception of the human place in the moral universe.

Those of us who advocate such a Galileo-like change, holding that there is more to the moral universe than human beings, are by no means united in outlook about what needs to be changed and what it needs to be changed to. The conviction that it is wrong to misuse the nonhuman world has very often preceded the elaboration of clear ideas about *why* it is wrong. There is a need, by no means satisfied, for a plausible and adequate moral theory by means of which we may give an account of, evaluate, and support such a broadening of our moral horizons. By and large there are two rather different schools of thought. One group of thinkers is primarily concerned with the welfare of sentient nonhumans. Animals can suffer and are therefore held properly to be objects of moral concern. The effects of human activities on animals are evaluated in terms of various relevant ethical theories. Human dietary preferences are criticized, together with scientific, social, recreational, and agricultural and other economic practices. Peter Singer's book, *Animal Liberation*, has done much to stimulate thought in this area of concern.

Another group of thinkers is less concerned with the welfare of individual animals and more concerned with the ethical significance of our actions affecting the environment. Their concern is with ecosystems, wilderness, species, objects of natural beauty or grandeur, and various environmental processes. By no means is all of this interest in environmental ethics, as it were, "Galilean" in orientation. Many people are very concerned about environmental issues primarily or exclusively because they are concerned about the consequences for humans of environmental problems. Pollution, the disruption of ecosystems, the extinction of species, and the depletion of economic, aesthetic, and recrea-

3

tional resources all have adverse consequences for humans. For such reasons, environmental ethics is vitally important in both theory and practice. Still, many people – and I am one of them – have an additional concern in environmental affairs. Although we share a moral concern for the fortunes of humanity, we also believe that there is intrinsic moral significance in wildernesses, ecosystems, species, and so forth, in addition to their significance for humans. Those who take such a viewpoint do not seek to exclude humans from the moral universe. That would be absurd. Rather, we see the moral universe as including humanity, but extending well beyond it. Aldo Leopold's *A Sand County Almanac* was a great impetus and inspiration to this line of thought in this century. Certainly his ideas and insights were a great inspiration to my own line of thought.

It is possible to be concerned about both the environment *and* animal welfare, but these may be quite distinct concerns and they may not go together. One may, for instance, hold that environmental affairs are morally significant only insofar as they affect humans and individual sentient beings. Tom Regan, who is very concerned for animals, writes (1983, 359):

> If . . . we had to choose between saving the last two members of an endangered species, or saving another individual who belonged to a species that was plentiful but whose death would be a greater prima facie harm to that individual than the harm that death would be to the two, then the rights view requires that we save the individual.

In Regan's scheme, what is morally significant is not the species, or the ecosystem of which it is a part, but only individual sentient beings. Let justice be done to the individual, though the species fall!

Unlike Regan and Singer, Leopold was a meat eater who loved to go hunting. Basically a kind man, certainly not a cruel one, his primary moral concern – beyond the human sphere – came to be with what he called "the land." In his use of the term, he included the whole biotic community, of which we are members but not sovereign lords. According to Leopold (1949, 224–5)

> A thing is right when it tends to preserve the integrity, stability, and beauty of the biotic community. It is wrong when it tends otherwise.

On this view, it would be wrong to permit a species to become extinct, particularly if we did so merely for the sake of a few individuals of a plentiful species. On the other hand, if we killed and ate a rabbit, we would not be acting wrongly, any more than would a coyote who did likewise. Regan would disapprove of a human doing so. He and Leopold, then, would each condemn some things the other condones.

Thus, considerable diversity of opinion exists among those who see the moral universe as extending beyond the human sphere. Even within the two major groups – those concerned with the welfare of individual animals and those concerned with the integrity of ecological wholes – there is much difference of opinion, but there seems to be a much wider gap between these two major groups. One group appeals to principles about respecting the interests of individual beings, while the other group appeals to seemingly unrelated principles about respecting the integrity of environmental wholes. While there is evidently this gap, it may be only a gap and not an incompatibility. Is there an incompatibility? Should there be any gap at all?

Once it is agreed that the moral universe extends beyond humans, it seems intuitively plausible, at least to many of us, that both points of view have some legitimacy. Animals ought, in some way, to be objects for moral concern and also we ought to have moral concern for the integrity and continuity of species, ecosystems, and the biosphere as a whole. How, though, are we to account for this intuitive plausibility? If we are to have sound ethics, rather than haphazard opinions, we must evaluate, criticize, and support our conclusions with viable principles. Do we indeed have adequate grounds for such intuitive conclusions? Is there one set of principles for our dealings with animals (and humans?) and another, different set of principles for dealing with the environment? That would be possible, but such moral and intellectual fragmentation hardly seems desirable. It is an outstanding question whether we can adequately support animal ethics and environmental ethics on the basis of a coherent unified theory. If we could, the gap would be closed and we would have good hope of resolving apparent conflicts between the different points of view.

In the following, I shall argue for a position that I believe does provide a coherent unified foundation for an environmental ethic and for an ethic governing our dealings with animals. First, though, I must give adequate support for the claim that the moral universe does extend beyond the human sphere. I start with the assumption that humans are in the moral universe, that we humans ought to be objects of moral concern. But what qualifies us to be objects of moral concern? Only a morally arbitrary line can distinguish between humans and nonhumans, because the interests of all that have interests are morally significant. Although this ground has been well covered, I shall be developing a concept of *interest* that goes beyond those concepts normally employed.

Moral consideration is due to us humans because we have interests. We can suffer or be happy, languish or flourish, be healthy or otherwise, whereas rocks and tractors cannot. Interests are not just something we *have*. Interests are a matter of the way we are, of the dynamic ongoing process that is a human life. Our interests are, as I shall argue, an integral feature of our life process. Those interests we have on the level of experience and desire are only the surface. We are complete beings with depth as well as surface, and we have interests to match. There is more to interests than merely favorable mental states such as pleasure or satisfaction of desire. I shall argue that favorable mental states are not the be-all and end-all, and that our (prudent) desires do not constitute, but follow from, our interests.

I am eventually led to the conclusion that animals, plants, ecosystems, and even species have interests, and that these

interests are, to the extent of each interest, morally significant. This will very likely seem a most astonishing claim. It
certainly astonished me when I first started to think about
it. No doubt some will consider it an illustration of Cicero's
observation that there is no opinion so absurd but that some
philosopher has held it. I ask the reader not to reject the
conclusion until after having evaluated the grounds I give
for it. I argue that if those grounds are rejected, we cannot
adequately account for morality even as it applies to humans.

It shall be presupposed throughout that there is such a
thing as morality and that it does apply to humans. Given
that, I shall argue that if there is a moral universe at all, it
must extend beyond the human sphere. Others have differed
in opinion, holding that we can draw the moral boundaries
so as largely or entirely to coincide with those of the human
race, or some portion of it. The burden of my argument here
is that there is no plausible, nonarbitrary way of character-
izing morally significant interests so as to support such a
conclusion. Neither is there any plausible, nonarbitrary reason for holding that only some interests are morally significant while others are not. We can no more maintain that
than we can maintain that some rocks are to count as having
weight while others are not. All rocks have weight, though
some weigh more than others. Indeed, if grains of sand had
absolutely no weight whatsoever, then neither would moun-
tains. If human interests are to have any moral weight at all,
then *all* genuine interests must be recognized as having some
moral weight – though some interests have more weight than
others. It is a matter of degrees. In arguing that the interests
of a mouse are morally considerable, I am not claiming that
setting a mousetrap is on a par with the premeditated murder
of a human being. Normally, a human being has more interests than does a mouse. Moreover, the interest of a mouse
in continuing to live is not the same as the interest of a human
in continuing to live. A mouse only has an interest in continuing a mouse life. That interest counts for what it is, but
only for what it is. Just how it is that we are to weigh off
differing interests of differing beings will prove to be a very

difficult matter. In the following we shall inquire concerning that, and concerning how we are to distinguish genuine interests from what might appear to be interests but are not.

Some may deny that there is a moral universe at all. Perhaps moral concepts are empty, or are merely expressions of our attitudes toward things. Personally, I find it very difficult to accept that all I can say about Adolf Hitler is merely that he and I have divergent attitudes with regard to interethnic relationships. To be sure, on any account I am permitted to record the fact that I have an attitude of hostility toward his attitude. Still, there is no logically necessary reason why anyone should have one set of attitudes rather than another (even though some of our attitudes may, in point of fact, make it difficult for us to obtain our various desires). We are logically entitled to have our attitudes for purely arbitrary reasons, or for no reason at all. Even so, many people prefer to have attitudes that, at least in the area of what might be thought of as moral attitudes, are in accordance with principles that are consistent and not subject to arbitrary restriction. I shall try to persuade such people that it is purely arbitrary to restrict their moral attitudes to the human sphere or to some part of it. However, I shall not really be addressing those who believe that the moral universe has zero radius.

What I shall attempt to do is to provide a *foundation* for, not a full articulation of, an environmental ethic. Neither shall I be giving a full articulation of an ethic regarding animals. In matters involving animals or the environment, there remains the problem of determining what particular interests are at stake, and, as was noted, the problem – a major one – of how we are to weigh conflicting interests. How, for instance, are we to weigh the interests of endangered species or ecosystems against the interests, human or otherwise, that conflict? I am not at all certain that these problems are entirely solvable, even in principle. Determining what is at stake and what the alternatives are is by no means easy, even within the purely human arena. This is so even within a comparatively simple ethical system, such as Benthamite utilitarianism which calls upon us to maximize the amount of just one good, pleasure. When there is more than one thing that is recognized as good, we have the old problem of comparing apples and oranges. How, for instance, are we to weigh utility, be it pleasure or whatever, against equity of distribution? There are several ways to do it, and no very sound reason for believing that any one particular way is the best.

Even if we cannot determine what all morally significant human interests are, and even if we do not know how to balance them all out properly, we do know that we ought to recognize their moral significance and take them into account as best we can. We cannot just disregard the interests of another, be it a person of another family, sex, race, religion, political persuasion, or socioeconomic group. Once we recognize that, we have come a long way, and we can at least start to learn how to act properly toward other people. So too, once we recognize that there are interests in the nonhuman world, and that they are morally significant, we will have come a long way. Then, we can at least start to learn how to act properly toward the rest of the world.

Will acting morally toward the rest of the world require a new ethic? Or will it just be an extension of old ethics to new territories? Something in between, I would think. Certainly we will need to elaborate and reinterpret the principles already inherent within human-centered ethics – and just as certainly those old principles cannot merely be discarded. Whether those principles will have to be supplemented with radically different principles is not something we can now determine. Certainly we will need more effective principles than we now possess for deciding between conflicting interests. That is true both beyond the human sphere and within it. We will learn only gradually what is needed and how to fit it together.

To say that our moral progress has not found the end of the road is not to say that we have failed to start. We have started and we have made progress, both in theory and in practice. Not enough, though. As a great and growing number of people are aware, we have gone a long way toward degrading our environment, and in many ways the situation is getting worse. That needs no elaboration at this point. It is, at least, heartening that there is coming to be such a wide awareness of this. It is also heartening that more and more people are concerned that in the process of degrading our environment we are acting wrongly toward other beings as well as injuring ourselves. Ecosystems are destroyed, species exterminated, and animals used unmercifully. Apart from repercussions to humans, where there are repercussions, it is wrong just because of what we are doing to the animals, species, and ecosystems themselves. It is my hope through this book to help us carry our moral progress further.

Chapter 1

Some background – much of which
is still in the foreground

> So God created man in his own image, in the image
> of man created he him; male and female created he
> them. And God blessed them, and God said unto
> them, be fruitful and multiply, and replenish the
> earth, and subdue it: and have dominion over the fish
> of the sea, and over the fowl of the air, and over every
> living thing that moveth upon the earth.
>
> Genesis 1: 27–8.

As I am arguing that the moral universe extends beyond
humanity, I shall start with the human sphere of morality
and ask what it is we are proposing to go beyond. There are
any number of human ethical systems, with a great variety
of supposed reasons why we should subscribe to them. All
of them, though, maintain that we ought to respect at least
some of the interests of at least some others in at least some
circumstances. The details and additional features vary, but
the central core has traditionally been consideration for other
people. What is there about people that makes them worthy
of our concern, that we ought to act morally toward them?
Let us first look at and criticize some of the leading traditional
ideas about the moral status of human beings. With that
background we can go on to investigate more closely the
question of just what calls for moral respect, and to tie it all
in with the question of the moral status of animals and the
environment.

"No evil," said Socrates, "can come to a good man" (*Apol-*

ogy, 41). On the face of it, this appears to be a preposterous statement. Good men can suffer pain, poverty, illness, bereavement, and other misfortunes. They can be persecuted and put to death. Socrates knew that full well. The point he was making was that the only true harm and the only true good befall the soul. Pain, poverty, and hemlock only affect the body and are only apparent harms. The soul, not the body, is the true self, and the only harm that can come to it is moral corruption. Tending and perfecting our soul are the first priority. For the most part, the classical thinkers emphasized the supreme value of the rational self.[1] Our rationality is what makes man, the thinking being, uniquely valuable. We are not only rational beings, though. We are complex, each of us a hierarchy of various levels. We have a range of physical needs, from the most simple, such as the need for nutrition, a need that plants have, on up to those we share with the higher animals. We have a range of passions as well, from our lowest impulses to our highest loves. At the highest level of our being is our rational soul, which makes us essentially human and gives us value, and here our highest good is to be found. The natural function of the lower part of our being is to be guided by the higher, and to serve it.

In the *Phaedrus*, Plato likens the soul to a charioteer driving two horses.[2] These horses, the lower part of our nature, are

1 For a more extensive discussion of the historical background, and as a general reference for much of this chapter, see John Passmore's *Man's Responsibility for Nature* (London: Duckworth, 1974); a second edition (1980) contains an additional preface in answer to certain criticisms. For a useful discussion, see Val Routley's critical notice in *Australian Journal of Philosophy* 53 (1975): 171–85. See also Passmore's "Attitudes to Nature" in *Nature and Conduct*, ed. R. S. Peters, Royal Institute of Philosophy Lectures, vol. 8, (London: MacMillan, 1975). I am very much indebted to Passmore for background material. Also see Robin Attfield's *The Ethics of Environmental Concern*, (Oxford: Blackwell, 1983), and *Animal Rights and Human Obligation*, ed. Tom Regan and Peter Singer, (Englewood Cliffs, N.J.: Prentice-Hall, 1976).

2 Plato, *Phaedrus*, 246ff. In the Hindu *Katha Upanishad* (1.3) there is also an analogy drawn between a person and a chariot, but it is significantly different from Plato's analogy. In the *Katha*, our rational faculty is still

our physical appetites and our passions. We go along well only if the charioteer keeps the horses under control. The one horse, representing our physical appetites, is unruly and must be kept constantly in check. The other, representing our passions, is of better breeding and can be an effective ally of the charioteer if properly guided. Depending on their guidance, our passions may descend to the meanest physical urge or rise in pursuit of truth, beauty, and goodness. In these higher pursuits the control and guidance of the char-ioteer, the rational soul, is indispensable. These are, of course, analogical horses. The attitude of Plato and most of the other major thinkers toward real animals was much the same. The natural function of animals was to be ruled by rational beings, humans, and to serve their interests. Animals were seen as good, bad, or indifferent according to their role, if any, in the scheme of things centered on the value of rational beings. Both within and without, the apex of the hierarchy was taken to be its moral center.

The ancients certainly were not unanimous in their views about what the good for humans was, or about how to achieve it. Far from it. Aristotle and the Stoics had their own ideas, which differed from those of Plato, and others differed even more widely. By and large, though, the prevailing con-ception was that value was intimately and intrinsically as-sociated with the sphere of rationality. Aristotle also held a hierarchical view of the human self, one according to which

the charioteer, but our soul is the lord riding in the chariot driven by the charioteer. Rationality is the highest part of the lower order but it is still a part of it, and is in the service of our soul, our true self, which is above all that. This expresses a different point of view not only about the self but about the importance of rationality. Moreover, according to the Hindu point of view an animal as well as a human may have a soul – a soul attached, for that period of its existence, to a being of a lower and less rational order. Indeed, a god may choose to become a monkey or a cow or some other animal, that being no more absurd than becoming a human. Clearly, animals fit differently into Hindu ethical systems. In consequence, many Indians follow a vegetarian diet. Still, the belief that animals have souls does not of itself provide a basis for an ethic for the treatment of animals. Neither does it say anything about the value of species, ecosystems, or environmental processes.

we are an interconnected complex of actualities, potentialities, and functions.[3] Our wellbeing, happiness, or *eudaimonia*
lies in the effective integrated functioning of that complex,
with our potentialities brought to their healthy development.
The rational part of our nature is the highest and the most
essentially human, and, naturally, much of its role is to guide
and control the nonrational part of our nature. Our very
highest good is the development and exercise of our rationality. This process makes us truly human. Here, the divine
part of us moves beyond our lower nature into a purely
intellectual sphere. The highest good of our lower nature is
to serve the good of our divine rational soul.

Animals, similarly, are of value, if at all, only to serve the
interests of humans. Aristotle tells us (*Politics,* 1254b and
1256b):

> It is clear that the rule of the soul over the body, and of the
> mind and the rational element over the passionate, is natural
> and expedient; whereas the equality of the two or the rule of
> the inferior is always hurtful. The same holds good of animals
> in relation to men; . . . Where there is such a difference as that
> between soul and body, or between men and animals . . .
> the lower sort are by nature slaves, and it is better for them
> as for all inferiors that they should be under the rule of a
> master. . . .
>
> Plants exist for [the sake of animals, while] animals exist for
> the sake of man, the tame for use and food, the wild, if not
> all, at least the greater part of them, for food and for the
> provision of clothing and various instruments. Now if nature
> makes nothing incomplete, and nothing in vain, the inference
> must be that she has made all animals for the sake of man.

Aristotle's ideas on the moral status of humans, and of animals, were quite in accordance with the thought of his times
and had considerable influence in subsequent centuries.
These days most of us would shy away from his inference
that the natural function of less gifted people is to serve their
superiors, but when it comes to nonhumans, Aristotle's line

---

3 In particular, see his *De Anima,* and *Nichomachean Ethics.*

of thought is not far removed from much of present-day opinion.

Stoicism, that era's leading alternative to Platonism and Aristoteleanism, was, if anything, even more convinced of the exclusive moral significance of rational beings. According to the Stoics, the universe is organized and guided by its active element, Divine Providence, the Reason that is inherent in all reality. The evidence of order and purpose in the world indicated to the Stoic that God had ordered the world for the benefit of his rational children, the human race. For the Stoic, the good, the purpose of life, was to live in accordance with the law of nature, the divine will or reason. Because reason makes us truly human, that also meant to live in accordance with our own nature. Since animals are not rational, they have no part in the good. The Stoics took wholly to heart Socrates' dictum that no harm could come to a good man. It is the inner life that is important. Goodness is a matter of reason, will, good intention, and resignation to divine law. We cannot control what happens to us, but we can learn to control how we respond to it. We may respond well or poorly, which is a matter of moral significance. What happens to us is only a matter of fact. This is the basis of the famous Stoic belief that pain is, in itself, morally indifferent. Insofar as moral goodness and badness are a matter of our rational soul, which animals lack, it followed that animals formed no part of the moral universe. They are in the physical universe not for their sake but for ours. Through his character, Balbus the Stoic, Cicero expressed this Stoic (and not only Stoic) point of view (*De Natura Deorum* 2.63):

> The things [of the earth] have been provided for those only who make use of them, and even if some portion of them is filched or plundered by some of the lower animals, we shall not admit that they were created for the sake of these animals also. . . . So far is it from being true that the fruits of the earth were provided for the sake of animals as well as men, that the animals themselves, as we may see, were created for the benefit of men. What other use have sheep save that their fleeces are dressed and woven into clothing for men? . . . oxen?

15

... their necks were born for the yoke and their broad powerful shoulders for drawing the plough.

Not all took such a point of view. The Epicureans did not,
and neither did Plutarch. The former were materialists and
put little stock in any divine transcendental rational soul.
They took the good to be pleasure, and recognized that animals as well as humans were capable of feeling pleasure and
pain. Humans are more intelligent than animals and thus
better equipped to think profitably about how to find the
optimum balance in life so as to maximize pleasure and minimize pain. By taking thought, they were able to act so as to
minimize the chances for discomfort and to lead the calm
and tranquil life advocated by true Epicureans. Reason, then,
is good for us because it *serves* our good. We do not live in
order to reason well, but reason in order to live well. Animals
may not reason as well as we do, pursuing their good through
other means, but they have their own lives, their own good,
and can suffer or be happy. They were not created merely
for our benefit. It was against the Epicureans that Cicero's
Balbus was directing his remarks. Though not an Epicurean,
Plutarch advocated kindness to animals and a vegetarian diet
out of compassion. These thinkers, who recognized the moral
status of sentient beings, whether human or nonhuman, expressed ideas that were to be revived in the nineteenth and
twentieth centuries. In ancient times, in the intervening centuries, and apparently in contemporary thought, such ideas
were and are a minority point of view. The view that humans
are of preeminent or exclusive moral significance, a view
buttressed by appeals to the supreme moral value of our
rational faculty, was the norm then and continued to be
predominant in the postclassical Western tradition. It was
reinforced by Christianity, which (usually) identified our rational soul as the soul, created in God's image, which God,
the origin of all value, anointed with moral value.

But if no harm can come to a good man, if harm and benefit
only occur in the soul, why should I not knife Socrates in
the back and steal his purse? To do so is immoral, and I

would therefore be injuring myself. But *why* is it immoral? Why is knifing him in the back any more immoral than giving him a friendly pat on the shoulder? To be sure, I would be transgressing moral rules against violence and robbery, but what makes them *moral* rules? Rules against violence or theft clearly give some moral recognition to the consequences of the act. Evidently, then, harm of some nonmoral sort can come to a good person. In causing this nonmoral harm I cause myself moral harm. Yet to be causing myself moral harm by acting this way, there must be moral significance to the nonmoral injury I am causing (or intending to cause) my victim. Willful injury, even nonmoral physical injury, to a rational being is evidently wrong (at least in some cases). Why might that be? If I were to kill Socrates, I would be cutting short his contemplation of the Good – at least in this life – and various other things I might do could have the effect of distracting his thoughts. Presumably, though, it would be wrong for me gratuitously to cause pain to Socrates or Aristotle even if there was no danger that it might distract them from thinking lofty thoughts. Those who are ennobled by reason are to be respected in their entirety, in their lower interests as well as in their rationality. Animals, on the other hand, and humans of a lower grade (whom Aristotle deemed to be slaves by nature) exist to serve their betters. It is not just that rationality is valuable, but that those who are rational are uniquely valuable, with even their nonmoral interests possessing moral significance. This seems to presuppose that reason has a metaphysical value that pervades the entirety of the rational being in both its rational and nonrational aspects. Historically, the rational soul has been identified with that immortal and supremely valuable God-given soul that Christians believed all humans to possess.

RELIGION

In the Old Testament we are given the injunction: "Thou shalt not muzzle the ox when he treadeth out the corn"

17

(Deuteronomy 25:4). This would seem to indicate that we are to have at least some minimal degree of concern for the welfare of at least some animals. But if souls are all that count morally, and animals do not have souls, why ought we to have any concern for the welfare of any animal? Why indeed? St. Paul (1 Corinthians 9:9–10) explains that preposterous-sounding suggestion for us: "Doth God take care for oxen? Or saith he it altogether for our sakes? For our sakes, no doubt this is written: . . . that he [a human] that thresheth in hope should be partaker of his hope." Clearly, then, this is a moral commandment about our treatment of humans, it being obviously absurd that God should actually care for oxen.

Many Jewish scholars have thought it quite believable that God should take care for oxen. Paul, however, was a Jew who was highly influenced by non-Jewish culture. He and other early church fathers such as Origen and Augustine seem to have imported elements of Greco-Roman thought into formative Christianity. Certainly they appear to have adopted such attitudes, particularly Stoic ones, toward non-rational beings and the mundane world. They expressed the belief that value flows exclusively from God, and – which is more problematic – that on earth value involves only humans, and concerns them only as it affects their relationship with God. Ultimately value is entirely on the vertical axis. The world around us, living and otherwise, is significant only to the extent that it affects our spiritual condition, and at best exists only as a resource to aid us during the earthly part of our career. At worst it may lead us astray. These attitudes were to prevail within Christianity. In the thirteenth century, St. Thomas Aquinas wrote (*Summa contra Gentiles*, bk. 3, pt. 2, chap. 112):

> The very condition of the rational creature, in that it has dominion over its actions, requires that the care of providence should be bestowed on it for its own sake; whereas the dominion of other things that have no dominion over their actions shows that they are cared for, not for their own sake, but as being directed to other things. . . . by divine providence

they are intended for man's use in the natural order. Hence it is no wrong for man to make use of them, either by killing or in any other way whatever. . . . And if any passages of Holy Writ seem to forbid us to be cruel to dumb animals, . . . this is either to remove man's thoughts from being cruel to other men and lest through being cruel to animals one becomes cruel to human beings: or because injury to an animal leads to the temporal hurt of man, . . . or on account of some signification: thus the Apostle expounds the prohibition against *muzzling the ox that treadeth the corn.*

Balbus would have approved.

John Passmore pointed out that there have been two major schools of thought concerning the dominion over the earth given to us in Genesis. There is the traditional view that we are entitled to be absolute despots over the earth, using it and lesser creatures as we see fit, by virtue of our rationality (the classical view) or by virtue of our soul and its special relationship with God (the usual Christian view). This version of things has predominated, at least until recently. Again, there are views according to which we are God's stewards and must recognize that we have duties as well as rights in our dealings with the rest of the world. Sometimes the further idea has been expressed that we have a mission to try, like good gardeners, to improve the earth and help to bring it as well as ourselves to a better condition.

In Genesis (2:15) we were instructed to dress the garden and to keep it. This has suggested to some that we have an obligation to do our job well – at least insofar as we are able to do so after the Fall. But if we are responsible to God for our government of the earth, what is to count as fulfilling our obligations properly or improperly? If our stewardship is merely a matter of maintaining or increasing the earth's productivity for the benefit of humankind, this really becomes a version of the "man as despot" view wherein we are told to get the most out of the earth on a long-term basis. This is a counsel of wise economic management, but it does not indicate any moral significance in the world we are to manage. Still, it can serve as the basis for an environmental ethic that calls on us to protect the earth for the benefit of other humans, present and future. There is such a thing as being prudent despots. On that basis alone we stand condemned.

God may wish to declare his glory through the wonders of the world, and the beauty of it may be for that end, or for our enjoyment, or the features of the world may be for our spiritual education. The medieval bestiaries taught that beasts, apart from any practical utility they might have, served the purpose of symbolizing various moral and spiritual points for our edification. The *Physiologus* (188), authoritatively quoted over several centuries, relates, with much other fascinating lore, that:

> The third attribute of the Lion is this: When the lioness brings forth her young, she brings it forth dead. But the Lioness watches over her cub until the third day, when the father comes and roars and breathes in its face and wakens it. So did the God and Father of the Universe waken the first born of all creation, our Lord Jesus Christ, his Son, from the dead. Well now spoke Jacob when he said of Judah the Lion's whelp: "Who shall rouse him up?"

Much later, George Berkeley, eighteenth-century bishop and empiricist philosopher, maintained that the world is not only organized for our benefit, but is an integrated system of signs for our instruction. According to such views the lion, as well as the ox, is a resource for the ultimate benefit of humankind. That, perhaps, is why lions get their meat from God (Psalms 104:21). Again, it may be that God has mysterious purposes that we do not comprehend. We ought not to interfere with those purposes or run the risk of doing so in ignorance. The general presumption remains that morality concerns only spiritual beings – God, the heavenly host, and humans. In whatever way, the world is an instrumentality, either for our ends or directly for God's. We may profit from the world, and we may be conscious that it is not to be wasted or destroyed, but there is no suggestion that it is anything more than an instrumentality. In such an outlook the idea that brutes or wildernesses might have moral significance in their own right would suggest that they had souls. That would smack of the old paganism that Christianity so firmly opposed.

There is still the possibility that God has attached some intrinsic moral significance to some things that are not spiritual. In spite of St. Paul and St. Thomas, there has been a persistent idea, as witness St. Chrysostom and St. Francis, that cruelty to oxen or other animals is morally wrong because of the effect on the animal itself. In recent years there has been increased interest on the part of religious thinkers in the idea that God might attach some intrinsic value to the natural world at large. Job (38:26–27) tells us that God has chosen "to cause it to rain on the earth, where no man is; on the wilderness, where there is no man; to satisfy the desolate and waste ground; and to cause the bud of the tender herb to spring forth." Would it not be presumptuous of us to think that what God does where there are no humans is entirely for human benefit? God is under no obligation to draw the moral line to suit our own self-important conceptions of our place in the scheme of things. Whatever beings an ethic might take to be morally significant, that ethic could still be interpreted within the sphere of Christianity or most other religions.

BACON, DESCARTES, AND REASON

In addition to the despotic position and the stewardship position, Passmore notes a third position that has had a powerful influence on Western thought: We are to use reason to perfect or improve nature. Most recently in secular garb, this view with its ideal of progress has had considerable impact on contemporary thought. Though less blatantly so, it is quite as human-centered as the despotic position, in that it tacitly turns on human ideals of progress. Indeed, I would consider that any position that does not recognize value in the non-human world is really only a more or less cautious version of the despotic position. They differ only in strategy as to

21

how we are go about getting the most from the world. Probably the rational-improvement approach, from the time of
Francis Bacon, has done the most to undermine the possibility of an adequate environmental consciousness in our
contemporary thinking about the world.

Bacon proposed that through the use of reason, particularly as employed in science and technology, we could go a
long way toward restoring the earthly dominion we enjoyed
before the Fall. In his day, around the start of the seventeenth
century, there already had been a revival of interest in the
ancient learning, and growing application to the practical
arts. Bacon's contribution was to criticize the then unsystem-
atic approach to increasing our knowledge, and to propose
a systematic approach, particularly with a view to practical
application. He thought that "if a man should succeed, not
in striking out some new invention, but in kindling a light
in nature – a light that should eventually disclose and bring
into sight all that is most hidden and secret in the universe
– that man (I thought) would be benefactor indeed of the
human race."[4] This new light he hoped to kindle through a
program of planned and coordinated experimentation and
observation – a program as revolutionary then as it is, thanks
in significant part to Bacon, commonplace to us now.

Bacon held that nature is a thing to be manipulated for
human benefit. It is not just that we might *use* nature, which
we have been doing for thousands of years, but that we might
change things, experimentally and in practical application,
harnessing nature to do our bidding. Here he was giving
articulation and further impetus to an idea that arose from
many sources during the Renaissance and continued to gain
strength through the Enlightenment and into our own times.
It is an idea that has borne multitudinous fruit – not all sweet
to the taste. In his own day there were religious misgivings
about Bacon's stated aim of attempting to restore our lapsed

4 Francis Bacon, in the preface to his *De Interpretatione Naturae*, as quoted
by Maurice Cranston in his article on Bacon in *The Encyclopedia of Philosophy*, Vol. 1, ed. Paul Edwards (New York and London: Macmillan,
1967), 235–240.

dominion through intellectual endeavor. The orthodox view was that our fall from grace was a moral problem, not an intellectual one. We need not be theologians to recognize that intellectual achievement is no guarantee against moral failure. Bacon's own shabby political career is proof of that. Also, there were worries that concentrating on means for manipulating nature may distract us from a consideration of ends. In Bacon's day the worry was that it might lead us to neglect our spiritual welfare. We must also worry that our apparent power over nature may lead us away from asking whether there are morally wrong ways of treating the non-human world. Moreover, we must not let a narrow concentration on means obscure from us the fact that we, too, are part of nature. When we manipulate nature we run the risk of unintentionally altering our own life conditions. Bacon, and many since, have been too concerned with individual factors and their close causal relationships, not fully appreciating that nature is complex and highly interconnected. In changing one factor, being concerned with one set of effects, we easily lose sight of the many side effects. As Barry Commoner so forcefully points out, it is impossible to change just one thing at a time.[5] Unexpected but environmentally devastating side effects have become by-products of many of our activities, injuring us as well as the natural world of which we are a part. All too many examples spring to mind.

Skepticism was rife in the seventeenth century, as old certainties were being called into question, and the new ideas that were constantly being proposed and challenged also seemed uncertain. The idea arose then that it might become possible to give an account of human beings in purely physical, even mechanical, terms. If that were so, we would presumably be on a par with the rest of nature. We needed, then, to reassess our place in the world, asking what, if anything, grounded our preeminent moral status. In re-

5 Barry Commoner (1972) draws forcefully to our attention that all things and processes of the living world are connected to all other things and processes, with the effects of our actions being multiplied accordingly.

sponse, René Descartes attempted to place philosophy on a firm foundation, reason, which would provide a means for acquiring secure knowledge, and which would provide security for our conception of ourselves as standing above the rest of the world. His attempt propelled philosophy into the modern era, but in spite of his overall contribution to philosophy, he left us with the heritage of severe blunders. His view of the difference between human and nonhuman nature widened the perceived gap between humanity and the nonhuman world to an unprecedented extent, and despite the subsequent erosion of its metaphysical foundations, has substantially persisted to the present day.

Reason is central to Descartes's conception of what a human is: "I think, therefore I am." This is his skeptic-proof starting point. We can neither doubt that we exist nor doubt that we think without the very doubt confirming what is doubted. Our first and most essential character is as thinking beings. He went on to claim that animals entirely lack minds, acting on a purely mechanical basis, just responding to stimuli. A dog's yelp when kicked is no more indicative of pain than is the noise of an automatic fire alarm when it responds to heat. One suspects that only a person as brilliant as Descartes could possibly manage to convince himself of such a conclusion. A less clever person would have known better. Even a child, unless corrupted by problematic philosophical theories, would know that kicking the dog causes it discomfort. In various guises, however, Descartes's theories on this subject have had a lasting effect on our thinking.

According to Descartes, a being cannot experience pain unless it is conscious of the pain. Feeling pain is a type of consciousness and therefore presupposes rationality. But why must consciousness involve thought of a high enough order to be deemed rational? For Descartes, there were no intermediate elements between rational consciousness and nonconsciousness. Rather, there were two radically different sorts of things in the world: material bodies, and minds, whose defining characteristic is rational (conceptual) thought. Physical properties only pertain to body, whereas

24

mental properties only pertain to mind. Rationality and the capacity to feel pleasure and pain are all part of the same thing. Not being rational, animals are not mental and therefore cannot feel pleasure or pain.

Yet, why can it not be that an animal has a lower-grade mind that thinks less rational thoughts and is yet able to feel pleasures and pains? After all, different humans have many different levels of rationality – and even very stupid ones are able to feel pain. The problem is that Descartes takes the mind as a very unitary sort of thing, with his version of rational thought as fundamental. As sentience and rationality are necessary and inseparable aspects of the mind, the absence of rational thought – as revealed by the absence of language – entails the absence of mind in animals, and therefore of sentience. He informs us in *Discourse on Method* (116–7) that:

> there are none so depraved and stupid, without even excepting idiots, that they cannot arrange different words together, forming of them a statement by which they make known their thoughts; while, on the other hand, there is no animal, however perfect and fortunately circumstanced it may be, which can do the same. . . . this does not merely show that the brutes have less reason than men, but that they have none at all, since it is clear that very little is required in order to be able to talk. . . . although there are many animals which exhibit more dexterity than we do in some of their actions, we at the same time observe that they do not manifest any dexterity at all in many others. Hence the fact that they do better than we do, does not prove that they are endowed with mind, for in this case they would have more reason than any of us, and would surpass us in all other things. It rather shows that they have no reason at all, and that it is nature which acts in them according to the disposition of their organs, just as a clock . . .

Mind is not so unitary as Descartes supposed. Among humans there are a considerable number of different mental abilities, problem-solving skills, and ways of having awareness and insight. No doubt they are somewhat related, but only somewhat. People are good at some things and not at others, with different people good at different things. Once we recognize that minds can occur in a number of different forms, two new possibilities are seen to be open: it may be that animals have a consciousness such that, without necessarily having any great intellectual ability, they are sentient and thus capable of experiencing pleasure and pain. Again, it may be that linguistic aptitude is a characteristically human form of rationality and that some animals have other types of rationality. The evidence is that these things are indeed the case.

Aside from all the behavioral evidence, and sheer common sense, the neurological evidence is that at least the higher animals can feel pain. They have brains with a well-developed subcortex, that being the region of the brain where the actual experience of pain evidently occurs. The cerebral cortex, the part of the brain that handles rational thought, did most of its evolving only after the subcortex had already nearly attained its greatest development. Thus, while the cerebral cortex of humans is more advanced than that of any other animal (except cetaceans?), the subcortex of most of the higher animals is at least roughly on a par with our own. Presumably their capacity to feel pain would be at least roughly comparable. Nowadays, few if any would deny that at least the higher animals feel pain, but there seems still to be something of a Cartesian holdover in the belief of many that animals feel pain significantly less than we do. This is a hard claim to argue against because it is rarely argued for. Most people who hold that opinion seem to merely assert it without argument – though I get the impression that the lower intellectual level of animals is supposed to have something to do with it. That the experience of pain occurs in the subcortical region, rather than in the cerebral cortex, destroys that claim in the case of most vertebrates. On average the Simple Simons of this world feel a broken leg as much as the Einsteins, and a sheep need not be a linguist to have a like unpleasant sensation. It is an area of factual inquiry what beings are subject to pain in what amount from what sources, an inquiry wherein residual Cartesian-style presuppositions only obscure the issues.

LANGUAGE, REASON, AND THE WORLD

Just what is the significance of language? What linguistic competence has to do with rationality, and what the moral significance is of either, are questions that have greatly influenced discussions of our ethical attitude toward the rest of the world. There is now substantial evidence that some primates, and possibly some cetaceans, do have linguistic capacities. The now-famous chimpanzee Washoe evidently was able to learn approximately 350 signs ("words") in American Sign Language, Ameslan.[6] She could use about 150 signs effectively, and was able to recognize the import of about 200 others. But why was she not just taught to use that much English? The fact is that the chimpanzee vocal apparatus, including nerves between the brain and larynx, is not as well developed as that of a human. No matter how bright a chimp might be, asking it to use speech is to ask the impossible. They just did not evolve that way – but they are quite able to make gestures. That Washoe and other chimps who have since learned some use of Ameslan were able to learn and use as much as they did indicates that they have some respectable degree of intelligence. Although a normal human can learn considerably more Ameslan than can a chimp, it is quite significant that chimps can achieve even the level of a retarded human.

To say of Washoe only that she meets the same standards as a retarded human is to do her an injustice. She is not *any* sort of human. She is a remarkable chimpanzee. Even among humans there are many different sorts of mentality, and the differences between species are undoubtedly even greater. One need only contrast dogs with cats. Although chimps are

6 See R. Allen Gardner and Beatrice Gardner (1969) and (1971), and also Eugene Linden (1974). I understand that there has been much subsequent research tending to reinforce the earlier findings.

remarkably similar to humans in many ways, we cannot just assume that their mentality is merely an image of our own – *man* writ small, as it were. We cannot just assume that rationality or any aspect of it is quite the same between chimps and humans, or that rationality of any sort fits in quite the same way into the overall chimp mentality and way of life. We humans are a linguistic lot. Because the chimpanzee mind is seemingly less disposed to linguistic communication, I would be inclined to think that Washoe's remarkable achievement is indicative of a *higher* intelligence, but of a different kind, than would be indicated by a retarded human who could attain only a similar standard of language usage. Washoe, after all, was playing *our* game.

Rationality is not a separate additional thing added on to the rest of us, like a driver in addition to the chariot. Nor is it just a cerebral cortex added on to the rest of the system.[7] The relationship is more organic than that. Washoe's rationality is that of a healthy, integrated, functional individual who is able to deal effectively with her environment. Unfortunately, we cannot say as much for the retarded human who can do no better at Ameslan than does Washoe. Such people are unable to function well in their own environment, and even if they could somehow assume a chimp's body, much less could they make a go of being a chimp. Nor, I think, could we make a human out of a chimpanzee, no matter how well educated. A human's rationality is an integral feature of what is involved in being a human, whereas a chimp's differing rationality is an integral feature of what is involved in the very different business of being a chimp.

7 At one time it was fashionable to refer to "higher" and "lower" portions of the brain, and "dominant" hemispheres. We are now coming to realize that the system – that is, we – are more functionally integrated, more *whole*, than that. Evidently we had been importing into our conception of the facts some of our own preconceptions and value judgments. This was what Peter Reynolds called "the Victorian brain." Such views are also connected with some wrong ideas about sexual differences. See Reynolds (1981). Also, see Stephen Walker (1983) and, for a briefer discussion, Mary Midgley (1985).

There is more to being human than just being rational and using language. There is also more to being Washoe.

If we conclude no more than that a chimpanzee can meet the same intellectual standards as a retarded human, we have reached a conclusion that is profoundly shocking to a great many people. It seems to threaten our special dignity as human beings – a threat once felt from the idea that we did not stand at the physical center of the universe. The Cartesian gap between humans and animals evidently closes to the point of overlap. What are the moral implications? Do we conclude that a retarded human and a chimp are on the same moral level? What level? Or do we assign chimps an inferior moral status just because they are not members of our own tribe? These suggestions may seem very disturbing. Attempts have therefore been made to find some firm ground on which to morally reestablish the Cartesian gap, something that actually does make a morally significant difference between even a smart chimpanzee and a stupid human. I doubt that many people would wish to maintain that Washoe has no moral standing at all. Perhaps she – and possibly other animals, to whatever extent – are worthy of some degree of moral consideration. However, unless we recognize that Washoe has just as much moral importance as the retarded human, we are still relying, to the extent of the difference in moral standing, on the principle that *merely* being a member of the human species carries moral weight. This is to insist on the Cartesian moral gap despite the failure of the Cartesian argument, retreating from bad reasons to evident circularity. To rescue the principle that any human has a higher moral standing than does any animal, we would have to find some plausible reason why humans are morally so important. I shall discuss such issues somewhat further in the next chapter. My point for now is that Cartesian-style presuppositions, often tacit, continue to influence contemporary thought in this area. Unless there are good reasons in favor of our presuppositions, we rest only on prejudice.

Washoe seemingly must have some moral status, given

that she has demonstrated a degree of intelligence and is able to communicate with us to a significant extent. Intuitively, these seem like morally relevant considerations. But why? Had Washoe been less bright, or not trained, would that have meant that her interests were morally less significant? Setting aside the question of rationality for the moment, let us ask why Washoe's communicational abilities might be morally significant. The mere fact that she does communicate with humans and has entered into personal relationships of trust and affection with humans does seem to me to carry some moral weight. For those who have dealings with Washoe, failing to act toward her with goodwill would, I believe, amount to betrayal of trust, a double-cross. Among humans, injuring a stranger, wrong as it might be to do so, is not held to be as wrong as doing so to a trusting friend. Nor need language mediate the relationship. If we encourage trust and expectation of goodwill, we acquire obligations. The family dog or cat has a claim on our goodwill, much more so than a strange dog or cat.

That being said, however, Washoe's linguistic skill seems to involve an *additional* morally significant dimension. Other animals enter into personal relationships with humans. There seems to be something *particularly* wrong about will-fully causing or allowing injury to a being that has entered into linguistic communication with us. Our use of language evidently has some importance as a means by which communicants are bound together into morally reciprocating groups. Many of the divisions, alliances, and antagonisms in the world today are associated with linguistic factors, and with the cultural factors so often associated with them. While Descartes stressed the importance of language use because of what he took to be its metaphysical implications, in effect he was stressing those factors that join us, and divide us, into groups.[8] The use of language in general distinguishes

8 In Papua–New Guinea, where there are said to be more than seven hundred languages, the pidgin term for a friend or comrade is *wontak*, based on the English "one talk." A friend, then, is someone who speaks

us from beings that lack language and culture, and gives us common ground as human beings even if we do not share the same language. Washoe, then, is something of an anomaly. As a language user, she seems to be in some way at least an associate member of the human tribe.

Washoe does not fit properly into our normal categories – which is a failure of our categories. She puzzles us because she is rational and language-using, to a point, and is capable of acquiring a rudimentary sort of culture. She seems to be a peculiar kind of just-about-human being, with some associated moral status. Much of the difficulty in knowing what to make of Washoe is the difficulty in knowing what to make of ourselves. What is it that is characteristically human? Why is it that *we* are morally significant? Is it *because* we are rational, use language, and have cultures? What we are runs deeper than that, and so, I believe, does our moral significance. These things are only part of what we are, and they fit into the rest of our nature in an integral and characteristically human way. Any other species – be it primate, cetacean, or extraterrestrial – that had language and culture would undoubtedly be very different from us and have them in very different forms. They too would be morally significant, as are beings that lack those assets. We must abandon the confused and patronizing notion that beings are morally significant to the extent that they are associate or honorary humans. Beings are what they are, whatever they are, and their moral significance is contingent on what they are in their own right, not on their similarity to us. As I shall argue in the following, our moral significance, and that of Washoe and of other beings, springs from the fact that we have interests, can suffer or flourish in our own right. Morality is not a matter of tribal membership, full or associate, however we conceive our own tribe to be characterized. Residual Cartesian-style elements in our thinking about the nature of mentality and moral significance only confuse the issues.

the same language. Morally, one has special rights and obligations with respect to one's wontaks.

31

Not only do Cartesian-style presuppositions continue to influence contemporary thinking about animals; they also influence our thinking about the nonhuman world as a whole. To be sure, Descartes did not share the medieval conviction that the world was created entirely for our material benefit or spiritual instruction. Knowledge of the scope and variety of the world had, by that time, precluded such a view (*Principles of Philosophy*, 271):

> Although it may be a pious thought . . . to believe that God has created all things for us in as far as that incites us to a greater gratitude and affection toward Him, . . . it is yet not at all probable that all things have been created for us in such a manner that God has no other end in creating them. . . . for we cannot doubt that an infinitude of things exist, or did exist, though now they have ceased to exist, which have never been beheld or comprehended by man and which have never been of any use to him.

In the midst of this he yet notes that "there is nothing created from which we cannot derive some use," and elsewhere he expresses the hope that (*Discourse on Method*, p. 119):

> we may find a practical philosophy by means of which, knowing the force and action of fire, water, air, the stars, heavens and all other bodies that environ us, as distinctly as we know the different crafts of our artisans, we can in the same way employ them in all those uses to which they are adapted, and thus render ourselves the masters and possessors of nature.

That Balbus was wrong about the world being tailor-made to suit our advantage is taken not to mean that the natural world is morally independent but that it is a moral vacuum. (But why should God create a moral vacuum?) Descartes's world is a mere mechanism. Morally, we are at liberty to use it as best serves our purposes, imposing our own purposes on its mechanism. The way to human progress is to take command of the machinery.

The place of humanity in the world, in Descartes's scheme of things, is largely analogous to the place of the mind in the body: different, alien, the sole source and center of value.

The body exists for the mind and is to be tended for its benefit. We are the natural lords over the material world, which we may utilize for our benefit. Whether or not we are sovereign by divine appointment, we are sovereign by metaphysical right – much as Shakespeare's Prospero, by virtue of his wisdom and goodness, was the natural lord over Caliban and over what previously had been Caliban's island. Just as Descartes's mind-body theory obscures our true being, this projection of the false dualism into the world as a whole obscures our place within it.

We are still influenced for the worst by Cartesianism not only in our attitude toward the natural world, but in our conceptualization of it. Descartes's world has only those properties that are subject to rational (i.e., mathematical) analysis, properties such as extension, mass, energy, velocity, and the like. Life itself is a mechanical process. Organisms and ecosystems are merely interacting aggregations of mechanical parts, rather than entities that have to be understood basically as wholes. The behavior of animals cannot be in any way understood in terms of the animals' mental states, since they have none. Even now, it is considered in some circles to be unscientific, and therefore improper, to conceptualize the behavior of animals (or even humans) in other than terms of purely physical behavior. Motives, desires, ends, and interests are dismissed without a hearing. Concerning animals individually or the environment holistically, this legacy makes it difficult even to ask the ethical questions.

Both Bacon and Descartes distanced humanity from a world taken as lacking moral significance in its own right, and saw our destiny in being the active manipulators of a natural world that is passive before the power of human rationality. It is not fair to blame them entirely. These ideas had other roots as well, and they gained strength through the subsequent development of science and technology. The secular humanism of the Enlightenment further contributed, as it often tended to stress the potency of the human intellect, to identify sin with ignorance, and to minimize the traditional conception of inherent human limitations. Still, the initial impetus of Bacon and the metaphysics of Descartes pushed these basic ideas into the channels leading to contemporary thought. The metaphysics has fallen by the wayside, but the point of view lingers on.

REASSESSING THE HUMAN CAREER

If anything, regard for reason and faith in rationality increased in more recent times, though not without occasional voice to the contrary. Reason was commonly seen as the great human value, and the means by which we would be able to solve any difficulty that might confront us. Rational progress, material progress, moral progress, progress toward civilization and humanization – for the past couple of centuries and to the present day, in various compoundings, the idea of *progress* has greatly influenced much of our thinking. Science and technology marched on from one triumph to the next, and there appeared to be a law of inevitable progress dictating that, led by reason, humankind would continually advance to ever higher levels. Some thinkers, such as Hegel, claimed to discover such a natural law. Not only did reason lead to progress and value, they held, it was their essence.[9]

According to Hegel and the other German idealists of the past century, the natural world is a morally latent thing in need of human help. Unlike Bacon and Descartes, they took nature to be something we actively create, and which we enfuse and ennoble with human spirit and value. This conception had an impact considerably beyond idealist circles, although it gains particular impetus from idealist metaphysical theories, which take ideas, mind, soul, will, or something of that general sort, to be constitutive of reality. Rationality – in effect, human rationality – is said to compose reality and give it determinate being and value. Spirit, rationality, being, and value are here largely identified. On this view, things

9 Immanuel Kant must certainly be mentioned in any discussion of the historical background of the question of the moral import of rationality. His views will be discussed in the next chapter, "Sweet Reason."

progress to higher levels of being and value accordingly as they incorporate progressively higher degrees of rationality and spirit. It follows that when we humanize nature, nature profits from our useful intercession. By taming a wilderness and creating a garden we create being and value, freeing nature from the fetters of its own indeterminate negativity by humanizing it and liberating it into the realm of spirit.

This line takes human-centeredness to the fullest extreme. It holds that the nonhuman world is not only without any moral significance in its own right, but that it does not even have its own being. Humanity, in a continuous process of creation, progressively raises nature from mere negativity to coherence, determinate being, and value. Indeed, for Fichte, nature exists only to provide us with an arena within which to pursue a moral career, and has no value or purpose save that which we create within it. By raising ourselves and nature above the original sin of nonrationality, we are to create a new Eden. In his *The Vocation of Man* (331), Fichte tells us:

> Cultivation shall quicken and ameliorate the sluggish and baleful atmosphere of primaeval forests, deserts, and marshes; more regular and varied cultivation shall diffuse throughout the air new impulses to life and fertility; and the sun shall pour his most animating rays into an atmosphere breathed by healthy, industrious, and civilized nations. . . . Nature [shall] ever become more and more intelligible and transparent even in her most secret depths; human power, enlightened and armed by human invention, shall rule over her without difficulty.

And so on. The point is not that we are to use or repress nature, but that we are to liberate it into the world of being, reason, and value. At first we may have to use considerable force, but as nature becomes more liberated we may guide it more gently. The values involved here are human values, of course, there being no other kind. To my ear, Fichte's remarks have the tone of a sales agent promoting a real-estate development scheme. Certainly they are quite naive. If nothing else, we now know that nature is more resistant to our manipulation, more independent in its being, than

Fichte gave it credit for. Often the results of our arrogance are tragic, as when we exploit and exhaust the land and turn it into a desert or reduce it to an all-but-sterile monoculture, or subject it to incongruous "development." On the moral level as well, I believe that Fichte and associates are fundamentally mistaken.

I do grant that there is some limited bit of value in their position. Sometimes we are able to husband and increase the fertility of the earth, developing and nurturing its latent potential. Those who are able to do that are good farmers, good foresters, good resource managers. They take natural material and develop its own natural potentials in accordance with human values. Those who fail to recognize and respect the potentials of the earth can only exploit it, and in the end will obtain the less from their labors. Humans can sometimes shape, as well as destroy, something of value. A world with people in it cannot entirely remain a wilderness, and the transformation is not entirely to be regretted. But does humanity have a moral mission to transform the world into a well-manicured garden? Fichte and a great many others have certainly thought so. Although the metaphysical theory that human rationality creates reality, or that it holds it together, is without a great deal of popularity these days, its moral cognate, the assumption that human values are the linchpin of moral reality, is very widely, and usually unconsciously, accepted. Throughout past ages, supposedly, nature has been building toward rational human civilization, and it is for us, then, to carry the ideal forward.

The ideal of progress was given great impetus by the idea of *evolution*, which is often thought to imply change for the better, in some evaluative sense. Change, particularly inevitable change, is often similarly understood to imply progress toward some better state. Herbert Spencer, the English evolutionary philosopher who coined the phrase "survival of the fittest," equated evolutionary fitness with normative value. He maintained that there is a law of evolutionary progress according to which the fitter (i.e., better) displaces the less fit, a law that works for the overall betterment of humanity. He expressed these ideas before Charles Darwin made public his ideas about biological evolution, though of course Darwinian ideas about biology were taken to lend support to Spencerian ideas about value. After all, since evolution started with slime and ended with us, it must be going in the right direction. Moreover, the human race has arguably made advances since the Stone Age. That there is a natural law of progress is a belief that has considerable intuitive plausibility for us humans, flattering our vanity and giving us comfort that in this precarious world things will turn out well in the long run.

One interpretation is the idea that we cannot in the long run stand in the way of progress, and morally we ought not to try. It is a pity when the less fit are squeezed out, but it is ultimately for the best. As Spencer tells us (1851, 322–3),

> The well-being of existing humanity and the unfolding of it into this ultimate perfection are both secured by that same beneficent, though severe, discipline to which the animate creation at large is subject: a discipline which is pitiless in the working out of good: a felicity-pursuing law which never swerves for the avoidance of partial and temporary suffering. The poverty of the incapable, the distresses that come upon the imprudent, the starvation of the idle, and those shoulderings aside of the weak by the strong, . . . are the decrees of a large, far-seeing benevolence. . . . under the natural order of things society, is constantly excreting its unhealthy, imbecile, slow, vacillating, faithless members.

Although nature's way may appear unfortunate, the end, both good and inevitable, justifies the means, which are natural, productive, and only apparently bad.[10] Just as the weak benefited from past evolution, so they must make way for a

10 In this vein, John D. Rockefeller, the megacapitalist and Standard Oil monopolist, is reported to have once told a Sunday school class that "The growth of a larger business is merely a survival of the fittest. . . . The American Beauty rose can be produced in the splendor and fragrance which bring cheer to its beholder only by sacrificing the early buds which grow up around it. This is not an evil tendency in business. It is merely the working out of a law of nature and a law of God." The quotation appears in R. Hofstadter (1944), 45.

better future. This law applies not only to society, but to the whole world. Accordingly, it is only right and for the best that humanity, the stronger, should impose its will on the rest of the world and so fulfill its destiny to create a better world. If any doubt remains, we may point to an evolutionary trend toward other things we approve of, such as greater levels of complexity, diversity, and organic interconnection. Evidently, the thing to do is to move along the path of evolution.[11]

The truth is just not that simple and easy. Although past evolution has been in the direction of things that humans consider to be superior, this is only contingently so, and our values must be given independent definition. Biological evolution offers us no guarantee of moral progress. There have been many different tendencies in the past, and future evolution may take a different path in the future. Once there was an evolutionary trend favoring large dinosaurs, and once before that there was a trend toward hard shells. Future natural selection may favor abilities to resist pollution and radiation. There is normally a reason when one thing replaces another, but usually the reason is only that the successor better fits a prevailing set of requirements. It does not mean that it is morally *better*. With all due respect, it does not seem at all plausible that that great evolutionary success, the cockroach, is the moral superior of failed Neanderthal man.

If we cannot find a necessary law of moral progress in the natural world, that in itself may be taken as a moral lesson. Perhaps the lesson is that we must ourselves develop newer and better values as time goes on, just as we developed other favorable adaptations in the past. Or, more grimly, perhaps the lesson to be learned is that nature moves against value,

11 It was not only laissez-faire capitalists and other right-wingers who appealed to the principle of evolution. Marxists and others on the left tried to establish that there was a necessary law of progress in whatever direction they approved of. At one time, *Kapital* and *The Origin of Species* were sold side by side in socialist book shops. For a further discussion of the subject of evolutionary ethics in general, see Antony Flew (1967), and Mary Midgley (1985).

that the struggle for survival actually favors the immoral. T. H. Huxley (1900, 218–21) drew conclusions quite directly opposite to those of Spencer:

> The thief and the murderer follow nature just as much as the philanthropist. . . . Social progress means a checking of the cosmic process at every step and the substitution for it of another, which may be called the ethical process; the end of which is not the survival of those which happen to be the fittest . . . but of those who are ethically the best. . . . The ethical progress of society depends, not on imitating the cosmic process, still less in running away from it, but in combating it.

Nor is there any guarantee that society must continue to progress, though it will certainly continue to change. Huxley called upon us to move contrary to what he saw as the way of nature (evidently not seeing instances of cooperation and even caring). Lesser men than Huxley drew the conclusion that the thing to do is to emulate nature's apparent lack of moral restraint – to follow "the Law of the Jungle," which is no moral law at all. Where once a Shakespearean duke saw "Sermons in stone, and good in everything," the nineteenth century – and, indeed, our own – was haunted by Tennyson's image of "nature red in tooth and claw." If nature is a savage and vicious jungle, and God is too far away, if there is no natural law of morality, then, individually or collectively, we must see to our own wellbeing. In practice, this point of view frequently became mingled with Spencerian-style views, according to which if there is any such thing as goodness at all, it is to be found through self-seeking.

Somewhat paradoxically, while the tendency of recent times has been to look upon morality as a self-interested and purely human invention, recent times have also seen the progressively wider acceptance, at least in lip service, of the principle that all humans *ought* to be accepted as full members of the moral community. Restricting membership to only some humans is considered to be very poor form. But why should all humans be members of the moral community? If morality is purely an in-house affair, there should be no moral constraint on whom we admit to or exclude from our moral community for whatever reason. There is no logical or practical necessity that the moral community must consist of exactly those who do or could potentially reciprocate. We may not wish to reciprocate with all comers. Indeed, if the moral community is a purely arbitrary arrangement contrived by us, we might decide to exclude any others according to convenience or whim. On the other hand, if the composition of the moral community is not arbitrary, if there is a moral reason why we ought to include all other people, then the same moral reason might call on us to in some way include other beings that might be affected by our actions.

In our thinking about the world, and about ourselves, I suspect that we would do well to give some heed to those thinkers who emphasize not just our mind but our inward being. Some of those romantic thinkers have undoubtedly gone quite off the rails but at their best, certain of them make some good points. They make a very good one when they remind us that we are not just rational beings, and that only. We would be poor indeed if we were merely Rational Man, Economic Man, single-mindedly measuring out our lives in theoretically "rational" utility. We have heart, we have soul, we have feeling, passion, spirit – we have *depth,* and it is in our depths, they stress to us, that true meaning and value are to be found. Reason alone can give us neither one. Our rationality is only the surface, and it is the servant of our soul.

Superficial pleasure is no more to be desired than empty rationality. Instead of those superficialities, most of the romantics emphasized such things as self-development, healthy growth, achieving potential, freedom from imposed and disruptive limitation, and the like. Their ideal was the full realization of the latent values within us. It is better for us if we can live in such a way as to coherently develop our potentials and satisfy our needs. I think that they are on to something there. As opposed to Sartre, who said that man invents himself with his choices, they believe that it is more than just a matter of our choices, our reason, or even our consciousness. We implicitly define ourselves by having, by *being*, our own particular life process with its own self-identity and needs, of which the rational, conscious, sentient surface is only an aspect. We thereby define what there is about ourselves that demands moral respect from others. At its best, having such a point of view will lead us to allow others (as well as ourselves) to live full and healthy lives in accordance with their own natures and potentials, and will prompt us to help them to do so. At its not uncommon worse, it may lead us to "help" others by pressuring them to live and develop according to *our* idea of what *their* needs and potentials ought to be. In our own time, a great many have been maimed by such good or supposedly good intentions.

When it comes to our dealings with nonhumans, much the same can be said. We have been much too inclined to ride roughshod over nature, imposing our own ideas of what desirable development ought to be. In that respect the Fichtean ideal is very much a part of the Western tradition, so much so that many of us have great difficulty even in conceiving that there could be an alternative. In welcome contrast are those romantics who recognized value in nature. Wordsworth's "vernal wood" was more than just something from which we might learn. It was something of value in its own right. For those akin to Wordsworth, if not to Fichte, nature has a value that is independent of us humans and goes beyond our human concerns.

Materially and morally, we are no more than part of the world. Many natural entities have goods of their own that are not defined by human needs or values. In all of their variety, natural entities, ourselves included, endeavor to live their own lives according to their own nature and potential. This is not a morally indifferent matter. I do not make the absurd claim that we must never interfere with the natural world, but I do claim that whether and how we do so is in some part a moral decision. Morally, we must learn to strike a living balance in a world of living balances. In what follows I shall draw on various elements in our cultural background, reject others, and attempt to build from there. I shall try to develop, more systematically and on the basis of adequate reasons – and, I hope, with vision – an account of the moral universe and those within, and of what it means to live a good life.

Chapter 2

Sweet reason

Reason is the mistress and queen of all things.

Cicero

But man, proud man
Dressed in a little brief authority
Most ignorant of what he's most assured . . .

Shakespeare, *Measure for Measure*

The day *may* come when the rest of the animal creation may acquire those rights which could never
have been withholden from them but by the hand of
tyranny. The French have already discovered that the
blackness of the skin is no reason why a human being
should be abandoned without redress to the caprice
of a tormentor. It may one day come to be recognized
that the number of the legs, the villosity of the skin,
or the termination of the *os sacrum* are reasons equally
insufficient for abandoning a sensitive being to the
same fate. What else is it that should trace the insu-
perable line? Is it the faculty of reason, or perhaps
the faculty of discourse? But a full-grown horse or
dog is beyond comparison a more rational, as well as
a more conversable animal, than an infant of a day
or a week or even a month, old. But suppose they
were otherwise, what would it avail? The question is
not, Can they *reason?* nor, Can they *talk?* but, *Can
they suffer?*

Jeremy Bentham, *Introduction to the Principles
of Morals and Legislation*

43

Only in comparatively recent times have ideals of moral egalitarianism achieved widespread acceptance – with practice lagging considerably behind theory. Not only did Aristotle, in his day, believe that the role of animals is to serve human needs; he took it as equally obvious that some humans are slaves by nature. Their natural role is to serve and be directed by their betters. Most barbarians and some Greeks were held to be of this nature, and to be capable of no better condition. Similarly, women, being only incomplete men, clearly should have only limited autonomy. Aristotle was by no means idiosyncratic in holding such opinions. Throughout most of human history, the prevalent view, in one form or another, has been that some humans are morally more important than others. Differences in social rank, age, sex, religion, tribal membership, language, race, and so on often made a very great difference to the moral standing one was accorded. Justifications for discriminatory beliefs and practices, when justification has been thought necessary, have frequently made reference to the supposed superiority, moral or otherwise, of the favored group. Such claims have often been buttressed by appeals to religious authority or, as in the case of Aristotle, to the natural order of things. Sometimes it has been held, consciously or otherwise, that questions of morality simply do not arise in the case of outsiders. It just would not occur to a Yanomamo warrior in the South American jungle to think of a member of another tribe in moral terms, any more than it would occur to you or me to consider the moral status of a pebble.

The idea that animals (and sentient beings in general) ought to be recognized as having full moral standing – that their interests ought to be treated on an equal moral footing with those of humans – has frequently provoked reactions very similar to those previously provoked by the suggestion that all humans were to be treated on the same moral footing. The range of negative reactions has indeed included total incomprehension, religious indignation, selfishness, and bad logic. Yet responses have also included serious discussion and opposition by formidable thinkers, raising genuine is-

44

sues that deserve our most careful consideration. Real conceptual problems to be resolved, and real moral issues at stake must be dealt with in terms of a viable overall ethical theory. I propose to investigate now more closely what is involved in the claim that animals ought to have full moral standing, and to survey the key reasons for and against. I shall take Peter Singer's *Animal Liberation* as my point of departure.

ALL CREATURES

Singer was hardly the first to suggest that animals were morally significant, but his book contributed greatly to the current interest in this matter. Opening the inquiry with a consideration of his views will provide a convenient entry to the issues as they appear in contemporary discussion. Although our primary focus at this point will be on the moral status of animals, I shall be working toward a clearer view of broader questions concerning the nature and moral significance of interests and of the entities that have them. I shall eventually argue that Singer's theory, despite going a long way in the right direction, is inadequate. We will need a more comprehensive theory.

Animal Liberation caused quite a public stir, as well as considerable philosophical debate, by arguing that one ought to give the same moral consideration to the interests of animals that one ought to give to the equivalent interests of human beings. Causing unnecessary pain, for instance, is held to be morally wrong, and to be no less so when the pain is felt by a pig rather than by a human being. Now, the idea that it is wrong to cause unnecessary pain to an animal would probably be accepted by most people – though most people seem to have very flexible ideas about what constitutes necessity. I suspect that just about anything that contributes to any human end, other than the end of sheer amusement at causing pain, would be widely accepted as being necessary. What many people found shocking was Singer's conviction that the interests of animals are on the *same* moral footing as the

45

equal or equivalent interests of humans, together with the conclusions he drew therefrom. He proposed that most research involving animals ought to be discontinued and that we ought to discontinue eating meat. In support, *Animal Liberation* graphically and arrestingly details the pain animals can endure in the causes of research and meat production. Singer also argued that most such research is unnecessary, and that we can feed more people, and feed them better, on a vegetarian diet. However, his overall point is that even if carnivorous diets and research causing pain to animals were of real benefit to humans, such activities would be justified only if using humans with equivalent overall result would be justified.

A great many readers of the book found the account of the pain inflicted on animals disquieting, agreed that such actions were morally improper, and concluded that the plight of animals ought to be alleviated. This is by no means the same as concluding that the interests of animals have the same moral significance as the equal or equivalent interests of humans, however, and Singer's own conclusions generated a great deal of resistance. Much of the resistance to the idea of extending the principle of equal moral consideration to include animals has taken the form of arguments that, as we noted, have historically been deployed against extending the principle of equal moral consideration to all humans. Indeed, Singer's title, *Animal Liberation*, was chosen because of the parallel he drew between racism and sexism, and what has come to be called *speciesism*. Just as we have had to expand the sphere of moral concern to include blacks and women, we must now expand it to include animals. For all such purposes, liberation movements have proved useful.

Some of Singer's less perceptive critics have spoken as if this notion of liberation indicated that he advocated giving full civil rights to animals. The ridiculous idea of giving dogs the vote and of extending equal employment opportunities to pigs was taken by some to be a *reductio ad absurdum* of Singer's ideas. Of course Singer advocated no such thing, nor are such programs required for the consistent application of his principles. Animals cannot vote or enter into employment contracts, and it is therefore not within their interests to do such things. Humans have interests that animals do not, and animals evidently have interests that humans do not. To treat an animal morally is to respect that animal's interests as they actually are, not to engage in some silly game pretending that the animal is human, that it can be treated like a human, or that it has the same interests humans do. That would be not only to overestimate the animal, but to underestimate it as well, failing to recognize its own particular character and interests.

It is well worth remembering that we humans differ enormously among ourselves. To treat people on an equal moral footing is not to presuppose that they are equally intelligent, capable, sentient, or pleasant to be around, or that they have the same interests. The point is that we are, as best we can, to treat the equivalent interests of different people on the same footing. It is not easy to determine how to do this, since different people have different interests, with differing priorities among their own interests. Simply having the same set of rules and procedures for everyone is not necessarily to affect everyone equally. The laws that prohibit rich and poor alike from sleeping under bridges or urinating in public streets are more of a hindrance for those without dwellings. While it is difficult to know how to give equitable consideration to the differing interests of very different people, it is even more difficult to know how to do this in the case of nonhumans. Still, insofar as what we do has effects on other beings, human or nonhuman, Singer believes that it is our duty to consider the interests of all affected beings as equitably as possible.[1]

1   In the early days of the civil rights movement it was frequently urged that blacks were just like whites, except for trivial differences largely concerned with pigmentation. Similarly, women's liberation movements proclaimed that women were just like men, except for differences arbitrarily imposed by role learning, and trivial differences of a physiological nature. As these movements approached their maturity, the

Singer concentrated his discussion on one basic interest that we evidently do share with all of the higher animals: the interest we all have in avoiding unnecessary pain. This is not the only interest animals have, and in *Practical Ethics* (and in several articles) Singer gives a wider discussion of the interests of animals. But avoiding unnecessary pain is in the interests of any being that can feel pain. That is a good place to start. Certainly it provides a point of focus for asking why, morally, we ought to care about the interests of animals. It will also lead us further into the question of the nature of interests. Why should pain in a nonhuman be as morally significant as pain in a human? Indeed, why should pain in a nonhuman be morally significant at all? Singer's basic argument can be summarized quite simply:

Pain is bad.
That pain happens to an animal is irrelevant to its badness.
<u>We ought to minimize the occurrence of badness in the world.</u>
Therefore, we ought to avoid causing unnecessary pain to animals
(as we ought to avoid causing unnecessary pain to humans).

It is of course the second premise that is the focus of the greatest controversy. Before we get into that debate, though, let us review the overall argument.

From the time of Epicurus to the modern age, hedonists have told us that pleasure and pain are of intrinsic moral value, positive or negative. One need not be a hedonist, however, to accept the point that, in the case of humans at least, pleasure and pain do in some way count morally. Per-

idea became more frequently expressed that similarities between blacks and whites or between men and women were morally irrelevant: blacks and women were not obliged to be like anyone else in order to have full moral standing. People have a perfect right to be themselves. Concerning animals, it may be a useful tactic to point out similarities between animals and humans – though one runs the risk of lapsing into a sentimentality that thinks of animals as little furry people – but I certainly hope we can get well beyond that stage. To treat an animal morally is to respect it for what it is in its own right and to respect the interests it does have, not to pretend that the animal is like us or that its interests are like ours.

haps they are not the only things that count morally, but certainly they do count in some way. How they are to be counted is controversial. On the one hand, utilitarians maintain that, whatever makes things good or bad, we ought to act in such a way as to maximize the amount of goodness and to minimize the amount of badness. Deontological ethicists on the other hand maintain that certain rights, rules, or principles take precedence over utility. (They may, for instance, hold that equity of distribution takes precedence to some degree over maximization of utility, or they may hold that some rights must be respected regardless of utility.) Whether one takes a utilitarian or a deontological line, though, pleasure and pain in some way have to figure in. Inflicting pain must be wrong under some circumstances, and pleasure must sometimes count as a benefit. Granted, there is still the question of whether (and how much) they are to count in the case of animals. First, though, a quick sketch of how utilitarianism enters into Singer's theory is in order.

Historically, hedonists and utilitarians – particularly those who are both – have been the most receptive to the idea that pleasure and pain retain their moral significance (even) when it comes to animals. If pleasure is intrinsically good, and pain intrinsically bad, then they are intrinsically so whatever being experiences them – or so it would seem. This line was taken by Jeremy Bentham, who founded modern hedonistic utilitarianism (in 1789). As indicated in the passage quoted at the start of this chapter, he took the capacity for suffering as the moral dividing line separating morally considerable beings from other beings. Pleasure is pleasure and pain is pain, other things being of only instrumental importance. Except insofar as they have to do with pleasure and pain, the various characteristics of a being are morally irrelevant. Rationality, for instance, is of moral importance only insofar as it might affect one's balance of pleasure over pain. As a utilitarian, Bentham advocated that one should act in such a way as in the long run to maximize the overall balance of pleasure – wherever found by whatever being. Singer, a twentieth-century utilitarian, follows roughly this line, though the intrinsic good he wishes to maximize is the satisfaction of (prudent) preferences. The preferences not just of humans but of any beings that can have preferences are to be taken into account. Singer's preference utilitarianism, calling for the satisfaction of all (prudent) preferences, is somewhat broader than Bentham's hedonistic utilitarianism, but incorporates it because all sentient creatures would normally prefer pleasure to pain (in the aggregate).

I shall subsequently discuss preference utilitarianism in greater detail – and argue that it is inadequate. At the moment, though, I would point out that utilitarianism in whatever form is not critical to the argument. The utilitarian principle of maximizing the balance of good over bad certainly lends itself to treating animals as objects of moral concern – a point well worth noting – but utilitarianism is not necessarily presupposed in recognizing the moral standing of animals. Granting that pain is bad for a being, one can recognize the moral significance of pain in humans and animals without being a utilitarian. So long as our ethics are concerned with what we do to others, pain will have some moral significance for us. As it happens, many of those who argue for the moral standing of animals – Tom Regan, for instance – are not utilitarians. We should bear in mind, then, that the argument Singer presents for the moral considerability of animals is not closely and necessarily tied to his utilitarianism. The principle of equal consideration would not demand that we treat interests only on a utilitarian basis. Let us set aside questions about utilitarianism for the time being, and concentrate on the principle of equal consideration and the issue of whether, specifically, the interest of nonhumans in avoiding pain merits consideration alongside the like interests of humans.

Once we accept the point that pleasure and pain are morally significant in the case of humans, the onus is on us to provide some morally adequate justification if we are to exclude from equal consideration any other being that can feel pain. We cannot claim with Descartes that animals do not feel pain. Every indication is that they do. If we exclude animals on the grounds that they are not human, that is as arbitrary as racism or sexism unless we can show that the differences between humans and animals are morally relevant. Humans differ from most animals in having opposable thumbs and naked skins, but these hardly seem like morally significant differences. What could be morally significant? Perhaps the immortal soul that humans are often said to possess? Souls certainly seem morally significant, but this line requires us to take it on faith that humans have souls. It also requires us to take on faith that animals do *not* have souls. Many religions have found it easy to believe that animals can have souls. The bald assumption that only humans have souls itself seems to be an example of speciesism. Even if we accept both of these points on faith, the conclusion still does not follow. That a being lacks a soul seems like a very poor reason for holding its suffering to be morally indifferent. Indeed, if the animal has no prospect of eternity as compensation for current suffering, that is all the more reason for being considerate of it in the here and now.[2]

Rationality, in one form or another, appears to be the currently most popular candidate for being a morally significant difference between humans and animals. Setting borderline cases aside for the moment, humans do seem to be more rational than animals – whatever that is worth. The suggestion now is that pleasure-in-a-rational-being and pain-in-a-rational-being, rather than just pleasure and pain per se, are morally relevant. This seems more than a little

2 It is reported of Cardinal Bellarmine that he permitted vermin to dine upon him unmolested, saying "We shall have heaven to reward us for our sufferings but these poor creatures have nothing but the enjoyment of this present life." This is the same Cardinal Bellarmine who was instrumental in creating difficulties for Galileo and also, more fatally, for Giordano Bruno. There is no doubt some trite point to be made here about how people may be more liberal in some areas than in others. With thanks to Peter Singer, I quote from W. E. H. Lecky's *History of European Morals: From Augustus to Charlemagne*, 2:172n. Lecky in turn cites "(Bayle. *Dict. Philos.*, art. Bellarmine)."

odd to start with. If one's rationality does not make a difference to how pain feels, why should it make a moral difference? Is causing pain to a Nobel Prize winner worse, everything else being equal, than causing pain to an average or dull person? Do intelligent people have more moral rights than stupid people? Or is there some all-or-nothing cut-off point in rationality above which pleasure or pain for a being is morally significant and below which it is not significant? The first problem here is to draw the line in such a way that it is not morally arbitrary. Opinions may differ on this. Whatever line we take, Singer confronts us with the question of whether we would morally approve of doing painful research on eating, or otherwise using, a brain-damaged human infant. If not, on what grounds can we morally approve doing so to an animal of equivalent or higher intellectual standard? To be sure, the infant is a member of our own species, but if we would not be justified in giving preference to a member of our own *race*, how can we be justified in giving preference on the grounds of species comembership? Just to posit that species comembership, unlike racial comembership, constitutes adequate grounds for such discrimination is to beg the moral question. Alternatively, we might exempt neither the damaged infant nor the animal from such treatment. For instance, if we are utilitarians, we might possibly condone using either being for such purposes if we were convinced that the overall beneficial consequences would outweigh the adverse ones. For other reasons, we might decide to exempt both beings. There are various conclusions to which a utilitarian or a nonutilitarian might come. Whichever way we go, though, one thing we cannot justify is trying to have it both ways. If rationality is what makes the basic moral difference, then we cannot maintain that the brain-damaged infant ought to be exempt from utilization just because it is human while at the same time allowing that the animal can be used if utility warrants.

It is not good enough to try to take a halfway position, recognizing that pleasure/pain is morally significant in the case of animals while yet claiming that their interests, but not those of the brain-damaged infant, can sometimes be overriden. Giving animals *some* consideration is better than giving them none at all, but trying to take such a halfway position is still to beg a moral question. *Any* degree of discrimination in the way we treat beings requires some morally adequate justification. Singer concludes that there is no way that is even remotely justifiable, to discriminate in favor of the brain-damaged human infant over the animal of equal intellectual level.

There may be other interests as well to be considered. Perhaps the parents of the brain-damaged infant would be themselves pained by their child being used for painful research, and other humans might be distressed by such an activity. Their distress is a factor to be considered, even if it stems from pure prejudice. It is very possible that fewer other beings would suffer if the animal were utilized, since it might well be that fewer other beings would know or care. Yet the animal may have a mate or young that would be distressed by the loss. Again, the infant, being biologically human, might make a much more useful subject for medical research, which would give us that much more of an interest in utilizing it. Perhaps the brain-damaged infant's parents would be delighted to rid themselves of a great burden – particularly if they could do so in such a good cause. Whatever the case might be, we have to take all relevant interests into account. What we ought not to do is to discount or put a premium on particular interests merely because of the species membership of the one who has the interest.

What are we to conclude? As a utilitarian, Singer is committed to accept the theoretical possibility that the balance of utility might be such as to justify eating or doing research on either the damaged infant or the animal. He does not advocate that we should (or should not) in fact eat or do painful research on brain-damaged human infants, but does maintain that we ought to give equal consideration to the equivalent interests of *all* beings. Both infant and animal merit our moral concern. This does not require us to treat the animal and the damaged infant the same way we treat other beings, nor does it even require that we treat them like each other. They must have different sets of interests. As Singer puts it (1976–7, 22): "The basic principle of equality does not require equal or identical *treatment*; it requires equal *consideration*. Equal consideration for different beings may lead to different treatment and different rights." The conclusion Singer invites us to draw is that the interests of the animal are as morally significant as the like interests of the brain-damaged infant, and that the interests of the latter are as morally significant as the like interests of a normal human. The infant's interest in not feeling pain is to have the same weight as my similar interest – even though the infant may lack some of my intellectual interests and may have other interests (such as an interest in having a guardian) that I do not have. The similar interest of an animal is to have similar weight, even though they have yet other interests. All of these interests must be taken into consideration.

Even if we accept the point that there are no morally significant grounds for discriminating between the brain-damaged human infant and the animal on the same intellectual level, we need not accept Singer's suggested conclusion. We might take a hard line and maintain that both the damaged infant and the animal lack morally significant interests because they lack a minimum degree of intellectual capacity. Recall that this idea was dismissed earlier on the grounds that pain is not any more or any less painful according to one's intellectual capacity, and that it seems wrong that one's moral standing should be a function of one's IQ. It has been argued that such dismissals are too quick. Perhaps the morally important dividing line is that between those beings that think cognitively and those that do not – a line putatively separating superior beings from those that cannot understand abstract ideas, conceive of propositions, or distinguish truth and falsity. This line does not follow the boundaries of the human race. It does not include the brain-damaged human infant in the class of beings with moral standing, while Washoe and possibly many other beings might well be included within the class of beings with moral standing. These means of division are not necessarily speciesist, although there would be speciesist motivation in taking this position if its primary attraction was that it followed our species boundary as closely as possible. In point of fact, many people have proposed reasons for taking such a line. I maintain that these reasons are not ultimately sustainable, but they are certainly worthy of our more thorough consideration.

From here there are a number of different things I want to do, all of which center, in one way or another, on interests and their moral significance. The rest of this chapter is devoted to considering claims that rationality is a necessary condition for moral considerability. Rationality, taken as the ability to think cognitively, separates us from at least most other animals, and a number of different reasons have been offered for taking this ability as a morally adequate dividing line separating those who have (full) moral status from those that do not. Investigating these various interrelated rationales in more detail may help us better to understand what is involved – and what is *not* involved – in moral considerability. I shall conclude that rationality is not a necessary condition for being morally considerable. The subsequent chapter further investigates the nature and moral significance of interests. On that basis, I proceed into some issues of special concern to me: those of whether nonsentient beings, and entities that are not individual organisms, have morally significant interests.

THE MORAL COMMUNITY – SELF-APPOINTED

One reason for taking cognitive capacity as the critical factor is that only beings that can think cognitively can take part in an arrangement according to which the individual has various rights and responsibilities relative to the other members of the moral community. According to the contractarian theory of ethics, right and wrong – indeed, all of morality – come about as the result of mutual agreement, tacit or explicit. Even stupid people (above a very minimal level) can understand the basic rules and thus can be members of the moral community, being members just as much as brilliant people. Noncognitive beings, however, are incapable of taking part in the reciprocal arrangement. Such beings are of moral concern only to the extent that members of the contracting group might choose to be concerned with them. Animals, brain-damaged humans, normal but prerational infants, and very senile adults would all be excluded from the group of beings with direct moral standing. This is not to say that they would be morally defenseless. Any or all such beings might be of concern to members in good standing of the contracting group. We might, for instance, wish to protect the senile out of pity, or for our own long-range self-protection. For sentimental or practical reasons, we might wish to protect infants (at least our own). Nonmembers of the contracting group might be given various levels of protection as, so to speak, honorary members in the moral club. This would be entirely at the discretion of the full members. Such a scheme easily accounts for the limited and rather selective moral status commonly granted to animals, and the less than full status that infants sometimes seem to be accorded. That dogs are granted a higher moral status than pigs would presumably be partly because dogs enter into a limited sort of reciprocal arrangement with us, and partly just because those who are full members of the moral club choose to grant dogs a higher status.

If the contractarian theory of ethics is correct, then there is little sense in saying that animals – or the land, or anyone or anything else – ought or ought not to be included in the moral sphere. On that account, *ought* is just a discretionary matter for those who are already members of the moral community. I cannot accept a contractarian theory of ethics, as it seems to me to reduce morality to the level of a cynical political trade-off. That, of course, is a reaction, not an argument. There are other objections. One is that the contractarian theory itself seems to presuppose at least one moral imperative that does not arise from contract: namely, the obligation to keep contract. (It cannot just be that Item One of the contract is "We all agree to abide by the contract," as there must be something to make Item One binding.) If we take the line that we are to keep the contract not because we ought to but because it is convenient for us to do so, this seems to me to omit the moral element entirely. It also seems to condone the strategic double-cross, when double-crossing can be done profitably and with sufficient discretion to avoid being bad for business. No convenience, no obligation. For our purposes, a more important line of objection concerns those beings that are left out of account. Because other beings count only insofar as they are of concern to those who are actually reciprocating members of the moral community, not only are animals and brain-damage cases left out, but normal human infants are also excluded. (Of course, the child is a potential member of the moral community, but that means merely that the child potentially has standing – whether we elect to give it actual standing being another matter.) To be sure, many people would care about the child, but on the contractarian theory we cannot argue that those who do not care ought to care. It seems odd to many of us that the child should have no moral standing in its own right.

Let us push the contractarian theory further. Instead of taking the moral community to be composed of every person who is capable of comprehending the rules, let us be somewhat more selective. The moral club will now consist of people selected on the basis of race, religion, nationality, language group, social or economic group, sex, sexual preference, age, political affiliation, or you name it. Others are to be of no direct moral concern – though perhaps they are of some limited concern to those who are members of the moral community. (It might be considered poor form to beat one's slaves too savagely.) Clearly, such a scheme just will not do. But *why* not? On the contractarian theory we cannot brand an arrangement of this sort as immoral, since what is immoral, and what is not, are defined by the contracting group. We might try to persuade insiders to adopt different rules and, at most, we could try to convince them that for some reason it would be preferable to admit outsiders into the moral community. We might appeal to sentimental or practical considerations, but we cannot appeal to morality without tacitly admitting that morality has some foundation other than the social contract of the group.

It seems much too arbitrary that people should be denied moral standing because of skin color or native language, or because of some feature they have or lack that seems to be of equal moral irrelevance. People who might be excluded can still feel pain, they can benefit and suffer, they are capable of decent behavior, and they could, if permitted, take part as reciprocating members of a moral community. In the old days, of course, the exclusion of Outsiders was justified by tales that suggested that they were inherently incapable of anything approaching acceptable behavior. Now we know better. Denying moral consideration to other people on arbitrary and irrational grounds seems quite disgusting to just about all of us. Most of us (belong to moral groups that) despise the idea of denying moral status to people merely because they are different. As a moral stance, this goes beyond the contractarian theory. After all, according to the contractarian theory, the group defines what is nonarbitrary and relevant. Ultimately, we go beyond argumentation. If some group of people wants to make tearing wings off butterflies – or killing foreigners – the center of its moral order, there is no way we can argue with these people so long as they are consistent in the values they adopt.[3] Indeed, as we noted previously, there is no way to argue with one who denies morality and values altogether. As stated then, it is to be taken for granted in this book that there is a moral sphere – of nonzero radius – and that there are moral con-

---

3 Douglas Adams writes (1982, 99) of the people of the planet Krikkit who believe in "peace, justice, morality, culture, sport, family life and the obliteration of all other life forms." Strange, but not inconceivable.

straints on our actions. Those who do not share this assumption need not have read this far.

I invite you now to share with me a further assumption: There is such a thing as a morality that is not generated merely by group agreement. Instead, moral communities act – recognize it or not – against a moral background. To be sure, we may have special obligations to those who are close to us, and different groups may properly decide on different procedures, but there are limits on what groups may enact and we do have moral obligations to others independently of what groups dictate. Because no one may arbitrarily be excluded from the moral sphere, I take it that the moral sphere includes all who can meaningfully be included within it, with equal consideration to be given to equivalent interests. Those who can be members of the moral community are to be full members, with differences in the treatment extended them to be due solely to differences in their interests and capabilities, or to differences in their objectively relevant circumstances. We may not discriminate on arbitrary grounds. To be sure, sometimes grounds for discrimination are not morally arbitrary. We may debar convicted criminals from voting and prevent ignoramuses from performing brain surgery. Yet we may not injure them capriciously.

The assumption I am now inviting you to make does not *logically* follow from the assumption that there is such a thing as morality. As we noted, it is not logically impossible for there to be a moral community selected in some way, with outsiders being granted limited or no moral standing. This is so, even though it does seem counterintuitive that we should be morally entitled to discriminate against people for seemingly arbitrary or selfish reasons. That morality is not a matter of in-group legislation is an additional assumption. For now, I am only asking you to make this additional assumption in the case of humans. By accepting this assumption in the case of humans we implicitly agree that the contractarian theory is incorrect, that the edict of some in-group is not sufficient to define who is to have moral standing. In that case we can hardly rely on that rather unattractive theory as a plausible excuse for ruling animals out of moral consideration. Such discrimination requires better justification if it is to be justified at all.

THE MORAL COMMUNITY — THE REALM OF REASON

Whereas the contractarian theory is implausible, and rather unsavory in its aspect of selfish mutual back scratching, Kantian ethics offers a much more attractive means of drawing the moral boundary so as to separate those beings that do have cognitive capability from those that do not. Instead of denying moral status to noncognitive beings on the grounds that they cannot (and therefore do not) take part in some contractarian alliance, Kantian ethics maintains that noncognitive beings lack moral status because they cannot understand moral principles and therefore cannot act from moral principle. Those beings with moral status, members of what Immanuel Kant called the Kingdom of Ends, are those beings who live according to the principles of reason. For Kant, the rational sphere is the moral sphere. Let us see whether his attempt to draw the moral boundary along these lines is morally adequate.

Kant was a true representative of the Enlightenment era in that he had a very high regard for the power of reason to improve the human condition, and in that he was a firm believer in what was then known as the brotherhood of man. Certainly he believed that discriminatory moral rules and differential moral status within the moral sphere were contrary to reason. He held not only that morality must be compatible with reason but that it can be derived from it. For him as for the Enlightenment in general, that which is rational is that which follows necessary universal principles. A rational ethic, then, is an ethic that follows necessary universal principles, and we are to follow only such principles. Telling the truth, for instance, can be taken as a necessary universal principle of behavior. Telling lies as a universal principle, however, is an incoherent notion, since ultimately there would be no communication, and hence no lies. For Kant, the morally important thing about an act is not what it accomplishes but the motive from which it is done. The motive must be one of acting from moral principle. There would be no moral virtue in saving the life of another person, for instance, if doing so were just a matter of a desire for fame or monetary reward, or if saving the life were merely the accidental by-product of other pursuits. One would be acting morally only if one were trying to do the right thing because it was the right thing. One would then be acting morally, regardless of whether one succeeded in actually achieving the desired result. Placing the emphasis on motivation seems quite proper to me. What I think is questionable is Kant's claim that acting morally requires acting from moral *principle* and thus that only cognitive/rational beings can act morally, and also his claim that only beings that are capable of acting on moral principle are beings whose interests have moral standing. These are independent points, and I shall argue against both.[4]

REASON AND MORAL AGENCY

Intuitively, there is a *prima facie* case that some of the higher animals are capable of acting morally. One can point to instances in animal behavior of concern, kindness, loyalty, and even a more or less rudimentary sense of justice. Dogs certainly seem to be able to develop a conscience and a sense of duty. According to Kantian ethical theory we must deny that the animal acted morally or in:morally, as the animal did not act from principle per se. Similarly, if a human were to save the life of another human, being moved to do so merely by compassion, this act would be morally neutral. On the Kantian scheme, the *only* action that is morally right is acting in accordance with a proper moral principle *because* it is a proper moral principle. Just doing what the principle

4 Much of what follows is adapted from my discussion in "Can Animals Be Moral Agents?" References to Kant are primarily concerned with his *Fundamental Principles of the Metaphysic of Morals*.

calls for is not good enough, and neither is doing so merely because one happens to want to. This scheme seems much too hard-nosed. I shall argue that Kant has overlooked some important factors here, and that some animals sometimes do act morally.

One important thing to be noted is that there must be more to morality than just acting on principle. For one thing, not all principles are worth acting on. Hitler was a man of principle, and so was Khomeini. One wishes they had not acted from principle. Kantians, of course, claim that evil or misguided people act only from principles that cannot be adopted as necessary and universal. It suffices to point out that some principles can be adopted as necessary and universal, yet have no moral content at all or even have negative moral content. Unlike the principle that we should universally tell lies, we can adopt as necessary and universal the principle that all tea drinkers should use lemon when available. We could, but it seems morally vacuous. Worse, we can contrive universalizable principles that seem quite immoral – that all people are to be tortured to death at age forty-five, for instance. The moral value of acting on principle is suspended in mid-air unless there is some moral value to give one's principle moral content. Otherwise, why should, say, being kind as a matter of principle be better than drinking tea as a matter of principle? Hume criticized this style of ethics prior to Kant in *A Treatise of Human Nature* (3.2.1) and pointed out that "To suppose that the mere regard to the virtue of the action, may be the first motive . . . is to reason in a circle. . . . An action must be virtuous before we can have regard to its virtue." There must be more to morality than merely acting from principle: there must be some additional factor that makes the principle *moral*.

Seemingly, this additional factor or moral content would likely have something to do with the effects of one's actions on other beings (with moral status). Kant eventually went beyond the simple appeal to universal principles, coming to a conception that was much richer: We ought to treat all people as ends-in-themselves and never only as means to

62

our own ends. All people have moral status on a par with oneself and are to be treated accordingly. We are not just to *use* them. Here we have a principle that is universal and appears to have significant moral content, being at least roughly equivalent to the Golden Rule. But what contributes the additional moral content? Why should we not treat other persons only as means? And why are we not obliged to animals as ends-in-themselves? Kant appeals to reason, or the value of reason, to support his scheme of ethics. Rationality, in the form of autonomous reason, is that which gives value to moral principle. Moreover, this rationality, which he more or less identified with the capacity to act in accordance with moral principle, is taken both as qualifying us as moral agents, and as qualifying us as objects of moral concern. He seems to suggest that his results are consequences of reason, though he does not actually spell this out. Underneath lies an insufficiently articulated presupposition of the moral value of reason. Kant, then, depended on reason to fulfill many and varied roles in this scheme. Reason is supposed to validate his moral principles, to make us (rational beings) moral agents, and to make us objects of moral concern because we can/do follow rational moral principle. This is asking quite a lot of reason. The point I intend to make now is that there is more to *moral* principle than Kant recognized, and that acting in accordance with the other factor(s) can by itself qualify a noncognitive being as a moral agent. Then I shall go on to the separable question of what qualifies a being as an object of moral concern.

Moral imperatives are not logically necessary. They are not tautologies, nor are they even conclusions unless we have at least one suitable statement of values as a premise. What makes a valid moral principle valid is not *that* it commands or *how* it commands, but *what* it commands. In adopting a moral principle, we are making a moral judgment that cannot be distilled from pure reason. Does valuing, even so, presuppose rationality? If not, then given that a being does value correctly, is rationality in any way a necessary condition for moral agency? I shall argue that correct valuing does not presuppose rationality, and that rationality is not a necessary condition for moral agency.

For our action to be morally right, we must do it for the right reason – valuing the right value. Of course any right action is formulable in terms of some moral principle commanding it. Kant maintained that what we must value is acting-in-accordance-with-a-proper-moral-principle-because-it-is-a-proper-moral-principle. Otherwise we would be acting for a nonmoral reason. But suppose I just act from valuing whatever factor gives the principle moral content. Why must I value, or even be aware of, the principle itself as well as whatever gives it content? For example, suppose I feel compassionate toward someone and act accordingly. I value the compassionate act, or place a negative value on the other's suffering. I do not act from a desire for reward, or from some other extraneous motivation. Kant evidently falls prey here to the fallacy of black-and-white thinking. Because we must not act from bad or neutral motivation, we must, he concludes, act from devotion to principle itself. He by-passes the possibility that one might act directly from regard for whatever factor gives the principle moral content. (Indeed, he had to bypass it since he was not aware that there was such a factor.) It seems at least plausible that one might directly respond to that factor. It might even be that animals sometimes respond to whatever gives content to a moral principle, without being aware of the principle.

Experiments have shown that many rhesus monkeys tend to avoid giving electrical shocks to other monkeys in circumstances that have been contrived in such a way that their obtaining food causes shock to other monkeys.[5] Some mon-

5 James Rachels discusses the case in his "Do Animals Have a Right to Liberty?" in Regan and Singer (1976). The experiments are described by the experimenters, Stanley Wechkin, Jules H. Masserman, and William Terris, Jr. (1964). They give the following abstract: "This experiment confirms and extends an earlier finding that a hungry rhesus monkey (O) will avoid securing food if this subjects another monkey (SA) to electric shock. In the present series this "sacrificial" behavior was manifested in 6 out of 10 animals independently of the relative position of the two animals in the dominance hierarchy. It was also

keys will go hungry for a considerable length of time rather than shock, or run the risk of shocking, their fellow monkeys. Interestingly from a "do unto others" point of view, monkeys that have previously been at the receiving end of the shocks are particularly reluctant to cause shocks to other monkeys. Seemingly, a monkey who is reluctant to cause pain to its fellow monkey is acting in accordance with something like the Golden Rule or the Kantian principle of treating others as ends-in-themselves. The monkey certainly seems to be motivated by morally commendable compassionate inclinations and to be acting as a moral agent. Not being a language user, however, the monkey cannot *state* the moral principle according to which it was evidently acting. The Kantian claim is that the monkey therefore has no conception of right or wrong, and no reasoned conviction that it is acting rightly. Having no language, it cannot be rational, and hence cannot be a moral agent. It merely acts from a morally neutral aversion to its fellow monkey having to suffer. The monkey, could it find the words, might well lament with Schiller's thoughts in *Die Philosophia:*

> Gladly I serve my friends,
>> but alas I do it with pleasure,
> hence I am plagued with doubt
>> that I am not a virtuous person.

To be sure, critical thinking about what we do, based on some conception of right and wrong, can be an extremely useful aid to moral agency. If we do not think about what we do, even the most benevolent impulse can go astray. Still,

found that while prior shock of the O resulted in inhibition of responding following the introduction of shock to the SA, this variable was not correlated with the final manifestation of a sacrificial pattern." Relative position in the dominance hierarchy, sexual differences, noise from the SA monkey, and acquired aversion to the experimental apparatus itself were all experimentally ruled out as influencing factors. The familiarity of the monkeys with one another was a significant factor, O monkeys being less willing to shock a former cage mate. The stronger than normal unwillingness to cause shock found among previously shocked O monkeys did tend over a period of time to erode toward more normal levels of unwillingness to cause shock.

reason is not enough to make one a moral agent. (Some psychotics are highly rational, yet accept few if any values as values.) To act morally, one must, at some point, be aware of and act with regard to some morally sufficient differentiating factor. Not only is this a necessary condition for being a moral agent but, I maintain, it is sufficient. Consider: Why is it that rational, language-using, concept-forming people accept a moral principle – for instance, the Golden Rule? As we noted, even if it were necessary that moral rules be universalizable, we would still need to recognize which universal rules had moral content. One accepts the Golden Rule as a guide to action because the acts it endorses or condemns appear to be good or bad. At least in the first instance, we do not agree to applications on the basis of the rule, but accept the rule on the basis that the sort of application it commands or forbids seems to be, directly, good or bad. To be sure, we very often make moral applications on the basis of rules, and accept rules on the basis of other rules, but sooner or later, rules are grounded on their applications. Of course, the Golden Rule, in its Christian, Kantian, or other formulations, goes beyond rules of the do so-and-so variety in that it provides a means for testing directly whether a proposed act is appropriate. We are, so to speak, to put ourselves in the other's place. Still, the point remains that we accept such a test, rather than some other test, because it gives good results. Tests or principles must have some grounds for being accepted. We can no more spin ethics out of *a priori* reason than we can physics. At least some acts have to be right before we can sensibly ask which principles are right.

Let us go back to the point about the monkey not being a moral agent because it does not intend to do the right thing. There is an ambiguity in this notion of intending to do the right thing. It can mean either

(a) intending to do whatever act is right (based on a concept of rightness, with the intention of doing the right thing because it is in accordance with that concept); or

66

(b) intending to do that particular act which, as it so happens, is the right act.

As Kantians point out, one can do (b) from a wrong motive. For that reason they have maintained that moral agency requires doing (a). Certainly doing (a) is sufficient for being a moral agent. Still, one might do (b) from a *right* motive – indeed, by the preceding argument, being able to do that is necessary for being able to do (a). We can do (b), motivated by an awareness of the factor that makes the right act right. We can do this even if, like the monkey, we cannot state what the critical factor is, and even if we have no abstract conception of right and wrong.[6] From this point of view, the monkey acted rightly from the right motivation, and could be said to be a moral agent.

Another way of making the logical point may be useful. Note that there is a related ambiguity in the notion of intending to do the right thing *because* it is the right thing. This can mean (a), or can mean certain things that come under the (b) heading. One might do (b) for any number of different reasons, but we might distinguish cases of what I shall list as (b'), which is doing (b) in response to whatever factors make the act in question morally indicated. One may do (b') from nonmoral or even immoral motivation, as when one wishes to be thought virtuous – perhaps even to ingratiate oneself with an intended victim. Or maybe it is just that the sound of screaming disturbs one's relaxation. We can call those cases of (b_1'), doing (b) from a nonmoral motivation in response to the morally relevant factors. Again, there is (b_2'), doing (b) from a moral motivation in response to the morally relevant factors – as when we put a negative value on the suffering of others. Intending to do the right thing *because* it is the right thing can be a case either of (a) or of (b_2'). One acts as a moral agent if one does either. In effect, I have argued that there cannot be cases of (a) unless there are cases of (b_2').

6 As Rawls pointed out (*A Theory of Justice*, 47), one may follow the rules of grammar without knowing what they are. Leibniz made a similar point.

Humans and possibly other rational beings exercise moral agency more extensively than less rational beings insofar as they can better understand the nature, ramifications, and consequences of a given act, and they can better understand their own motivation. Whether rationality is always an asset in acting morally is highly doubtful, but that it can be useful is beyond dispute. Rational beings can understand things that less rational beings cannot, and this clearly affects their moral agency. Those who know facts and understand issues have a greater opportunity, and greater responsibility, to do right than those who do not. So much is obvious. Moral responsibility and opportunity are greater among wise men than among dolts, and greater among (at least most) humans than among nonrational beings. Kantians and others who stress the moral importance of rationality argue that since only rational beings can *know* that what they are doing is right, only they, at their varying levels, can be moral agents. The compassionate rhesus monkey does not know that it is acting morally – and neither does a young child. (At most, they have what Plato called "right opinion" – if they even have opinions.) But *why* must a moral agent be aware that it is acting rightly? So long as it does act rightly, caring about the relevant differentiating factor that makes the right act right, why must the moral agent know *that* anything? Once we recognize that morality is not just a matter of acting on principle for the sake of principle, we have no persuasive reason to believe that a being must know that it is acting morally in order to act morally. Neither is there persuasive reason to believe that a nonrational being cannot be aware of, value, and act on those factors that give moral content to concepts and principles. It is only with such awareness and valuing that we can distinguish moral principles from morally neutral ones. Even with this awareness and valuing the monkey cannot derive a principle, but it can act morally on this awareness and valuing.

There remain possible grounds on which one might deny that nonrational beings can be moral agents. One might argue that morality does indeed require something *in addition to* rationality: it requires caring/valuing, and the willingness to be bound by rational moral considerations. It requires adhering, by *choice*, to a moral frame of reference. As Kant put it, we legislate ourselves into the Kingdom of Ends, which according to him we do by willing freely to abide by moral principle. No doubt Kant overestimated the importance of adhering to principle as such, but it is arguable that morality involves freely valuing whatever factor it is that makes a moral principle moral. Perhaps we legislate ourselves into the Kingdom of Ends by freely so valuing. If nonrational beings act only on instinct or in accordance with conditioning, we might exclude them on the grounds that they do not make free choices. Not having tasted of the fruit of the tree of the knowledge of good and evil, animals do not belong in the moral sphere after all, citizenship in the Kingdom of Ends being a matter only for higher beings capable of moral choice.

What are we to make of the argument based on the claim that animals follow behavior patterns that have been positively reinforced in the past, or which are based on instinct? Both humans and animals, we must not forget, can be conditioned to act in certain ways, and we can at least raise the question of instincts in humans. Animal instincts range from the very closely circumscribed instincts of the lower animals, such as those controlling the social behavior of ants, to the much more flexible instincts of higher animals, such as those prompting the hunting behavior of coyotes.[7] That humans also have instincts, presumably instincts that are very flexible in their manifestations, is not a possibility that can be ruled out of court. This raises some important questions: Can all of the seemingly morally significant behavior of animals be ascribed to instinct or conditioning? Can instinctive or con-

7 In her admirable, "The Concept of Beastliness," Mary Midgley explains the distinction between closed and open instincts, and illustrates the gradations between them. There and in a subsequent book (1979), she demonstrates that the difference between beastliness and humanity is not what it has often been thought to be, and that we have been guilty of some very confused thinking in that connection.

ditioned behavior be morally assessed? In the first place, the apparently moral behavior of animals cannot always just automatically be written off as instinctive or conditioned. In the case of the compassionate rhesus monkey, for instance, the tendency to refrain from causing pain cannot just be written off to instinct or conditioning, since the situation was (fortunately) unprecedented, unless we appeal to some general conditioned response or instinct toward compassion toward one's fellow monkey. Even so, the fact that monkeys previously at the receiving end of the shocks showed more of a tendency to refrain from causing them would suggest that an active sympathy, sharpened by painful memory, was at work. Can all of this be ascribed to conditioning or instinct? If so, we could make a parallel and equally strong case that human compassion springs from such sources. Most of us had some training in that direction, and it may be that as social beings we have some instinctive predisposition toward sympathy and toward learning certain socially useful behavior patterns. It is sheer dogmatism to attribute all behavior, animal or human, to instinct or conditioning, but it is even worse dogmatism to make such an attribution only in the case of animals. Even if we were to attribute all of the seemingly moral behavior of animals (and humans) to instinct or conditioning, though, there is still the question of whether such behavior can be morally assessed.

I answer in the affirmative. If a human being were, through conditioning (or instinct), to come to put a negative value on the suffering of others or to subscribe to the principle of avoiding it, and acted accordingly, I would certainly not refuse to recognize that person as a moral agent. What is important is whether one's heart is in the right place, not how it got there. Otherwise we would rule out most of the human race as moral agents. If the instinctive or conditioned behavior of humans does admit of moral assessment, we can as well make such a claim on behalf of animals.[8] This argument, then, provides no good reason

8 Someone, I forget who and where, has pointed out the oddity that the

for rejecting animals but not humans as moral agents. Because I accept that humans can be moral agents, I do not rule out animals.

Now for the negative side. It might be argued that a being can act morally only if it can act immorally. If an ignorant animal cannot be blamed for acting immorally, then how can we claim that it is prompted by morality when it does seem to act rightly? (I am indebted to Tom Regan, who raised this point in a letter.) Is it ever in order to morally *blame* an animal for the way it acts? I would certainly agree that one is reluctant to condemn an animal morally – setting aside those unsophisticates who think of animals in human terms. One cannot morally blame the wolf for taking the sheep, though it might be bad for the sheep and grazier. More relevant is the question of whether we should morally condemn the rhesus monkey who does not show inhibition about causing shock to other monkeys. I am not certain whether such an animal is to be morally condemned, although I am inclined to think it is not to be condemned.

In defense of the sometime moral agency of animals, it might conceivably be maintained that any good act that can be done by an animal is an act of supererogation. On this line one could sometimes praise but never blame an animal morally. Yet it seems improbable to me that a being that could ever recognize moral value would never have obligation. I think it more plausible that an animal that does not recognize the moral value of acting in a certain way is not *normally* to be morally blamed, insofar as there is normally no reasonable expectation on our part that it could recognize the moral value of acting that way. When there *is* good reason to think it could recognize the moral value of acting the right way, we could then hold the animal blameworthy. Establishing blameworthiness is logically much more difficult than establishing praiseworthiness. In either case we must estab-

---

well-ordered family life of wolves is often written off as "mere instinct," whereas a woman is given moral praise for acting in accordance with her "maternal instinct." Instead of taking credit from human mothers, perhaps we should give more credit to the wolves.

71

lish to a sufficient degree that the animal was aware of the relevant moral consideration, or that it could have been expected to be aware of it, but (as in the case of the rhesus monkey) the fact that the animal acts in accordance with the morally relevant consideration can be very strong evidence that it is aware of it (and acted for that reason). On the other hand, if the animal does not act in accordance with the morally relevant consideration, it may act either in spite of an awareness of it or in ignorance of it. If we cannot establish that it acted in spite of an awareness of the morally relevant consideration, we have not established that it is blameworthy. I believe that our reluctance to condemn animals is in some part a reflection of our reluctance to claim knowledge of animal awareness and motivation, as well as, in some part, a reflection of our belief that they are unable adequately to understand the situation. If a sufficient number of its conspecifies were to act in accordance with a morally relevant consideration, we might then very well come to the conclusion that an animal that did not act in accordance with the morally relevant consideration was indeed acting immorally. Unless it were retarded or had some other excuse, it would seem probable that it was acting contrary to a moral consideration that it could and ought to have recognized. The plausibility of the condemnatory conclusion would increase with the proportion of its conspecifies that did act in accordance with the morally relevant consideration. The logic of the matter seems to dictate that *before* we could morally condemn an animal, we would have to be able to morally praise a similar animal. Although I would be cautious, I think there might be circumstances under which I would blame an animal morally.

If moral principles have genuine standing in the real world, it can only be because of something about the real world that makes them moral, and animals can possibly be aware of and value those factors in the concrete. A theory according to which value judgments have moral force purely on conceptual grounds alone, and not because of the way things are, has, I submit, no claim to standing in the real world, and is binding on neither man nor beast. I conclude then that some animals can act as moral agents and that a monkey who is reluctant to cause pain to its fellow monkey is morally better than a monkey who does not care. Such an animal displays moral agency even if it cannot make the proper decision in all cases, and even if it cannot write up its successes in a manner acceptable to journals of moral philosophy. Like most humans, it would never do as a metaethicist, but it might be able to do the right thing on the basis of the morally relevant factors in a given situation. In general, a being acts as a moral agent when it respects the interests of (some) others as well as or, to some degree, in preference to its own.

Where are we? I have attempted to show that morality is not the exclusive domain of rational beings, that subrational animals *can* act morally, and sometimes do so. A single example suffices to establish that point. I make no claim that animals of any sort act morally (or immorally) any great proportion of the time. Animals most of the time just live their lives, acting amorally. So, most of the time, do humans. When I decide whether to eat one sort of cereal rather than another in the morning, or to walk to the university by a variant route, I am not normally making a moral decision. Animals act morally or immorally with even less frequency. Still, once we are receptive to the idea that animals are capable of moral agency, I think it is not difficult to locate numerous examples, particularly among the social animals.

Although some level of awareness of situation and probable consequences is clearly necessary in order to perform a morally significant act, this need not involve principled moral deliberation. Undoubtedly, the application of human levels of intelligence is often of very great instrumental value in moral agency – yet no amount of instrumental utility can add up to a moral prerequisite. (Not only is rationality not necessary for morality, but we all know the lamentable fact that it is also not sufficient. The world would no doubt be a better place if all villains were stupid.) Since rationality is not nec-

73

essary for moral agency, the moral sphere is not to be defined merely in terms of the reciprocal interaction of rational beings. If nonrational beings can even occasionally enter the moral sphere as moral agents, we cannot dismiss any of them as objects of moral concern merely on the grounds that morality is exclusively relevant to rational beings. However, Kant did dismiss them on just those grounds. He did not really distinguish between being a moral agent and being an object of moral concern, taking the Kingdom of Ends to be the community of rational beings/moral agents. Indeed, that a moral agent should be an object of moral concern seems so thoroughly in order as scarcely to be worth remarking. If a being acts morally toward others, it seems quite improper that its own interests should be disregarded by another moral agent. Still, it is quite another matter to ask whether a being need necessarily be a moral agent in order to merit our concern. Kant glossed over this point, because he largely identified rationality, moral agency, and being of intrinsic moral concern – all in the name of the value of reason, and supposedly as a consequence of reason. One becomes a member of the Kingdom of Ends by exercising that very faculty that makes one a moral agent. However, since it turns out that rationality is not the glue that holds the moral universe together after all, we can legitimately ask why moral agency or rationality is required in order for one to be of moral concern. We have already noted that the moral sphere cannot be merely the interacting community of those who find it convenient to interact. Now we see that the heart of morality is not respect for principle but respect for interests. How, then, can we refuse to recognize the moral significance of the interests of any being that has interests? It seems simple enough that we are obliged to give due respect to the interests of all beings that can benefit or suffer.[9]

9 As did Aquinas before him, though certainly not Descartes, Kant seemingly felt somewhat uneasy about leaving animals entirely out of account morally. As did Aquinas he resorted to the argument that although animals are not morally significant in their own right, we still ought not to be cruel to them, because that might lead us to be cruel

LANGUAGE AND INTERESTS

Unfortunately, the matter is not so simple as to be beyond the complication of ingenious but misdirected philosophy. Even if we agree that being a moral agent is not necessarily required for being an object of moral concern, and even if we agree that all interests, wherever found, morally require equitable consideration, we still have a long way to go. There remains one formidable argument against the moral status of animals. R. G. Frey argues that the principle of equal consideration of equivalent interests does not require us to consider the interests of animals, for the marvelously simple reason that animals do not have interests to be considered (1980). He maintains that the division between those beings that have interests (in a morally significant meaning of the term) and those that do not is the division between those beings that have a linguistic (and therefore cognitive) capacity

to humans. The practical conclusion is welcome, but it seems strange that being cruel to a dog is wrong because it might lead to bad habits, but is not wrong because of what it does to the dog. Moreover, we might well ask why kicking dogs but not dirt clods would lead one to be cruel to humans. Would it not be just because it hardened one to be indifferent to things that indeed are morally significant? If animals really did have no more moral importance than dirt clods, would not the best policy be simply to remind people that humans were different from animals and dirt clods, rather than to confuse the issue by advocating some particular treatment for animals?

In any case, there is no necessary correlation between cruelty to animals and cruelty to humans. In one of his short stories, O. Henry (William Sydney Porter 1910) tells of a Kentucky sheriff who was trying to extradite a fugitive on a charge of having murdered his wife. To confuse the sheriff, who was supplied with only an imperfect physical description of the murderer, the fugitive and a friend *both* claimed to be the wanted man. The sheriff, of course, could not run the risk of returning with the wrong man. Eventually, the resourceful lawman resorted to the expedient of giving a sharp kick to a friendly dog which frequented the company of the two friends. One of the two sprang to his feet protesting vociferously, and was promptly arrested. It turned out that the sheriff had indeed made the right choice. As he explained, "I'm a Kentuckian, and I've seen a great deal of both men and animals. And I never yet saw a man that was overfond of horses and dogs but what was cruel to women." The story reveals a number of different attitudes one might have about animals and people.

75

and those that do not. Beings lacking linguistic capacity lack interests. I shall go into his argument at some length because of the importance accorded his argument in the literature and, more generally, because of the importance accorded language. Whereas Kant told us that the moral sphere is defined by moral principle, which presupposes rationality/linguistic capacity, Frey tells us that having morally significant interests presupposes having linguistic capacity. We need a better conception of what it is to have an interest.

In outline, Frey's argument is as follows:

(1) All those and only those beings that have interests have a right to have their interests considered.
(2) Having an interest requires having desires and self-consciousness.
(3) Having desires and self-consciousness requires linguistic ability.
(4) <u>Animals lack linguistic ability.</u>

Therefore, animals lack self-consciousness, desires, interests, and moral standing.

Premises (2) and (3) are clearly the critical ones. Concerning (1), Frey remarks – correctly, I believe – that the rhetoric of rights is overused and often tends to confuse the issues. Such terminology, he observes, can be deleted from moral discussions without loss of meaning. In referring to rights, Frey adopts what he takes to be the usage of those whom he calls "animal rightists," though in fact only some of those to whom he is referring use the term "rights." Singer and others have denied that the concept is central to their arguments. Premise (1) can be rephrased so as to omit all mention of rights. The important issue concerns what is involved in having interests that require moral consideration. Against premise (4) we might cite the seemingly linguistic accomplishments of Washoe et al. Frey spends a few pages debating whether Washoe properly could be said to have linguistic ability, taking a rather negative point of view. There are, of course, various ways in which the boundary between those who do and those who

76

do not use language can be gerrymandered to suit our point of view. However, the most that could come out of debating this is that we might have a few more or a few less apes and cetaceans within the moral sphere – which would leave quite unaffected the moral status of the great mass of non-linguistic animals. Let us turn now to (2) and (3), which are the key points in Frey's argument.

Frey (1980, 78–9) follows Regan (1976) in distinguishing two senses in which a being might be said to have an interest in something. "B has an interest in X" can mean either that X is/would be conducive to the good or wellbeing of B, or that X is of interest to B (i.e., B wants or desires X). According to Frey, only interests of the latter sort are morally significant. He argues that if interests merely of the former sort were morally significant, we would then have the absurdity that such things as tractors, cave paintings, and plants would have morally significant interests. After all, lack of oil and prolonged exposure to rain can harm tractors, excessive carbon dioxide can harm prehistoric cave paintings, and plants need water, but their interests, he says, are not morally significant. Frey goes on to argue that only beings with linguistic ability can have interests in the second, morally relevant, sense. Before we go on to consider interests of that type, though, a few points about interests of the other sort need to be worked over. It is not at all obvious to me that tractors and cave paintings have a good or wellbeing that can be harmed or benefited. According to Frey, it is quite obvious that a tractor can be harmed (1980, 80–1):

> It must be emphasized, moreover, that it is these objects them-selves which are harmed, and that their owners . . . are harmed *only* in so far as and to the extent that the objects themselves undergo harm. . . . Surely a tractor is harmed by prolonged exposure to rain? And surely the harm the tractor's owner suffers comes through and is a function of the harm to the tractor itself?

I will certainly grant that excessive exposure to rain or in-sufficient motor oil can cause extensive changes to a tractor.

We customarily do say that such things harm tractors. Referring to it as "harm," however, and not just as "change," is to presuppose some values. Whose values, the tractor's, or the farmer's? What seems obvious to me is that while the change is to the tractor, the harm involved is to the good or wellbeing of the farmer. Suppose now that I plan to use the tractor as part of a rural tableau I am constructing, and which I intend as a work of art. To gain a more picturesque quality for the tractor, I try to see to it that it suffers as much exposure to the elements as possible. Each patch of rust I regard as an artistic triumph. Has it been damaged? One might say that I have damaged the tractor for artistic purposes. As a tractor it has been damaged, but as an *objet d'art* it has benefited from the exposure. To ask whether it has *really* been harmed or benefited is to ask whether it is really a tractor or really an *objet d'art*. Which it is is what we choose to regard it as. In itself, it is neither the one nor the other. Were such an object to appear as a highly improbable freak of nature on an uninhabited planet, it would merely be an object that was neither harmed nor benefited by its subsequent corrosion.

I believe that Frey is making a basic mistake in assuming that things always come in *kinds*, and that a thing's kind is a feature of the thing itself. He writes (1980, 80):

> anything, including tractors, can have a good, a well-being, I submit, if it is the sort of thing which can be good of its kind; and there are obviously good and bad tractors. . . . Just as John is good of his kind (i.e., human being) only if he is in health, so tractors are good of their kind only if they are well-oiled.

Certainly a thing can be harmed or benefited as something of a given kind – but who gives the kind? Whether, to continue our example, the thing is a tractor or an *objet d'art* is a function of our intentions and not a feature of the thing itself. The thing does not define itself as one or the other. However, I suggest that *some* things, particularly living things, do, in an important sense, define themselves. John is a human being and can be harmed or benefited as such, however he

78

might be regarded by others. This is not just a matter of how he regards himself. Any living being, whether or not self-conscious, has an identity, an internal integrity, which mere objects and artifacts lack. I shall use the term *self-identity* to indicate that what an entity is and what serves to maintain it is determined by its own nature. Now, if we cease to regard a tractor as a tractor, then it ceases to be so – though of course it remains a particular object with the make-up it happens to have. If it changes then it changes, but there is no harm that it suffers, no self-identity that it loses. A living thing, on the other hand, does have a self-identity and does have a wellbeing that can be harmed or benefited, no matter how we regard that being.

To be sure, it is quite possible for us to regard a living being as having a kind that is different from that of its self-identity. It is even possible for the being to be harmed under one description by what benefits it under another. Calves, considered as beef cattle and as an economic investment, might be improved by being castrated and branded. At some point they are improved by being slaughtered. Are they benefited by being castrated, branded, or killed? They are improved as an economic investment, and the stock owner is benefited, but these things are of no benefit to the calves in their own right. They are harmed in their own right. I am not claiming that something can be described only one way, used only one way, or be of only one kind. There is no incompatibility in saying that the calf is an economic asset *and* that it is a living being, and both of these things are undeniably true. I do claim that a thing can be harmed or benefited in its own right only if, as it were, it has an "own right" – only if it has a self-identity according to which it can be harmed or benefited. A tractor is not even a tractor in its own right, and therefore cannot have needs or be harmed or benefited as a tractor in its own right. Any harm or benefit to a tractor is harm or benefit according to a human point of view. Tractors in this way are quite different from calves and other living beings, which do have needs and can be harmed or benefited. In Kantian terms, a living being can be treated as being an end-in-itself as well as a means. Tractors and the like can only be treated as means, when they are treated at all. Unlike calves and trees, tractors and other nonliving things do not come in predetermined kinds. Their kinds are assigned to them by those who take an interest in them. In contrast, animals, trees, and all other living beings have optimal states that the life process of that thing functions to achieve or maintain. My point, though, is not just that living things come in kinds. *Kinds* are not ultimate moral categories. Rather, the point is that by having optimal states, living things inherently define what is in their interests. Tractors do not.

What conclusions are we to draw now in terms of Frey's argument? He argued that we cannot take interests-as-needs to be morally significant, on the grounds that this would involve us in the absurdity that such things as tractors and plants must then have morally significant interests. He then drew the further conclusion that what is morally significant must be interests-as-desires. I do not concede that this argument is sound. To start with, taking interests-as-needs to be morally significant does not entail that tractors have any moral significance in *their* own right. Tractors do not have needs, although farmers do. Still, the farmer's calves have needs in their own right, and so does the wheat. Whether the calves have any interests that are morally significant is one of the points at issue, and so is not to be presupposed one way or another. But what of the wheat? I certainly agree with Frey that plants have needs, though I am not at all certain that Frey and I agree for the same reasons. Although we agree that wheat needs water and various other things in order to do well as wheat, I believe that Frey and I have different conceptions of what determines what it is to do well as wheat. Be that as it may, does the conclusion that plants do have needs reduce to absurdity the proposition that interests taken as needs are morally significant? It is not at all clear to me that it does. To accept that all interests, taken as needs, are morally significant does not entail that they are equally important.

It may be that a plant's needs for the necessities of life are morally significant, on some level, while not as morally important as a human's needs for the necessities of life. I see no reason to assume that interests are atoms that all have the same moral weight. That a dandelion had the same moral weight as a human is something I would take as a reduction to absurdity of the principle that interests, taken as needs, are morally significant – if that were an implication of the principle. It is not an implication of the principle. That plants have some minimal moral weight is not something I am prepared to reject, without argument, as being absurd. Frey does not give any argument, but merely assumes that it is absurd. I believe that it is true rather than absurd. I shall have more to say about that subsequently.

We need not follow Frey to his conclusions, even if we were to agree that it is quite as absurd that plants should have interests as it is that tractors should. One alternative would be to sidestep the absurdity by denying that plants do have needs, maintaining that they no more than tractors have an identity that determines needs and interests. Still, to make such a claim in the case of plants would appear to be to deny a manifest truth. Plants clearly do have needs in their own right. A more promising line would be to maintain that only certain sorts of need interests are morally significant. Perhaps only needs concerned with pleasures or pains, with desires, or at least with sentience, are morally significant. One might say that while plants as well as dogs need water, it would not matter morally if I decided not to water my philodendron, but it would matter if I were to allow my dog to die of thirst. Virtually everyone who maintains that animals have moral status agrees that the capacity to feel pain is sufficient to give a being moral standing. Singer takes it as a necessary condition as well: if a being cannot feel pain it cannot suffer a morally significant hurt. Some of us deny that it is a necessary condition, claiming that some beings that cannot feel pain nevertheless have morally significant interests. Frey, however, denies that sentience is a sufficient condition for having morally significant interests. Although he agrees that animals can feel pain, he denies that they have a morally significant interest in not feeling pain. He does this because he takes interests-as-desires rather than interests-as-needs to be morally significant. His claim is that animals lack language, and therefore lack beliefs, and therefore lack desires, and therefore lack morally significant interests.

Can animals have desires even though they are unable to entertain their desires linguistically? If animals can have desires, and if interests-as-desires are morally significant, then the class of beings that have moral significance is considerably broader than Frey recognizes. If this is so, the desire criterion draws the boundary between those having and those lacking moral status along much the same line as does the criterion based on the capacity to feel pain, since presumably any animal that can desire anything whatsoever will desire not to feel pain. Focusing on desires, though, gives a somewhat more comprehensive conception of a being's interests. I shall argue that Frey is incorrect in his conclusion that having desires requires having linguistic capacity and that animals therefore fail to have desires. I shall also argue that he is incorrect in his claim that the mere capacity to feel pain is not sufficient to give one morally significant interests. If it can be shown that Frey's arguments on these points are not sound, then one can allow that some animals do have moral standing on the basis of morally relevant need interests, without following me to my ultimate conclusion that all beings with interests have moral standing. That is a point to be argued later. For now I shall first attack the claim that animals cannot have desires and then go on to attack the claim that the capacity to feel pain is not sufficient to give a being moral standing. My current objective is to argue that beings are entitled to moral consideration if they have desires or can feel pain. In a subsequent chapter I shall argue that these things are not necessary in order for a being to have a morally significant good.

Frey argues that a being cannot have desires unless it has

the linguistic capability to express those desires (1980, 104–
7). Following Frey, suppose that a dog desires a bone. Either
the dog is not aware that it desires the bone or else it is aware
that it desires the bone. For a being to desire something, it
must at least occasionally be aware of the desire, because the
notion of unconscious desire is parasitic on that of conscious
desire. (Whether there can be purely unconscious desires is
a very debatable point. However, let us grant Frey his assumption. The interesting issues are yet to come.) For the
dog to desire the bone, then, it must at least sometimes be
conscious that it desires the bone. "If the dog is aware that
it has this simple desire, then it is aware that it simply desires
the bone; it is, in other words, self-conscious" (1980, 105).
Frey then attempts to show that the use of language is necessary in order to have self-consciousness. He then invokes
Kant, Strawson, and Wittgenstein in order to argue "that the
meaningful ascription of [desire] to oneself is only possible
if one can meaningfully ascribe it to others and that one can
meaningfully ascribe it to others only within the context and
confines of a public language" (1980, 106). Thus, self-
consciousness presupposes the ability to use a public language. He backs up this argument with the claim that "there
is nothing in either my or my dog's behavioral repertoire by
which we can indicate the possession of self-consciousness"
(1980, 106). In contrast, we supposedly know about the self-
consciousness of other people because they tell us.

The main points in Frey's argument are subject to considerable debate. The debate should not even get started. There
is no reason in the world to believe that a dog, in order to
desire a bone, must be aware of *itself* having the desire or
aware *that* it has the desire. Frey just assumes, without benefit of argument, that there is no middle ground between not
being conscious at all, and being self-conscious. It does not
seem to me to be obviously impossible that a dog might be
aware of a bone and consciously desire the bone – being in
that sense aware of the desire – without being aware of the
self that desires the bone, and without being aware *that* it
desires or aware *that* anything at all. Indeed, if anything

seems absurd, it is the thought that a dog must be a linguist to desire a bone. Frey is tacitly assuming that awareness must be awareness *that* something rather than awareness *of* something, which is tacitly to assume that awareness must have a linguistic referent. That premise is at least as much in need of an argument as is the conclusion.

We now move on to Frey's main argument for his contention that having desires requires having language. This is the argument that having desires presupposes having beliefs, which in turn requires having language. Though a better argument, it is possible to challenge it on a number of points. Even granting that it seems much more plausible that a belief must be a belief that so-and-so than that an awareness must be an awareness that so-and-so, we may question whether beliefs may occur *only* in linguistic form. Although desire may presuppose some sort of belief or awareness, a very critical question is that of whether desiring requires having beliefs in such a strong (linguistic) sense that the rest of the argument follows. Let us look at Frey's argument in more detail. Suppose that a being has a need for food, a need that results in its eating. There are various ways in which the need might conceivably be connected to the eating. Perhaps the need leads directly to the action without any consciousness whatsoever. Insects and other lower animals likely eat in this fashion. If one is a Cartesian or a behaviorist, one might maintain that all other creatures go from stimulus to response without benefit of mental states, there being no beliefs, no desires, no awareness, no feelings. (Indeed, if I wanted to be really hard-nosed about it, I could deny that there is adequate evidence that other people have mental states.) Frey, though, does not take his stand on such extreme behaviorism. Although we cannot be antiskeptically certain of this, or of hardly anything, let us follow Frey in assuming that animals can have mental states of some sort. Suppose that an animal feels hunger. Let us presume that the animal is conscious of the hunger, though it is not necessarily self-conscious. Let us even suppose that the feeling of hunger prompts the animal to eat. Frey is willing to concede as much as this. Even so, all of this may happen without the animal having a desire or a belief. Frey points out, at considerable length, that behavior cycles can be identified, individuated, and accounted for without reference to beliefs or desires. We do need to identify and individuate behavior cycles in some way, but we can do that on the basis of needs alone. Need, then, can lead to a given behavior without desires or beliefs being present, even when feelings are present. There is no logical reason to assign desires, beliefs, or even feelings any causal role – improbable as that might seem intuitively. Of course, the fact that we need not rely on beliefs or desires does not prove that there are none. Frey's next step is to try to show that desires and beliefs are ruled out in the case of nonlinguistic beings.

A feeling is only a feeling, not a cognitive but a conative state. Frey's point is that a desire for food, unlike the feeling of hunger, is cognitive. It involves some thinking about ways and means and things. There is some presumed connection between the feeling of hunger and the obtaining and eating of food. Indeed, having the very idea of food involves having some abstract thought about the world. To be sure, the mere desire for food does not require thought as structured and as highly conceptualized as does a desire for a T-bone steak, medium rare, with Worcestershire sauce and a baked potato. Still, the bare desire for food does require at least some rudimentary beliefs. Are they beliefs that are necessarily tied to language? Frey claims that all beliefs are necessarily tied to language. According to him, when we believe something, what we believe is that a certain sentence is true. This has the implication that beings that lack language, and so cannot have beliefs about sentences, consequently cannot have beliefs about anything. This seems quite odd to me. Even though I do use language, it seems to me that I very often have beliefs that are not about sentences. Indeed, I think that I sometimes have beliefs that are not, at that moment, wrapped up in a sentence. Let us look at Frey's argument.

According to Frey, "In expressions of the form 'I believe that . . . ,' what follows the 'that' is a sentence, and what I believe is that the sentence is true" (1980, 87). Similarly, in the case of "He believes that . . . ," the "he" in question believes that some sentence is true. That rules out animals as believing or having desires (1980, 88):

> If what is believed is that a certain sentence is true, then no creature which lacks language can have beliefs; and without beliefs, a creature cannot have desires. Such is the case with animals, or so I suggest; and if I am right, not even in the sense of wants as desires, then, do animals have interests.

This strikes me as quite amazing. It should not amaze me, as philosophers have been going off the deep end about language for quite a long while. Perhaps my amazement is really at the fact that there is so little amazement at this sort of thing. We are asked to believe that there were no beliefs, let alone desires, before the advent of public language. It seems preposterous to me that we should have beliefs only consequent to our having a language. (Is this the first and ultimate manifestation of Parkinson's Law?) More believable is that we developed language because we had things to say (and a desire to communicate them). Let us consider this further.

Animals seemingly do have forms of nonlinguistic "communication," wherein noises or gestures on the part of one animal in some way trigger covert or overt responses in other members of its group. This may not involve thought or consciousness at all, as when one ant causes a particular response in a nest mate by exuding a specific chemical (a pheromone). The other ant responds to the odor much as does a machine that had had the appropriate button pushed. Higher animals have systems that are more elaborate and more flexible, and probably involve some form of consciousness. Frey concedes that animals most probably do have some form of consciousness. Still, it is difficult to see how, on his scheme, consciousness can have any significant role in animal "communication." Frey denies to animals beliefs, desires, emotions, and all forms of perception that involve comprehension. Supposedly, there is nothing animals want to communicate, and nothing they understand when it is communicated. Animal "communication," on this scheme, is evidently still a matter of stimulus and response, with animals being credited with very little more than Descartes was willing to concede. What role is there for consciousness to play? Yet it must have been out of this that human linguistic communication developed. Was there a sudden leap into the realm of language, and therefore of belief, desire, and so forth, or was this a matter of gradual evolution?

That there was a sudden leap into language is quite absurb. For that to have happened, some cave person (or whatever) must have first started using noises or gestures linguistically. This would have been an amazing accomplishment, particularly for a being without beliefs or desires. Even that would not have been enough, as language must be public. Some other cave person must have been a party to the very same language. But of course they could not have worked out their system together before the advent of their language, when they had no means of communicating ideas, and no ideas to communicate. That there was a sudden leap into language is not a reasonable belief.

Could linguistic communication have evolved gradually out of nonlinguistic interaction? This would mean that beliefs, desires, ideas, and so forth, gradually came into focus out of nonlinguistic forms of consciousness, with no dramatic gap separating linguistic from prelinguistic consciousness. The gradualist hypothesis does not seem at all implausible to me, even apart from the fact that the alternative, sudden language, is ridiculous in its own right. Flexibility being a major virtue of both, language and thought – whether or not they are separable – do not necessarily come in precise, rigidly defined units. That being so, thought and language as known to philosophers might well have been preceded by less structured instances of belief and expression. Now, it may well be that an animal cannot have a belief as precise and well articulated as, for instance, "the lion concealed in that tall grass is very dangerous." Still, Frey does grant that

87

animals have sensory data and moods of a sort. Certainly an animal can have feelings of apprehension concerning a thing or an area. I shall not presume to try to imagine how the evolution of language went, but it is not obviously impossible that a belief such as that about the lion might have been successively approximated – in previous times, in previous beings – by a number of more primitive thoughts. Being aware of a sense of danger felt to have to do with a particular thing is to associate ideas, and such an association of ideas might well be a step on the way to a more precise and linguistic way of thinking. Certainly it does seem quite likely to me that a nonlinguistic association of ideas might precede an articulate linguistic expression. Whatever line we draw between language and nonlanguage will probably be somewhat arbitrary. However we draw the linguistic line, the line between what is and what is not a belief need not coincide with it. Common sense suggests that belief precedes language. I may, for instance, be aware that a particular person is acting peculiarly, and I may be substantially aware of what is peculiar, before I am able to put it into words. Having thoughts that we cannot quite, or quite yet, put into words is not at all uncommon. It may well be that animals have beliefs and desires that, while not fully linguistic, are sufficiently well developed to count as beliefs and desires. If Frey is going to claim that these things are inseparable from language, the burden is on him to provide solid reason for believing that this is indeed the case.

Frey's support for his claim is, in essence, that the only way we can express or describe a belief is via language, and that to believe something is to believe that it is true, truth being a notion necessarily tied to language. Interestingly, Frey acknowledges that to know that a belief/sentence is true is to "possess an awareness . . . of an intimate link between language and the world" (1980, 91). To know that a sentence is true is to be aware of something in the world that makes it true. But in that awareness, we evidently have a nonlinguistic knowledge of, or belief about, that which makes the sentence true. That being so, we might well have a belief without any linguistic expression (even an internal one). For that matter, for a child (or a chimpanzee) to start to learn a language, it must gain some awareness of expressions being connected with beliefs and reality, for which it must first have some awareness of reality. Although Frey leads us up to these issues, he never addresses himself to them.

Neither can I at all accept Frey's argument based on the fact that arguments can only be stated or described via some language. He tells us (1980, 87):

> Now what is it that I believe? I believe [for instance] that my collection lacks a Gutenberg Bible; that is, I believe that the sentence "My collection lacks a Gutenberg Bible" is true. In expressions of the form "I believe that . . . ," what follows the "that" is a sentence, and what I believe is that the sentence is true. The same is the case with expressions of the form "He believes that . . . "; The difficulty in the case of animals is this: if someone were to say, for example, "The cat believes that the laces are tied" then that person is holding, as I see it, that the cat believes the sentence "The laces are tied" to be true; and I can see no reason whatever for crediting the cat or any other creature which lacks language, including human infants, with regarding the sentence "The laces are tied" as true.

It is an obvious truth that a belief can be stated or described only in some language. That does not mean that what is believed is a sentence. The belief that so-and-so is one thing, the belief that a sentence stating so-and-so is true is another. What Frey believes about his book collection is one thing; what he believes about a sentence describing it is another. To be sure, any being that is adept at language and believes something will have to agree to the truth of a sentence that states the belief (in a language relevant to the language user). Normally, then, *in the case of a language user*, the two beliefs will be true or false together. It does not follow that the two beliefs are the same, or that only a language user can believe. It simply begs the question to assume that what a believer believes is that some sentence is true – even though that sentence might necessarily be used were one to report the belief.

Frey gives a supplemental argument centered on what it is that is believed (1980, 89–90):

> I do not see how the cat can be correctly described as believing the laces are tied unless it can, as I do, distinguish between the beliefs the laces are tied and that the laces are untied and regards one but not the other as true. But what is true or false are not states of affairs which reflect or pertain to these beliefs; states of affairs are not true or false (though sentences describing them are) but either are or are not the case, either do or do not obtain. If, then, one is going to credit the cat with the belief that the laces are tied, and the cat, in order to be correctly described as believing this, must be able to distinguish this belief from the false belief . . . and states of affairs are not true or false, then what exactly is it that cats are being credited with distinguishing as true or false? Reflection . . . forces one to credit cats with language, in order for there to be something true or false in belief.

In effect, this argument is that

What is believed is held to be true rather than false.
<u>Sentences are true or false.</u>
What is believed is a sentence.

To start with, the argument is invalid on purely formal grounds. It needs a premise of the form "Things that are true or false are sentences" in order to be an admissible argument. The needed premise is much stronger than the premise given. The premise that is needed to make the argument formally valid claims that *only* sentences are true or false, and rules out other things as being true or false. That is, it rules out the possibility of there being nonsentential beliefs that are true or false. That is too much to assume. This premise, which would be required in order to make the argument formally valid, simply begs the question. Aside from the major shortcoming, the argument is unsound because the first premise happens to be false. To believe, for instance, that a particular lion is dangerous is to believe something about the lion, whereas to believe that it is true that

90

the lion is dangerous is to believe something about a belief (or a sentence, or whatever it is). There may be various implications to what we believe, implications that would be readily apparent to a sufficiently rational language user, but it by no means follows that a believer must be aware of everything implied. If the cat, to continue Frey's rather bizarre example, believes that the laces are tied, then that is what the cat believes. It does not have to believe that the belief is true (or that it is true that it is true), or that some incompatible belief is false. Moreover, neither a cat nor any other believer needs to distinguish its belief from every or any other belief, although we might have to do so were we to give an account of what the believer believes. (And of course we could give an account only in some language.) Semantic adroitness is not a prerequisite for belief. Frey has given us no sound reason to think that nonlinguistic beings cannot have beliefs and desires.

There remains one last and very important link in Frey's case: he argues that the capacity to feel pain is not a sufficient condition for the possession of interests (1980, chap. 11). To start with, he points out that Singer et al. have not given arguments for their claim that the capacity to feel pain is a sufficient condition for possessing interests. That much is true, but for his part Frey does not provide any argument for believing that the linguistically held desires of humans determines interests in a morally significant sense. Singer's strategy is to argue that there is no morally significant difference between human and nonhuman pain – whether or not the being in question can linguistically formulate its aversion to it – and to assign the burden of proof to those who deny that the capacity to feel pain is a sufficient condition for the possession of morally significant interests.

Frey offers a two-part argument against the claim that the capacity to feel pain is a sufficient condition for the possession of interests. Suppose that it were sufficient. If it were the one and only sufficient condition, then it would be necessary as well. However, it is not necessary, as Frey argues,

91

and so cannot be the sole sufficient condition. Subsequently, he argues that it cannot be one among a number of sufficient conditions. First necessity: Frey argues that the capacity to feel pain cannot be a necessary condition for the possession of interests, as humans have interests even in cases wherein, by reason of ignorance or insentience, the capacity to feel pain has nothing to do with it. A person has, for instance, an interest in not being slandered, even when that person never hears about it. The late Karen Ann Quinlan had interests – though it is not clear whether her interests were in having her life-support system turned off, or in having it left on. Unfortunately, it is also not at all clear *why* Frey believes people have interests in such cases. What are the reasons that would support an ascription of interests to nonrational and even nonsentient humans that would not support a similar ascription in the case of many animals?

Frey gives us only a hint. We are told that a "desire for good health is one important desire typical of human beings (in respect of their general well-being), so, even if comatose, John can and will be deemed to have a stake and so an interest in good health" (1980, 157). But why do desires typical of humans count in the case of perpetually comatose John? Even if typical, they are not John's. What is lurking in the background, as well as a scarcely concealed speciesism, is the view that the desires that one *would* have, if thinking clearly and aware of the relevant facts, ought to count. This view, defining one's good in terms of prudent desires, I shall consider and reject in the chapter on interests. (Perhaps I should add that I am not absolutely certain that Frey is ascribing interests to comatose John on the basis of hypothetical desires. Frey is not clear on that point. If he has other reasons, let alone more plausible ones, I can find no indication of what they are.) For now, I merely point out that if we take recourse to what humans who cannot desire would desire if they could desire, then we could just as well draw conclusions about what animals would desire. Rhetorically, it is tempting to poke fun at Frey by suggesting that one might as well go on to draw conclusions about what rocks would desire. Still, I can find no reason for ascribing any particular hypothetical desire to a rock, since there is absolutely nothing that would contribute to its welfare and nothing, not even being ground into gravel, that would injure it. The difference, I am suggesting, is that unlike rocks, animals as well as humans have welfare needs, and therefore would normally have corresponding desires – to the extent that they were able to formulate desires in response to their interests. It is perfectly sensible to think that an uncomatose John would desire health, and that Fido would desire a bone. Unlike Frey, though, I hold that one's interests are determined not by any sort of desires, real or hypothetical, linguistically formulated or otherwise, but by our wellbeing needs. More of that later. My point now is that Frey has given us no good reason to believe that John has interests while Fido does not.

Where are we? Frey has pointed out quite correctly – as we are both convinced, for different reasons – that the capacity to feel pain is not a necessary condition for the possession of morally significant interests. If the capacity to feel pain were the sole sufficient condition, it would also be necessary. If the capacity to feel pain is a sufficient condition at all, then, there must be other sufficient conditions as well. So far, I can accept the argument – and I do think that there are other conditions that are sufficient. From here, though, Frey's argument declines rapidly. He takes refuge behind a burden-of-proof demand. Singer is challenged to produce any other sufficient conditions there might be. By the preceding argument, the capacity to feel pain cannot be the *only* sufficient condition, if it is sufficient at all. If Singer cannot produce *other* sufficient conditions, Frey claims, we have no reason to believe that the capacity to feel pain is at all a sufficient condition for having morally significant interests.

Burden-of-proof arguments are risky at best, and this one is quite inadequate. It is quite open to Singer to sidestep it by claiming that the capacity to feel pain is the one and only, necessary and sufficient, condition for having interests. That would require him to deny that comatose John and Karen Ann Quinlan have (or had) interests. Frey is aware that Singer does deny that they have interests (1980, 148n). Certainly it is absurd to think that Frey's believing that there are other sufficient conditions is a fact that requires Singer to produce some of them in order to preserve his own pain-capacity condition. Another approach to avoiding Frey's conclusion, being the approach I would take, is to suggest wider criteria. I believe that having wellbeing needs, of which pain avoidance is but one aspect, is a sufficient (and I think necessary) condition for having morally significant interests. For that reason, I believe that comatose John and Karen Ann Quinlan, as well as normal people and animals, have (or had) morally significant interests. Frey has given us no convincing reason for believing that animals do not.

Oddly enough, Frey readily concedes that animals can be wronged. (Certainly I never got the impression that he was one who would be unkind to animals.) We are told that "even with no rights posited, acts can still be morally wrong," and he concedes that animals can be wronged morally (1980, 170). If not interests, desires, or rights, animals can at least have painful sensations. I find Frey rather mysterious here. He seems to be tying interests to rights, then saying that animals have a moral status of some sort even without rights and interests. For my part, I am content to leave the problematic concept of rights out of the account altogether, as being more rhetorical than illuminating. I tie interests directly to injuries and benefits, and argue that anything that can be injured in its own right has an interest in not being injured, and that anything that can be benefited in its own right has an interest in being benefited. I certainly would like to know more about Frey's view about the morality of our dealings with animals, a matter on which he leaves us to dangle.

I agree with Frey that we humans, with our greater conceptual apparatus, have many interests that animals lack. Cattle, whatever else might distress them, are not tormented by a knowledge of what will happen to them at the slaughterhouse. Nor do they enjoy playing word games. Is it merely that Frey and I use different terminology for describing a common belief that animals can be wronged and that normal humans have more highly developed interests? I think there is more to it than that. Frey and, for that matter, Kant take rationality as making a *qualitative* difference to an interest, a qualitative difference that gives it moral significance, whereas I take it as (roughly) making a difference to what interests it is that we do have. Although we may have intellectual interests that an animal lacks, our pain is no more painful, no more contrary to our interests, no more a wrong to us because we linguistically conceptualize our dislike of it. An animal's interests are not diminished *merely* because it does not think about them as we do.

Toward the end of his book, Frey raises another point which is well worth noting (1980, 164–7). He cites with approval John Rodman's observation (1977, 91) that making sentence the criterion of moral significance is still too human-centered, being biased in favor of those beings that most resemble us in their mode of being:

> In the end, Singer achieves "an expansion of our moral horizons" just far enough to include most animals, with special attention to those categories of animals most appropriate for defining the human condition in the years ahead. The rest of nature is left in a state of thinghood, having no intrinsic worth, acquiring instrumental value only as resources for the well-being of an elite of sentient beings.

This is a very good point, though it seems to me that Frey is being even more and more arbitrarily, human-centered with his emphasis on linguistic capacity. Even so, his unelaborated-upon recognition that some nonhumans can be wronged does point beyond that.[10] I have discussed Frey's view at some length in order to bring out some important

10 In Frey's subsequent work, *Rights, Killing, and Suffering*, he does recognize that nonrational beings which are sentient have *some* sort of moral standing, though they lack interests and rights. Yet having made this concession, it seems to me that he minimizes it with very little in the way of explanation, let alone justification. Human interests are to take absolute priority in anything like normal practice.

points about what reason and linguistic capacity do *not* have to do with moral significance, and to lay some of the ground-work for a more positive account. I shall now set myself to the task of trying to develop broader and clearer conceptions of what morally significant interests are, and of what sorts of beings have them.

Chapter 3

A matter of interest

They that be whole need not a physician, but they
that be sick.

Matthew 9:12.

Thus far we have found no morally sound reason for holding
that only humans, or only rational beings, have moral standing. From considering the major unsound reasons that have
been offered, let us turn now to the closely related question
of the nature of interests that are morally significant. If we
can give an account of what it is to be a morally significant
interest, that would, among other benefits, shed light on the
question of what beings have moral standing, and on the
question of why they have it. It might also shed some light
on the question of how we are to treat such beings. Different
ethical theories advocate different ways of treating such
beings, but all ethical theories, of whatever stripe, agree that
the interests of the individual (with moral standing) are morally significant, if not morally decisive. If we first work out
what morally significant interests are, and what sorts of
beings have them, we might be better placed to evaluate
alternative ethical theories about how we ought to treat
beings with moral standing. I shall start with us humans,
whom we all agree do have morally significant interests.
Money, food, clothing, seeing enjoyable movies, collecting
stamps, and a host of other things may be in our interests,
or at least we may take an interest in them. Yet these things
are good for us, when they are good for us, only insofar as

97

they are instrumentalities toward whatever is of intrinsic value for us. What is good for us in its own right? Various things have been proposed as constituting the good of the individual. Things have been proposed as being good accordingly as they are desired or, alternatively, accordingly as they are desirable (whether or not they are actually desired). I shall argue for a version of the latter alternative, and against the claim that what is good for us is good for us because we desire it. I shall explain why I reject hedonism and any other theory that identifies the good with a mental state, and why I reject the identification of our good with the satisfaction of our desires or preferences. Then I shall go on to develop a view that identifies our good with the satisfaction of our wellbeing interests.

MENTAL STATES

According to hedonists pleasure is the one thing we desire for its own sake, all other things having value in proportion to their contribution to our balance of pleasure over pain. Clearly, there is some truth to that. Our pleasures and pains are important to us, and the effects we have on others in terms of their pleasures and pains is morally assessable. We ought not to cause pain to others without good reason. Important as pleasure might be, however, reflection suggests that there must be more to the story than just that. If pleasure were our only good, then *Brave New World* would be the ultimate, and the disquietude many of us feel in the face of its apparent pointlessness would be unfounded. Hedonism's too-narrow identification of good and evil with pleasure and pain leaves out of account much that has been held to be of great intrinsic significance for their own lives by very many sincere and thoughtful people. Love, knowledge, achievement, and various other things have been knowingly and thoughtfully preferred over pleasure. Pleasure and pain, while important, are not the sole content or measure of a good life.

If we wish to go beyond simple hedonism, the major op-

98

tions seem to be to identify the good more broadly in terms of what we prefer, or else to identify our good with, in some sense, our overall wellbeing. These alternatives overlap in considerable part. Pleasure will frequently be among the objects of our preference, and it, or at least the absence of pain, will normally tend toward our wellbeing. Again, the objects of our preference will clearly coincide to a considerable degree with those things that serve our wellbeing, and we will frequently prefer the pleasurable. Accounts of our good based on either wellbeing or preferences are commendable not only in that they go beyond hedonism but also in that they do not tie the definition of the individual's good exclusively to any sort of experience or mental state. Wellbeing accounts take our good to extend beyond our mental states, and the preference account identifies our good as being the actual satisfaction of our preferences, not just as the experience of their being satisfied. As it happens, there is very good reason for allowing that the individual's good may be something beyond mere experiences and mental states.

A strong case for seeking beyond mental states and experiences in our conceptual quest for the good emerges from Robert Nozick's fascinating thought experiment of the "experience machine" (1974, 42–5). Imagine we have a device that could give us any sort of experience we might wish – intensely pleasurable experiences, experiences of love, great achievement, aesthetic contemplation, or whatever else we might care to nominate. The experience machine could even be programmed in such a way as to give us experiences appropriate to us and our responses. In that field of experience we might act as autonomous beings, acting with moral agency, reciprocity, and all that, quite unaware that those with whom we were dealing were not real people, and that we were experiencing unreal events. This machine would obviously be a very valuable resource, and no doubt it would render television sets and electronic games obsolete. Could the experience machine give us the good life? While having gratifying experiences is at least normally good in itself (and certainly it would be bad to be attached to a sadistically programmed machine), it seems quite hard to accept that experiences are the only things in which we have interests worthy of moral consideration. Such a machine would provide an enticing diversion, but few would willingly be attached to it on a permanent basis. It seems quite absurd, for instance, that the experience of loving and being loved (perhaps with an imaginary person) should be what counts, with an actual love relationship with a real person being an optional and irrelevant extra. Having an ideal love relationship with a wonderful but nonexistent person, experiencing great but unreal achievement – at best they seem hollow and pointless, and at worst an obscene joke. This is not a logical objection, but if we agree that it would not be preferable to have our real life shrivel while we entertain mental states divorced from reality, then we must accept something other than mere experiences/mental states as the good of the individual. They are undoubtedly significant, but there must be more to the story than that. It seems, in brief, that reality ought to be involved.

The reason why we cannot identify our good as any set of experiences and mental states is that we are beings of whom our experiences and mental states constitute only one level. We have a set of interests to match our complexity. Our good, in a morally relevant sense, is not just the experience of having our interests satisfied, but actually *having* our interests satisfied. I am not making the absurd claim that our experiences and mental states are irrelevant. Obviously, many of our interests are centered on our experiences and mental states, and are morally important. Even so, this is not always a necessary condition for an interest to be an interest and to be morally significant. Suppose that I were to have the experience of some great achievement. I might have such an experience because that was actually what was happening, or because I was hooked up to an experience machine, without my being able to tell the difference. With regard to identical experiences it would still clearly be in my interests that the former should be the case, and the *difference* between the two is morally significant. This indicates that in some cases there is a dimension of our good beyond experiences/ mental states. In those cases, the mere experience/mental state is not sufficient to satisfy the interest. (Indeed, a *difference* in experience is neither sufficient nor necessary.) Hedonism, then, and any other account that locates our good solely in our experiences/mental states is inadequate.

It will not do to claim that what is required for the moral significance of an interest is both the experience/mental state and the reality. The lack of the experience/mental state may not deprive the reality of its significance in all cases. It is not always a necessary condition. Suppose an Olympic athlete runs a very close race and collapses crossing the finish-line. The runner briefly recovers consciousness in the hospital, then dies before anyone tells her whether she had won the race. It would be very nice for that person if, having won, she could be told of the victory so that she could have a victory experience before death, but failing that, the runner, while still alive, clearly still has an interest in winning the race. We may have interests that are morally significant even when they do not involve experience/mental states.

If we are to identify the good of the individual, we must go beyond hedonism and beyond any other view that is entirely concerned with experiences/mental states. If we are to define the good in terms of what is desired, much the best approach is just to leave out all further conjecture about what might be desired, pleasure or anything else, and just take the good as whatever is desired. That is less risky and has the further advantage that, at least in principle, our relative interests can be given appropriate weightings according to our choices. This approach is becoming very popular, particularly among utilitarians. I shall argue against this sort of account and in favor of an account based on wellbeing interests. Before we get into that, I would note another point raised by the preceding considerations. If we recognize that experiences/mental states are not always a necessary factor in the individual's good, then the way *starts* to open up for even nonconscious beings to have morally significant interests. Perhaps insects, trees, and even species and ecosystems have morally significant interests. I have not established this, certainly, but it now seems less unlikely that nonconscious beings might have a good and be entitled to some sort of moral consideration. Of course, if one's good is a matter of one's preferences, then nonconscious beings, having no preferences, have no good to be considered. However, if our good is a matter of wellbeing, then perhaps – just perhaps – the wellbeing of nonconscious beings is morally significant. But that is getting ahead of the game. For now, the question is whether our good should be understood in terms of preferences or in terms of wellbeing.

PREFERENCES

There are complications if we are to take one's preferences as constitutive of one's good. Sometimes we prefer something that is not good for us, though we do not yet know it. If it kills us, we may never know it. So, a particular preference may be for something. We can try to get around that problem by defining one's good in terms of that which results in the greatest overall amount of preference satisfaction. After all, if things backfire on us, that is not what we want. Still, there are problems concerning infants and people with various forms of mental incapacity who may be incapable of forming some preferences. They may prefer things that are (presumably) bad for them, and may not avoid that which will kill them – resulting in no unsatisfied preferences. Accordingly, recourse is normally made not just to the subjective but to the subjunctive, invoking that which *would* be preferred if one were well informed and thinking clearly. As Singer puts it (1979a, 80), "we make the plausible move of taking a person's interests to be what, on balance and after reflection on all the relevant facts, a person prefers." (Perhaps Singer should say "would prefer.")

Given our limitations these prudent preferences, or prudent desires, as they are frequently termed, may not be actually preferred, and what is actually preferred may not be prudent. The class of prudent desires, then, contains quite divergent things, some prudent desires not being desires at all. The desires we do not have, but could have under ideal circumstances, are taken to be of equal moral importance with our actual prudent desires.

I shall argue that defining the individual's good in terms of prudent desires, while a considerable improvement over hedonism, does not go far enough. What makes an object of actual or would-be desire good for us, when it is good for us, is that what is or would be desired contributes to our wellbeing. At best, reference to prudent desires can serve only as a criterion of an individual's good, not as its definition. Such a criterion is of only limited utility and dependent on the wellbeing factor. Indeed, as I shall argue, the prudence that is needful in our prudent desires, a matter of relevant knowledge and clear thinking, is prudent only with reference to our wellbeing. The prudent-desire account (as I shall hereafter refer to the identification of the individual's good as the satisfaction of that individual's prudent desires) draws much of its strength from the fact that that which we do or would prudently desire is commonly coextensive with what contributes to our wellbeing.

There are a number of attractions to the prudent-desire account. For one thing, such an approach takes account of our nature as cognitive, rational, autonomous beings. Rightly, we tend to be very suspicious of paternalistic theories which try to tell us what is good for us and which advocate that we do what is right for people – whether the beneficiaries like it or not. This is a problem for any attempt to define the good of the individual in terms of wellbeing, pleasure, or anything else other than what the individual prefers. Certainly it would seem that people, if not animals, when they are well informed and thinking clearly, should know better than anyone what is good for them. They, rather than theories about their interests, would be their own best judges of their interests. The prudent-desire account takes cognizance of our capacity for self-determination, and it also shows a commendable liberal respect for the values of widely differing people with very divergent backgrounds, conceptual schemes, beliefs, needs, and emotions. We – in whatever logical order – have different goods, make different choices, and have different sorts of wellbeing to which different things contribute. All of this must be taken into account. In consequence, the prudent-desire account has the additional advantage of greater practical convenience. In determining what is good for ourselves, what we can most readily get a handle on is what our desires are in various instances, or what we believe they would be. Similarly, in the case of other people the easiest (and in many ways the safest) way of finding out what is good for them is to note their express or implied desires. Most directly, we ask them.

Another attractive thing about defining the individual's good in terms of prudent desires is that it seems to offer a halfway house between the view that being valuable is a matter of being valued, and the view that some things are valuable and therefore ought to be valued whether or not they actually are valued. It inclines toward the former, however, since it invokes desires. Yet the prudent-desire account is not simply a version of the former view, in that it invokes *prudent* desires in recognition of the obvious, that some desires are better than others, and that we can be mistaken about these things. Even so, the prudent-desire account certainly does not go on to take the objectivist position holding that some things are valuable regardless of whether they are valued, since what we would desire is the last word. There is no appeal from what we would desire, when we knew the facts and were thinking clearly, to what we ought to desire, regardless. As a halfway position between problematic alternatives the prudent-desire account has a certain attractiveness. Still, this attractiveness is misleading.

I intend to argue that the good of the individual is not to be defined in terms of prudent desires but in terms of the individual's wellbeing, which in turn must be defined independently of prudent desire. To do this, I must distinguish adequately between having one's wellbeing served and having one's prudent desires satisfied. While distinguishable in principle, they are difficult to separate in practice. Normally, those things that are the objects of our prudent desires and those things that contribute to our wellbeing are quite the same. Even so, I shall argue that there are cases where they do not coincide. In those cases it is easier to see that things are or are not good for us accordingly as they serve our wellbeing, and not accordingly as they satisfy our prudent desires. Even in cases where they do not coincide, the wellbeing factor, as I shall argue, is what makes what is good for us to be so.

Let us ask how prudent desires are related to wellbeing. It is worth noting that we generally do not desire *ad lib.* Sometimes we do, and what we then desire is, to some extent, contributory to our wellbeing. After all, having frustrated desires is contrary to our wellbeing, even in cases where it works out to our ultimate benefit. There are a range of cases wherein it matters little what we choose – which movie shall we see?– and one thing rather than another contributes to our wellbeing by virtue of our desiring it. (That our desires do tend somewhat to shape what is required for our wellbeing makes it all the more difficult to distinguish our wellbeing needs from the objects of our prudent desires.) More commonly, however, when there is more riding on it, we have desires not *ad lib* but because we think, rightly or otherwise, that what is desired will contribute to our good. A fairly straightforward example is that old utilitarian standby, pain – which we all prefer not to experience (except for good reason). Avoiding pain contributes to our immediate wellbeing, though some pains contribute to our long-term wellbeing, and this is no doubt why we are so unanimous in our desire not to feel pain (except for good reason). This desire is not arbitrary, but grounded in what we are and what contributes to (or detracts from) our wellbeing. It is for such a reason that we can be so confident that a being of whose desires we had no experience would prefer not to experience pain (except for good reason). Pain avoidance, then, seems to provide a clear example of something that contributes to our wellbeing giving rise to our prudent desire. We desire not to feel pain unnecessarily *because* that would detract from our wellbeing. Moreover, I take it as evident that the pain is bad for us primarily because it is immediately contrary to our wellbeing, and only secondarily because it is contrary to our prudent desire. In general, it is by no means the case that our primary values spring from our desires, as from some sort of axiological Unmoved Mover. Our most central desires spring from our most central being, and are a matter of what contributes to its wellbeing.

This is not to say that our choices are unimportant or that they are predetermined by our wellbeing needs. Our choices play a major role in determining what our wellbeing needs are, what form they take, and how our priorities are ordered. They are important to us in much more than just the rather trivial sense in which it contributes to our wellbeing to see a particular movie when we decide we want to. Our prudent desires and what is conducive to our wellbeing – which may or may not be the same thing – are at least partially inde-terminate. Many things can happen to us and a person has a great many potentialities, by no means all of which are mutually consistent. Accordingly, our prudent desires and that which would contribute to our wellbeing may take a number of different forms and do not entirely take any par-ticular form. One series of events or course of personal de-velopment might lead to one set of needs, capacities, desires, and satisfactions, whereas another line might lead to other needs, capacities, desires, and satisfactions – other benefits at other costs. We have alternatives, and opening some doors closes others. What contributes to our wellbeing varies ac-cording to chance and circumstance and, very importantly, according to the choices we make. We may make choices that affect our entire life, bringing a whole series of needs, desires, frustrations, and satisfactions in their train.

Jack Benny at one point in his life decided to become a comedian, and became a very good one. That choice entailed that he not concentrate on becoming a top-grade violinist. Probably he could have become one. He adopted one life strategy rather than another, and we might even say that he became a different person. Certainly he acquired a different set of needs, desires, and potential satisfactions. Certainly the prudent desires he arrived at changed what was good for him in life. Even so, a viable life strategy must be based on what we are and what would contribute to our wellbeing. Being a comedian or a musician would be foreclosed to us if we lacked a sense of humor and had a tin ear. Moreover, such an idea would not just come to us out of the blue. Being one or the other would be a more or less viable means of pursuing one's wellbeing in terms of self-development, self-expression, self-esteem, social esteem, aesthetic satisfaction, and the income by means of which one might attain other satisfactions. Were there no such benefits, it is hardly possible that one could have such an aim as a prudent desire.

As we change, which is to say as we live, some things become more important to our wellbeing, while other things become less important. It is not merely that for various reasons, internal or external, we come to have a different set of means to our ends. We come to have different ends, and to assign our ends different relative priorities. Our choices in some part determine the overall balance of what does or would constitute our wellbeing. But are there not limits to how much our choices can determine our wellbeing needs? It seems to me that there is a normal presumption that people, in order to count as being prudent, must have *some* good reason for having desires contrary to what is, or otherwise would be, their wellbeing. To be sure, people sometimes exhibit self-sacrificial behavior for moral reasons, or out of love for someone or something. I see no reason to believe that people value things other than themselves only out of ignorance or confused thinking. But let us ask whether it is possible to prudently desire for *oneself* something contrary to what is or otherwise would be one's own wellbeing. To some extent the question is closed from the start, since anything we actually desired would serve our wellbeing to some extent, if only because frustrated desires are contrary to our immediate wellbeing. We must also bear in mind that something can serve our overall wellbeing, even though it might conflict or apparently conflict with some isolated aspect of our wellbeing. Satisfaction of whim is probably a good enough reason for sticking a pin into one's finger. The concerns of a whole person obviously go far beyond a momentary minor sensation. Yet the more there is riding on it, the better the reason has to be. If an active healthy person were to decide to undertake a course of action bound to result in the loss of a leg, and could offer no better reason than that he or she desired to do so, that would be proof that the person was either ignorant of the consequences or mentally unbalanced.

The interesting cases are harder to determine. Suppose that a person desires to smoke and drink to an extent that detracts from his or her physical wellbeing. Such activities, if they exacerbated an existing physical condition, would certainly not be good for the person from a physical point of view. One can well imagine a smoking drinker who believes that the joy received from accustomed activities outweighs the probable benefits of better health and longer life. It is of course highly possible that the person is not both well informed and thinking clearly. Wishful thinking is all too common. (As distinct from that, a person might just lack the willpower to stop. If this were really so, then being miserable trying to do what one is unable to do would only make matters that much worse.) If the person is correct in thinking that his or her psychological wellbeing would be served by continuing in such habits and judges that this would outweigh the adverse consequences, physical or psychological, then the desire of the individual concerned to continue smoking and drinking – at least in the most cost-efficient manner – is a prudent desire. And if the individual came to the opposite conclusion, then that alternative would likely be correct. In assigning priorities among the various things that do/would contribute to our wellbeing, choice clearly has a significant role. One priority can be higher than another just because we choose for it to be.

It is evidently not possible, then, to determine what the overall wellbeing of a given individual is without making reference to that individual's choices or desires. There are any number of differing ways of balancing ends and assigning relative priorities, that being a matter of individual cases. To get a definite determination of an individual's wellbeing, we would have to know what things meant in terms of that particular individual. Even if we had a godlike omniscience, knowing everything there was to know about an individual, we would still have to make reference to the individual's desires in order to give an adequate account of his or her wellbeing. Our desires, in the case of those of us who have desires, are an uneliminable element in our wellbeing needs. As well, then, as the epistemological point that knowledge of desires is prior to a full knowledge of wellbeing – and the libertarian point that people must be accepted as their own best judges of what is good for them – there is the inescapable substantive point that satisfaction of our desires is inherently involved in our wellbeing. Even so, as the leg-loss case indicates, our priorities and our wellbeing requirements are only partially determined by our choices.

Where does that leave us? Certainly we must recognize that prudent desires must be taken into account if we are to give an account of our wellbeing and/or our good. The smoking-drinker case, however, raises a deeper problem that we have not yet resolved. It is logically possible that a person might know the facts and be thinking clearly, yet will do something contrary to his or her wellbeing. By definition, such a desire would be a prudent desire. But are all prudent desires prudent? We have already noted that not all prudent desires are desires. Maybe some are not prudent. Could a person have such a perverse desire? We might try to dismiss such a case on the grounds of logical impossibility, claiming that if a person were in command of the facts, then a failure to desire that which would contribute to the overall balance of one's wellbeing would be an ipso facto proof that the person was not thinking clearly. (The only excuse would be that one recognized some external good.) It would, of course, suit my argument to employ this rather arbitrary expedient, since it implies that considerations of wellbeing determine our prudent desires and therefore, directly or via prudent desires, determine our good. Again, we might try to rule out such cases by claiming that they are psychologically impossible. If this questionable claim were true, it would still put wellbeing at the root of prudent desire and therefore at the root of our good. Although it would be convenient for me to rule out such cases, I just cannot believe that our will is as closely yoked to fact and reason as this would assume. I believe that there are cases wherein we are aware of the relevant facts and think about them clearly without willing, perhaps without being able to will, that which would serve our wellbeing. We may even will something to the contrary. (Our smoking drinker may be a case in point. Sometimes people do not, or cannot, will to stop such activities, even though they know quite clearly that they should and why they should.) If I am wrong in thinking that there are such cases, then so much the better for my claims about the primacy of wellbeing needs in determining our good. But what if I am correct in believing that there actually are such cases?

According to the prudent-desire theory, as advocated, our good is delimited by what we do/would desire when well informed and thinking clearly, and that which we do not desire under such circumstances is not good for us, no matter how much it might contribute to our wellbeing. For all practical purposes we certainly should operate on the working assumption that competent people know (and will) what is good for them. But is it really plausible to claim that our wellbeing is not good for us when it is not desired or is contrary to our desire? My intuitions tell me that when we fail to will our wellbeing we are failing to will our own good, this being some sort of a failure of the will, and that what is good for us is that which would contribute to our wellbeing. (That, of course, is no excuse for interfering in the lives of others against their will.) Yet these are only my intuitions. How can we decide the issue?

We have a range of cases to take into account here. In some cases our desires are only slightly at variance with what would otherwise serve our wellbeing, and our desires slightly redefine our wellbeing interests insofar as we have a wellbe-

ing interest in having our desires satisfied. There is no problem here – and no help in solving our problem. Skipping
over intermediate cases for the moment, let us return to the
extreme ones. Although we cannot rule out *all* cases where
prudent desire is at variance with wellbeing, some things are
so *grossly* at variance with our wellbeing interests that they
truly can be ruled out as impossible. Either they are psychologically impossible or they are irrefutable evidence of unclear
thinking to the point of insanity. Undeniably, some people
are very self-destructive. It is significant that we can rule out
some desires as being necessarily imprudent or not good for
us. It seems quite absurd that our good should be determined
by our prudent desires, no matter how much they might
diverge from our wellbeing interests, right up to the point
where the divergence is so gross as to justify a verdict of
insanity. We can conceive of a series of intermediate cases
of perverse will, where our prudent desires diverge from our
wellbeing interests but not to an extent that would justify a
finding of insanity. In these intermediate cases, by hypothesis the person is well informed and thinking clearly but
desires something contrary to his or her wellbeing. Only
when we get to some extreme range of cases can we claim
that the person of the perverse desires is unhinged. (I believe
that there are these intermediate cases, but remember, if
there are none, that would tend to support my claim that
our good cannot conflict with our wellbeing.) In those cases
that fall short of insanity, the person must still, according to
the prudent-desire account, be counted as thinking clearly,
and the object of desire would have to be counted as good
for that person. But then we come to some point beyond
which the person is suddenly out of his or her mind. That
is too ridiculous to permit belief.

What is really going on is something that is much more a
matter of degree. There is more to having a sensible set of
desires than being well informed and thinking clearly –
though these things are obviously important. In the sort of
perverse-will cases being considered here, it is not a matter
of thinking clearly (logically, rationally) up to the point of

going massively illogical. One can be thinking logically well past the point of insanity. What is significant here is that there is a point beyond which having self-destructive values constitutes being mentally incapacitated, no matter how logically one might be thinking. The problem with one's thinking in such a case is not a cognitive defect but a conative defect. The intermediate cases are a matter of having one's values out of kilter to some degree, whereas in the extreme cases, one's values are very much out of kilter. This is a matter of prudence to a greater or lesser degree – prudence being a matter of how well one's desires are in accordance with one's wellbeing interests. That a viable notion of prudent desire must be tied to the notion of wellbeing seems to follow inevitably, then, once we recognize that having grossly self-destructive desires is proof of mental incapacity. I shall therefore take it as established that a prudent desire, to be prudent and to have our good as its object, must be consistent with our overall wellbeing interests.

There is a correlative point to be made here. Not only is there the prudence of actual desires to be considered, there is also the sort of case where one fails to have a prudent desire for something that would contribute to one's wellbeing. (Of course, I am again setting aside cases where one is respecting some external good.) Extreme cases of nondesire count as evidence of mental incapacity, just as much as do extreme cases of perverse desire. The grounds that force a decision of mental incapacity in the extreme cases are that one is neglecting one's wellbeing and one's own good. Here as well, we can posit a series of intermediate cases, short of insanity, where one is well informed and thinking clearly, yet one fails to desire one's wellbeing. (And, of course, if there are no intermediate cases, that can only be because a prudent desire must result from a wellbeing need – when one is well informed and thinking clearly. Though incorrect, such a claim would be quite convenient for my argument.) In the intermediate cases of apathy, one is still imprudently neglecting one's wellbeing and one's own good, while well informed and thinking clearly, though not neglecting them to the point of being mentally incapacitated. The fact that there are cases of apathy (or that we can even imagine such cases), so extreme as to justify a claim of incapacity, gives us reason to believe that prudence and our good are tied to our wellbeing even in the absence of desire. Something is good for us if it is what we would desire if our desires were sufficiently in accordance with our wellbeing needs. As a more general point, I would observe that our will, like any other organ, can serve us well or poorly. It does not constitute our entire being. Our good is a matter of our whole being, not just a matter of our will.

These considerations lead me to conclude that our good is at least sometimes determined by our wellbeing needs in the absence of desire, and sometimes even contrary to what we desire when we are well informed and thinking clearly. In such cases, neither our wellbeing nor our good is determined by our prudent desires. If anything, the prudence of our desires is determined by our wellbeing needs. I shall now argue that, in general, our good is a matter of our wellbeing and only secondarily springs from the satisfaction of prudent desire. Our prudent desires concern our good only insofar as they are tied to our wellbeing interests – which they shape only secondarily and to a limited degree. In consequence, wellbeing is to be defined independently of prudent desire. I approach the question by trying to separate wellbeing and prudent-desire satisfaction enough to find room for some leverage between them. While our desires must be consistent with our overall wellbeing if they are to count as prudent and their objects as good for us, and while our choices go some way toward determining our wellbeing needs, what of *unmade* choices? How are we to assess purely would-be prudent desires? Often, what we would choose under ideal conditions is substantially determined by considerations of wellbeing. At most, we then would choose among alternatives that would contribute to our wellbeing in some way. The chosen alternative becomes further a matter of our wellbeing when we have chosen it, because it is then an actual desire. But suppose that we have not yet chosen it, and suppose that the object of would-be desire would not, unless chosen, contribute to our wellbeing. The prudent-desire account necessitates the conclusion that an object of purely would-be desire is good for us, even when it does not concern our wellbeing. Is that a reasonable claim to make? If there were a case where we would have a particular desire under conditions of knowledge and clear thinking, but where we did not actually have the desire and where that would-be desire was not entailed by our actual desires or other wellbeing considerations, would that object of would-be desire then be good for us? Of course, it is difficult to identify such a case before the desire is actualized. Normally, we identify what would be desired on the basis of what is actually desired or on the basis of other wellbeing considerations. If we know what would be desired, we know it on the basis of reasons. It is therefore difficult to find a really strong example of a prudent desire of the merely would-be variety that was not tied to wellbeing. If such a case could be imagined, where the hypothetical desire did not become actual, the nonsatisfaction of the would-be desire would, at least to my intuitions, appear to be valuatively neutral. This is because nothing, in such a case, would be eroding the wellbeing of the individual. To me, this seems decisive.

For a possible example, suppose that I have a child in my care who is happily playing. Suppose too that an ice-cream wagon is passing by. If I do not tell the child of this, the child will continue playing happily. I have reason to believe that, thinking clearly, the child would wish to be informed of the ice-cream wagon and, being informed, would form a strong desire for ice cream. The ice cream would neither help nor hurt the child, nor give it more delight than that received from the game in progress – plus any other *ceteris paribus* qualifications that might be appropriate. Were I not to tell the child, and not to buy ice cream, would I be neglecting the child's good? If the child actually desired the ice cream, I would be (perhaps justifiably) withholding a good if I did not buy the ice cream, but in the absence of knowledge or desire, and in the absence of actual utility for the child's wellbeing, it seems to me that the child is not being denied a good. (Nor, I think, would it significantly affect the case if it were an adult rather than a child. We might make up other stories, perhaps using a time-machine to find out what a person would desire under various circumstances – though having such a machine used on us is itself apt to go against our wellbeing.) In all such thought experiments, I am led to the conclusion that prudent desires do not concern our good unless and until they become actual or otherwise make a difference to our actual wellbeing.

A prudent desire, at least if it is to count so far as one's good is concerned, must be consistent with the wellbeing of the individual. Moreover we can no doubt agree that if something does/would contribute to the wellbeing of an individual, and if the individual has a prudent desire, actual or would-be, for that something, then whatever it is is a good for that individual. I have just argued that a purely would-be, nonactual, prudent desire is not morally significant when it is not tied to the wellbeing of the individual. All of this suggest that our good is a function of wellbeing rather than of prudent desire. Where the wellbeing area overlaps the prudent-desire area, there is good or bad for the individual. Where there is prudent desire but no effect on our wellbeing (that being a case of purely would-be prudent desire), there is no question of good or bad for the individual. Where there is a wellbeing need, what is needed is good for us even if we do not desire it, and our prudent desires are imprudent when they diverge from our wellbeing needs (unless directed toward some other good). I conclude, then, that our own good is that which serves our wellbeing interests, with wellbeing not to be defined in terms of prudent desires. It is our wellbeing that is basic.[1] Let us now pause to take stock.

---

1 T. M. Scanlon (1975) points out that we tend to put a higher moral priority on the need interests of other people than on their preference interests, even though they may attach more importance to a preference interest. For instance we may feel an obligation to give food to starving people, but not to help them build a religious monument, even though they may be willing to starve in order to build the monument. Is it

TAKING STOCK: RESPECT FOR INTERESTS

While it is agreed that humans do have morally significant interests there is at least a *prima facie* case that some other beings also have morally significant interests. This raises the question of what, in the case of humans, constitutes an interest, and the question of what makes them morally significant. We considered and rejected the suggestion that our interests are interests in having or avoiding certain experiences or mental states. To be sure, we often do have such interests, but an associated experience or mental state is not a necessary factor in our having a morally significant interest. We often have interests in things that do not involve that. The prudent-desire account was much more promising, taking us to have an interest in that which we would desire when well informed and thinking clearly. That recognizes the broader scope of our interests and goes further toward recognizing the role of interests in our overall scheme of things. From an anthropocentric point of view, it has the advantage of minimizing the interest of those who are less adept than we are at conceptualization. The account, though, is inadequate. To the extent that it is in any way adequate, it tacitly turns on considerations of wellbeing, which are fundamental.

One of the tasks before us is to investigate the moral significance of the wellbeing interests of nonhumans. We now take it as given that we humans have morally significant interests in that which (does or would) contribute to our wellbeing. While we rational beings have morally significant interests in things that involve our rationality, we also have significant interests in things that do not involve our ration-

that we reckon that the food is really *more* of a good for them, whether they know it or not? Or is it that moral importance is not a direct function of importance for the interest bearer – or that it is a function of only certain sorts of importance for the interest bearer? In any case, the moral significance of *their* interest, as we are to assess it, is not necessarily a direct function of the order of the interest bearer's desires. That, at least, seems to be suggested by our moral intuitions in such cases.

116

ality at all. There is no nonarbitrary reason why interests that do not involve rationality should be thought not to be morally significant. This is so whether or not the being that has the interest is a rational being, as that does not affect the interest in question. It is not right to say that an interest is or is not to count because of something irrelevant to that interest. That the beings belong to some sort of a nobility, or are members of a particular ethnic group or religion, that they have a particular sex, or that they are more or less rational does not affect the moral status of one of their interests, though it might well affect what interests they have. Because of his intellectual capacity Socrates might be subject to more pains than a pig, but in itself and apart from its effect on other interests, pain in Socrates is no more morally significant than the *same* amount of pain in a pig. Again, we humans have wellbeing interests that do not involve even our sentience, and these are also morally significant. By the same token, there is no nonarbitrary reason why the wellbeing interests of only sentient beings should be recognized as having moral significance. They are often connected with interests that do involve sentience – in the case of we who are sentient – but as we have seen, sometimes our interests do not affect our sentience (or intellectual capacity) or vice versa. Even then they are morally significant in their own right. Our under-lying whole being has wellbeing interests, and it is this, in fact, that led us, evolutionarily, to have sentience and then thought, and which gives them substance. Evolutionary priority is not necessarily moral priority, to be sure, but it is our whole being that gives moral significance even in the absence of sentience and thought. To be fair, then, we must conclude that although nonsentient beings clearly have fewer interests, the interests they do have, such as they are, have moral significance as well, to the extent of those interests. There is no significant difference to determine a difference in moral status.

While different beings have different interests, there is no viable and nonarbitrary reason why – when everything else is equal – the interests of one being ought to take precedence over the *equivalent* interests of another being. Much less is there reason why the interests of any being may be left out of moral account. I come to the following principle:

Give *due* respect to all the interests of all beings that have interests, in proportion to their interests.

This principle clearly requires considerable elaboration. Certainly we need to develop some sort of an account of what wellbeing interests are and what it is to have one, and we need to inquire about what sorts of beings have them. Then there will be many questions about what due respect is and how we are to determine how to give it in proportion to particular interests in particular circumstances. First, we shall inquire concerning individuals, asking what it is for an individual being to have an interest. Subsequently, I shall go on to the question of the moral standing of forms of life that go beyond the individual. I shall begin by probing further into *why* a wellbeing account is superior, and to show how such an account gives us a better understanding of the critically important matter of what, be we human or nonhuman, our good has to do with *us*. This will help us better to understand how to understand the good in the case of nonhumans. In this connection I shall elaborate somewhat on why I hold that interests are, very importantly, a matter not only of variety but of degree.

INTERESTS AND LIFE, AND ANIMALS

For most purposes involving competent human beings, there is no outstanding practical advantage in a wellbeing theory of the individual's good. In fact, it can be downright dangerous on a practical level. Well-meaning busybodies and not so well-meaning opportunists could use a wellbeing theory as a justification for imposing their own values on other people for the latter's own good – or allegedly for their own good. Examples will leap to mind all too readily, and there is no need to dwell on them.[2] People must be accepted as the best judges of their own interests for the practical reason that outsiders are not apt to know any better, and also for the practical reason that power-seeking individuals will otherwise all the more readily find excuses for their schemes. Still, the truth is the truth. We should not allow supposedly practical considerations to lead us to define the individual's good in terms of prudent desires. Rather, practical considerations should lead us to accept people's word about where their wellbeing lies. Taking the good of the individual to be a matter of wellbeing not only gives a truer and fuller account of a competent human's good, it also allows us to coherently employ the conception to cover nonhuman beings.

Not every being, nor every being that has a good, nor every human, is a competent human. We must be wary of theories that are too closely tied to a frame of reference designed around the paradigm of the competent human being. Descartes, recall, led himself to believe that animals were insentient, unable even to feel pain, because of their differences from humans. Frey was not so misguided as that, but he tried wrongly to tie interests and desires to language. His central mistake was not directly attributable to his identification of the individual's good with the objects of prudent desire, but even so, when it comes to beings that do not have a high level of conceptual awareness, the prudent-desire account distorts matters much more than it does in the case of competent humans. Quite apart from Frey's linguistic muddles, the prudent-desire account is much too closely tied to the human model. Humans characteristically conceptualize about things, particularly those things that concern their interests, but not all beings are conceptually oriented. Even if, unlike Frey, we recognize that animals can think about things and have desires, we do them an injustice if we identify their

2　After the Hungarian uprising was brutally put down, Janos Kadar told us that "The task of the leaders is not to put into effect the wishes and will of the masses. . . . The task of the leaders is to realize and accomplish the interest of the masses"; see *East Europe* (July 1957). No comment.

interests merely as lying in those things for which they have developed prudent desires.

The prudent-desire account of interests has misled even Peter Singer into denying that animals have interests they assuredly do have. I propose now to show how it led him astray on the particular question of whether animals have an interest in life – whether life is a good for them. My objective is not merely to answer the question of whether animals do have an interest in life, though that is an important topic in its own right. I hope to illuminate further the reasons for the inadequacy of the prudent-desire account, as it applies to animals in particular, and to work toward a better under-standing of why we need an account of interests based on wellbeing.[3] This will serve to lay some of the groundwork for a better understanding of wellbeing, one that can mean-ingfully be applied to various sorts of cases, human and nonhuman.

The question of whether killing animals violates their in-terests is to be distinguished from the separate (and less problematic) question of whether causing them pain violates their interests. Suppose we were to raise animals in such a way that they are able to live a pleasant and more or less natural life, then slaughter them painlessly. Would this be to fail to respect their interests? Singer is inclined to think that this would not violate their interests (1979a, 99–105; 1979). Although they would not experience future goods (i.e., the satisfaction of prudent desire), they would not exist to experience the deprivation. Not existing, they would have no interests to be respected or violated. To treat (normal) humans in this fashion, on the other hand, would be to violate their interests, since they have a desire to continue to live, whereas animals presumably have neither self-consciousness nor a conception of future time. Of course, killing them in the midst of a satisfying life would reduce the amount of interest satisfaction in the world, but we could

3 The following discussion is closely adapted from my "Do Animals Have an Interest in Life?" (1983).

make up for that by replacing slain animals with other animals living satisfying lives. Certainly we would replace them if we desire to remain in the farming business. This replacement gambit answers objections concerned with the maximization of interest satisfaction. In doing so, it displays one of the most objectionable, perhaps *the* most objectionable, of the features of utilitarianism: that it takes beings as more or less interchangeable bearers of interests to be satisfied. If some sort of interest satisfaction is *the* good to be maximized, then *we* are of value only as vehicles of interest satisfaction. This strongly suggests to me that something is very wrong. Our good is more a matter of us. The thing is that satisfaction of our interests is good for *us*, not that we are good for interest satisfaction.

Singer does not intend this line of thought to be a justification of the utilization of animals as normally practiced, to be sure, since most contemporary methods of animal husbandry involve significant degrees of pain. Perhaps it might serve as a basis for a free-range chicken operation where a chicken would meet a painless death after a good life. Michael Lockwood, quoting an unpublished paper by Christina Hoff, raises the point that to endorse such a practice would seem to imply that we must then condone practices that, at least intuitively, appear much more objectionable (1979, 168–9). Let us suppose that one were to buy a puppy to serve as a family pet. The family delights in the companionship of the young dog, playing with it, sharing walks and outings, and enjoying its affection. When it comes time for their annual vacation, they destroy the dog painlessly, since it would be inconvenient to take it with them or otherwise to make provision for it. On their return, they acquire another pet, making this an annual practice. Perhaps they engage the services of "Disposapup Ltd.," a commercial organization that provides well-bred puppies of good disposition, house-trained if one wants them a bit older, and attends to the annual disposal professionally and painlessly. There seems to be a high degree of parallelism between this practice and that of painless farming, insofar as in both cases, the animals live good lives and die painlessly to further human interests, and are replaced in due course by other animals living similarly good lives. If we do not violate the interests of animals in the one case, it would appear to follow that we would not be doing so in the other. Yet intuitively, the Disposapup procedure seems objectionable, if not downright disgusting. Does objecting to such a practice rest on more than an emotional prejudice? If so, what are the grounds? Do animals have an interest in continuing to live? What are the implications?

Certainly it seems like a dirty double-cross to enter into a relationship of trust and affection with any creature that can enter into such a relationship, and then to be party to its premeditated and premature destruction. (This charge would evidently not apply to the painless farming operation.) Still, it would be a morally objectionable double-cross only if Disposapup violated the interests of the double-crossed. If the redundant dog does not have an interest in remaining alive, then its interests would not be violated nor the dog betrayed. I shall argue that many animals do have an interest in remaining alive, except under some extreme circumstances, and that the prudent-desire account goes very widely astray. Then we can try to identify what is lacking.

As a subsidiary point I wish to argue, given that animals have such an interest, that it is a morally objectionable betrayal of trust to treat the family pet in the way suggested. I shall briefly consider this point before turning to the main points. If animals do have an interest in remaining alive, and if the Disposapup procedure amounts to a breach of faith, this would account for the intuitively felt difference between premature pet disposal and painless farming. I believe that the former *is* a breach of faith, holding that a relationship involving obligation need not be formalized (let alone expressed in a language). Dogs can, after their fashion, feel affection, obligation, expectation of goodwill, and trust. If we encourage such feelings in any being, human or otherwise, we have, I believe, entered into a tacit and morally significant undertaking that entails obligations on our part.

122

The fact that the dog cannot understand or conceptualize all of its interests does not diminish our burden of trust. If anything, the opposite. Double-crossing the family dog would, then, be morally objectionable – if it does have an interest in remaining alive. Whether or not one accepts this argument, however, the key and independently important question is that of whether animals do have an interest in remaining alive.

Let us note certain ways in which killing people would affect people's interests. For one thing, it would cause other people to wonder if their own number was to come up soon, occasioning a great deal of anxiety. Moreover, people close to the slain would suffer the pains of bereavement. Killing people *ad lib* would definitely violate interests. Killing dogs and chickens, on the other hand, would not normally violate interests in this way, as they would not be as aware of what was going on. However, this evaluation concentrates on the negative effects on survivors rather than on the interests of the slain. If the deceased were killed painlessly and without prior fear, these considerations would give us no reason for concluding that their own interests had been violated. More to the point, as far as the victims are concerned, is that people are self-conscious, have a conception of the future, and normally have a desire to continue to exist. We can argue therefore that if people have such a desire, they thus have an interest in having their desire fulfilled, and thereby an interest in staying alive. Killing them would violate this interest. Chickens and dogs, on the other hand, are presumably intellectually incapable of entertaining these desires. The prudent-desire account of the individual's good, then, entails that killing people contrary to their desires would thereby violate their interests, even if it were done painlessly and unexpectedly, whereas killing chickens or dogs in such a way would not violate their interests. Preference utilitarianism thus concludes that killing people is wrong, unless the total of other interests outweighs the interests of the slain, whereas painlessly killing and replacing animals is held to be morally neutral. This reason for not killing people seems too weak to many of us, since our interest in continuing to live is taken thereby as only one interest among many to be calculated into the cost-benefit analysis. That we are self-conscious and desire to live is held by some to provide a basis (with what other factors?) for a right to life that at least normally overrides other preferences. We might perhaps invoke a Kantian-style respect for autonomy. On any of these grounds, though, self-consciousness and a desire to continue to live are of central importance. That they are of great importance I would heartily agree, but I must argue that there is more to life, or to anything, being good for us than these reasons take account of.

We have already noted that our desires and our wellbeing interests may not be entirely in accordance with one another. (A thought to bear in mind: If we are not so good at recognizing or following our interests, what justification can we give for requiring that a dog recognize an interest before we concede it has it?) So, do we have an interest in life? Does even a happy person (one living a good life) have an interest in staying alive? Suppose that we were to unexpectedly and painlessly kill a happy person (replacing that person in due course with another happy person). Suppose, too, that the person desired to remain alive, and suppose even that this desire was one of the things that contributed to the person's good life. We might argue that so long as one is not killed, neither one's interests nor one's desires have been violated, and that when one is dead, one has neither interests nor desires to be violated. Singer is concerned to deny the force of such an argument (Singer, 1979a, 80–1):

> According to preference utilitarianism, an action contrary to the preference of any being is, unless this preference is out-weighed by contrary preferences, wrong. Killing a person who prefers to continue living is therefore wrong, other things being equal. That the victims are not around after the act to lament the fact that their preferences have been disregarded is irrelevant.

According to the prudent-desire account of the individual's good, employed by preference utilitarianism, to assume that

124

humans do have an interest in life would be to assume that they would, knowing all the relevant facts and reflecting on them properly, have a preference for continuing to live. This would be to assume, too, that they would not merely prefer, from such an enlightened viewpoint, to have the preference while alive, as contributing to the good life. This can be distinguished from having a preference in that enlightened state for actually continuing to live. After all, life might possibly be not in one's interests, even though while one lives it might be of practical benefit to have that desire. (As well, we must distinguish both of these preferences from preferences not to fear death, feel pain, have other people upset, and all that.) The satisfaction of the preference for having the preference while alive would contribute to the quality of one's life at least as much as would the satisfaction of the preference for actually staying alive, with the added element in satisfying the latter preference not evidently contributing to the quality of one's life while one is living it. It is not necessarily true that even most people would, under those unusual conditions of enlightenment, have the preference for actually continuing to live, as distinguished from other preferences, for it is possible that having such a preference is a matter of ignorance or confused thinking. If we would not have the preference for life under ideal conditions, there would then be nothing wrong with a suitably discreet Disposaperson procedure, as well as Disposapup. We need a reason for believing that people would have an interest in continuing to live. Of course, if we assume that prudent desires are based on wellbeing considerations, we can build a case that living, and not just preferring to live, is in one's interests. Let us assume, in any case, that humans would have such a preference under ideal conditions. The question we are concerned with is that of whether the assumption that humans would, and animals cannot, have a preference for staying alive warrants the conclusion that humans do and animals do not have an interest in life.

It follows from the prudent-desire account of one's good that animals that are not self-conscious or do not have a conception of the future, do not have an interest in continuing to live. In fairness, of course, before we disregarded an animal's possible interest in life, we would have to ascertain that it was not only linguistically incapable of expressing such a preference but also intellectually incapable of entertaining it. There is still a question or two about whether this really is being quite fair to animals. Is it unfair to animals to require that they should be capable of intellectually recognizing their interests by having conscious preferences? Even the preference utilitarian's criterion does not demand that we actually be aware of our interests, but only that we would be aware of them, were we aware of the facts and thinking about them clearly. It does no good, though, just to suggest that an animal would have a preference for continuing to live if it could entertain such a preference, for then it would be a person and not what it is, whereas a human can have an enlightened preference without being what it is not. What I do suggest is that the preference-utilitarian criterion is biased in favor of humans in that humans tend to conceptualize things more than do other animals. My claim is that humans and other animals alike, normally have a wellbeing interest in living – a morally significant interest – and that such an interest is the grounds for the human prudent desire. We conceptualize our interest in continuing to live because that is one of the things that we do with our interests, whereas other animals act in accordance with their interests in other ways.

I have already argued that what is good for us is not simply to be identified as what we prefer, and that in some cases we have preferences because of what is good for us. I shall now argue that it is conceivable that an animal can have a wellbeing interest in life, an interest that does not involve even a would-be preference. I shall then argue that the case for animals having an interest in continuing to live is as viable as the case for humans having an interest in continuing to live. There is adequate reason to believe that both humans and animals have such an interest. Moreover, as I shall argue, the interest springs from considerations of wellbeing in both cases. Preferences are not enough even to establish that continued life is good for humans. This discussion will serve to illustrate better how our good is a matter of our wellbeing interests, and it will serve as an entry to a further discussion of the nature of wellbeing interests.

Given that what we prefer and what is good for us are not simply to be conflated, and given that we humans sometimes have preferences because of our wellbeing needs, it becomes easier to maintain that an animal might have an interest (or a good) that did not result in a prudent desire. Normal humans – on the rather strong assumption that their will is behaving "properly" – will/would prefer what is good for them, except when concerned for some other good, but we cannot assume that animals will/would prefer what is good for them. *Prima facie*, there is at least the possibility that while a wellbeing interest may entail a correlative would-be preference by a person who has the interest, a similar interest may not entail a correlative preference by an animal that does have the interest but cannot conceptualize to the point of forming an appropriate preference. Pain, our previous example, can presumably be conceived of in some form by any being that can feel it, but we cannot just assume that all wellbeing interests (or goods) must manifest themselves so directly and conceivably. An interest (or good) must in some way make some sort of a difference to whatever being has the interest, but it is question-begging just to assume that the being must be able to conceive of the interest (good) that makes the difference to it. Something may make a difference to us without our being able to conceive of it. Suppose, to focus on our currently central question, that an animal *did* have a wellbeing interest in continuing to live (that it was good for the animal). It could act in accordance with this interest quite successfully by instinct or in pursuit of things it can conceive of (food, pain avoidance, etc.) without conceiving of the interest it was acting in accordance with. After all, humans can further their happiness without thinking about pursuing happiness at all. Certainly it is not logically necessary that to be an interest is to be perceived to be an interest.

Let us now ask whether animals, or some of them, really do have an interest in continuing to live. My strategy will be first to return to the question of whether humans have an interest in continuing to live, and if so, why. I shall argue that if the human interest in continuing to live is held to be merely constituted by our preference for doing so, the reason will not bear the weight placed on it. On the other hand, if the preference for continuing to live does not *create* an interest in continuing to live, but continuing to live is preferred because we do have such an interest, then any plausible reason for holding that humans do have such an interest would apply to some animals as well.

It is worthy of note that the human preference for continuing to live presents a case that is unique among our preferences. In the case of any other preference we might have, such as that for food, for the absence of pain, or for Balinese oil paintings, we can experience either the satisfaction of the preference or its not being satisfied, as the case may be. If having an unsatisfied preference is bad, one can only avoid that (while one lives) by changing or satisfying the preference. On the other hand, while one can experience the satisfaction of one's preference for continuing to live, one can never experience its nonsatisfaction. When we are dead we have no preferences to be nonsatisfied. Why, then, ought we to respect someone's preference for continuing to live? To be sure, if someone is killed, there is not the good of there being a satisfied preference for continuing to live, but on Disposaperson principles we can rectify the difficulty by bringing about another person with a similar preference. The argument that we should honor a preference for continuing to live because continuing to live is necessary for that person's attaining the satisfaction of further interests can be met on similar grounds, as we can again invoke the replacement gambit. It should also be noted that such an argument could be used in favor of killing someone to avoid their getting a severe disappointment. (Fantasy: Next time I flunk a student, instead of a felt-tipped marking pen I use a revolver.)

According to Singer, recall, the fact "that the victims are not around after the act to lament the fact that their preferences have been disregarded is irrelevant." He does not say why it is irrelevant. Can there be preferences where there is no preference haver? If so, is there any reason why we should respect a disembodied preference? Seemingly, unless we are to recognize the interests of nonexistent people, the point must be that what violates the victim's preference when I commit murder is not his or her death or my having caused it, but my act causing it, an act that I undertake during the last moments of the victim's life when he or she is still around to have preferences. This version conforms with our common intuition that there is, at least normally, something wrong with killing people. Too, it puts the moral emphasis directly on the act of killing (or allowing to die), rather than on the consequences, which would be problematic. Even so, not putting emphasis on the consequences seems more than a little odd in the context of Singer's utilitarianism. More to the point, it does not work if it is supposed to be a reason for concluding that humans do, and animals do not, have an interest in not being killed. If we take such a point of view, focusing on the act leading to death performed while the victim, however briefly, yet lives, we can argue that killing animals, however painlessly, is as much a violation of preference as it is in the case of humans. After all, the point is not simply whether one has such a preference against the act, but whether one would have such a preference if one were as aware as one could be of the relevant facts.

Although we assume that animals have no concept of death, they generally tend to have strong dislikes for acts leading to that result, or would if they knew more about it. A hunter or fisherman will tell you that animals learn fast about that sort of thing, and develop extremely strong aversions. A dog may not know that the gas chamber would kill it, but if it witnessed live dogs going in and dead ones coming out, it would soon acquire a very strong preference for not going in. It may have no concept of self, future, or death, but it has/would have a strong preference against any sort of thing leading to its death, and that is what counts according to this scheme. It might be objected that an animal does not understand the result of the process, whereas humans do – that animals form their aversions only in ignorance or by instinct. That does not cut any ice, though. Whatever might be the reasons for our basic preferences, whether instinct, further knowledge, or something else, it is our basic preferences that count on the given premises. So, on the one hand, if we interpret the prudent-desire criterion as militating against killing on the grounds that death violates a preference for continuing to live, the argument works for neither humans nor animals, as the dead have no preferences. If, on the other hand, we interpret it as militating against death-causing acts on the grounds that such acts violate the would-be preferences of those yet living, then the argument militates against such actions directed toward animals as well as against those directed toward humans.

If we take our interests to be defined by our preferences, the most we can say is that if humans have an interest in continuing to live, then so do at least most of the higher animals. We may not even say that much if we concluded that neither humans nor animals have an interest *that can be infringed* in continuing to live. If the consequences for living beings were the only morally significant considerations, there would then be no reason against the suitably surreptitious murder of the unloved, the only moral wrong in that case being indiscretion. That it would sanction the capricious murder of harmless hermits seems to me to be sufficient reason for rejecting that one. That our preferences against death-causing acts constitutes our interest in continuing to live seems, in my view, to be only slightly less unbelievable. At the very least, it seems counterintuitive that there is no more to our interest in continuing to live than a would-be preference against an act of which we may never know, and the result of which is irrelevant. It seems much more plausible that the act leading to death should be morally significant because of the end result – because it is *death* that really counts. Still, intuitions are not always the most reliable of guides. There is another, more substantive, point I would raise here. Given that preferences are the primary factors, I would ask why we should – per the prudent-desire criterion – make reference to would-be cases of knowing the (supposedly) relevant facts. In most cases, obviously, it is because we might otherwise become dissatisfied with the overall consequences in terms of our various preferences, but that could hardly be the case when it comes to death-causing acts. If I gave someone a suitable poison in her favorite drink, and she preferred, in ignorance, to drink it, she would have no dissatisfied preferences then or thereafter. It would seem that in applying the prudent-desire criterion to questions of death we are really giving tacit recognition to the significance of consequences. Death itself is significant. Once again we come back to the point that we have, or would have, preferences *because* of our interests.

Let us now take it that we humans do have an interest in continuing to live, and that we do not have the interest because we do/would have a preference for continuing to live, but have the preference, if we do have it, because of the interest. If this were the case, it would seem at least possible that an animal might have a similar interest, but not have such a preference because it was unable to conceptualize it. If it is not possible that an animal could have such an unconceptualized interest in continuing to live, this would have to be because animals lack something unique to humans. Presumably, unless we were to attach a great deal of moral importance to naked skins or opposable thumbs, that factor by which we have interest in continuing to live would have to reside in the human intellect. Something along those lines seems to me to be implicit in the prudent-desire account of one's good. This, of course, would slot in very nicely with the philosopher's prejudice that we live to conceptualize, rather than conceptualize to live. Now, though, we have concluded that our interest in continuing to live does not spring from our preferences, no matter how conceptually adept we are. If there is some additional, presumably intellectual, factor that gives humans an interest in continuing to live, what could that factor possibly be? Rationality or any other noble human quality, no matter how valuable, does not mean that *we* have an interest in our own survival (though others might have an interest in our survival). At most, it might mean that if we did have an interest in continuing to live, our interest should be given priority. But what could bestow on us an interest in continuing to live, so that our interests would be infringed by death? Perhaps we are looking at things the wrong way.

LIFE AND INTERESTS

Killing people is normally bad for them. Intuitively, one tends to think that this concept is at least as evident as any moral principle that might be proposed. We may even be inclined to think that being killed is bad for an animal, a consideration that may or may not strike us as a reason for not killing them. Even so far as humans are concerned, however, appeals to conceptualized desires and preferences cannot settle the issue one way or another. Such appeals cannot deliver the goods because concepts, desires, and preferences are not at the most basic level of what is good for us. We must search into our wellbeing to find the most basic level of our good. So far, I have not really said a great deal in explication of the difficult concept of wellbeing. We need some sort of a workable account that goes further, and which (at least in principle) gives us a basis on which we can determine whether something is in a being's interests. Certainly it must do better than the prudent-desire account. I would consider it a plus if it could do justice to the belief most of us have that being killed would be contrary to our interests.

It would be preferable not to think of beings as living *and* having interests, as if those were separable things, and we ought not to phrase our questions in such terms. An interest is not just something *had* by a being, but is a

132

more or less integral part of being that particular being. Living is not something a living being can stop doing while remaining what it is, and in general, interests are not something we can have or change like clothing. (To be sure, some of our more peripheral interests, like our interest in seeing a particular movie, can easily be changed or abandoned, but the more central an interest is to what we are, the more difference it makes to us.) A person or animal, we must remember, is not just a thing (which has things), but is a complex ongoing process as well, a life, encompassing various complex psychological and biological subprocesses traversing time and different bits of matter, events and states of affairs, incorporating thoughts, feelings, memories, pleasures, pains, urges, preferences and all the rest of us. The animal/person/life process does not just *have* interests; our interests are, I believe, inherent in the process itself. Certainly our interest in life is inherent in our being alive – the interest is part of our being what we are. A living being, unlike a tractor or a rock, is an ongoing coherent organic whole, a thing-process, with past, present, and orientation and drive toward the future. Our being killed frustrates the life process that we are, and therefore frustrates us. In general, what I take to be in our interests are those things that contribute to the overall effective functioning of our life process as a whole. This is so whether or not we are humans, and whether or not we are language users or even sentient. What we do/ would think about the interest is only part of the story, and not the central part. Our life defines our interests, each life on its own terms. What is in our interests is nonetheless in our interests if we are not aware of the interest, and even if we are not conscious of the interest's being satisfied. We need not have an awareness of being alive – which is quite an abstract concept – in order to have an interest in living our life. Whatever sort of being we are, whatever type of life we have, our own particular life is the center of our own particular good and it is, in its own way, worthy of moral consideration.

REVERENCE FOR LIFE

All life is morally valuable. In recognition of this, Albert Schweitzer was led to propose his widely noted ethic calling for reverence for all life. Schweitzer observed that "in the course of gradual evolution, man sees the circle of his responsibilities widening until he includes in it all human beings with whom he has any dealings" (1965, 13), and suggested that "only the kind of ethics that is linked with affirmation of the world can be natural and complete" (1965, 13). In a movingly eloquent, albeit somewhat vague, passage, Schweitzer tells us (1923, 253–5):

> True philosophy must commence with the most immediate and comprehensive facts of consciousness. And this may be formulated as follows: "I am life which wills to live, and I exist in the midst of life which wills to live." . . . A mystically ethical oneness with existence grows forth from it unceasingly. Just as in my own will-to-live there is a yearning for life, and for that mysterious exaltation of the will which is called pleasure, and terror in face of annihilation and that injury to the will-to-live which is called pain; so the same obtains in all the will-to-live around me, equally whether it can express itself to my comprehension or whether it remains unvoiced.
>
> Ethics thus consists in this, that I experience the necessity of practicing the same reverence for life toward all will-to-live, as toward my own. Therein I have already the needed fundamental principle of morality. It is *good* to maintain and cherish life; it is *evil* to destroy and to check life.
>
> As a matter of fact, everything which in the usual ethical valuation of inter-human relations is looked upon as good can be traced back to the material and spiritual maintenance or enhancement of human life and to the effort to raise it to its highest level of value. And contrariwise . . . evil, is in the final analysis found to be material or spiritual destruction or checking of human life. . . . A man is really ethical only when he obeys the constraint laid on him to help all life which he is able to succour, and when he goes out of his way to avoid injuring anything living. He does not ask how far this or that life deserves sympathy as valuable in itself, nor how far it is

capable of feeling. To him, life as such is sacred. He shatters no ice crystal that sparkles in the sun, tears no leaf from its tree, breaks off no flower, and is careful not to crush any insect as he walks. If he works by lamplight on a summer evening, he prefers to keep the window shut rather than to see insect after insect fall on his table with singed and sinking wings.

This is an attractive conception in many ways. It recognizes that we are all members of the community of life, interrelated and interdependent, and incorporates the ideal of moral community as well, seeking for the source and center of moral significance in life itself. The question then is not whether a being can feel pain or have prudent desires, but whether it has a life of its own.

From this, what follows in the concrete? Does this mean that we are to treat each life as being *equally* as valuable as every other life? If, as I have suggested, a life can be evaluated only on its own terms, it does seem to follow that we cannot properly discriminate between lives. Schweitzer appears to adopt just such a radical egalitarianism, taking life itself as the center of value. In doing so, he is in sharp contrast with those who take only humans to be centers of value. As well, by putting the emphasis on life, Schweitzer is also in contrast with many, such as Peter Singer and Jeremy Bentham, who are favorably disposed toward nonhumans but who give moral consideration to only limited aspects of our being. Human or nonhuman, there is more to us of moral significance than hedonism or preference utilitarianism takes account of. I applaud Schweitzer's centering his ethic on life. However, I believe his ethic is too simplistic and too egalitarian. I shall discuss and criticize it here partly because it is so widely noted – though it has little influence in philosophical circles – but mostly because it illustrates certain of the pitfalls into which a life-centered ethic may blunder. I shall use it then as a foil to show more clearly why I take the line I do in developing my own conception of moral significance. Although we ought to revere life, I shall argue that some life is more valuable than other life. This is not because only some interests count while some do not – all interests count – but because not all interests are equivalent. While lives can be evaluated only in their own terms, it is still the case that some lives are morally more significant than some other lives. Although an amoeba and a chimpanzee must each be considered in terms of what it is, the chimp has more of a life to live in its own right than an amoeba has in its own right. It is not to equal consideration for life that we must turn to ground our ethics, nor is it even to equal respect for interests. That, as I argue, is to cast a net with too wide a mesh. Interests vary widely in kind and degree, and the best we can do is to give equivalent consideration to equivalent interests.

The reverence-for-life ethic cannot provide adequate grounds for refusing ever to kill. If we do not kill, we cannot live. Even if we are not meat eaters, we could not live only from what we could gather from uninjured plants (gathering only from unweeded fields). We must also kill microorganisms to stay alive, and kill them we do, in countless numbers, whenever we wash our hands. Even so, we might perhaps revere life, and recognize and value its continuity, without absolutely prohibiting killing. After all, death is an integral part of life, and even killing seems to have some place in the scheme of things. Schweitzer in fact did allow that some killing for the sake of the wellbeing of other life is morally permissible. If we concede that some killing is permissible on the part of a conscientious moral agent, however, we are immediately confronted with the usual series of problems about what constitutes an adequate justification and where one draws the line. Yet Schweitzer tells us, such priorities as we might be able to assign must be in terms of a "wholly subjective standard. . . . How can we know what importance other living organisms might have in themselves and in terms of the universe?" (1965, 47). If ethical matters really are wholly subjective, then washing one's hands might be just as bad as Hitler's extermination programs – and the latter might be no worse than the former. It is impossible to believe that Schweitzer would allow that. Indeed, it should be noted that the first part of the quotation is at odds with the second part. If values really were wholly subjective, organisms could not have importance in terms of the universe, or in any other terms except insofar as subjective valuers might subjectively value them. Our ignorance would not be ignorance of anything. A more plausible line would be that our judgments (often) have a very subjective element because we (often) do not know the true importance of things – however importance is to be assessed. As it stands, Schweitzer gives no account of what it might mean for something to be morally important in terms of the universe, or in terms of itself, nor does he indicate what one might have to do with the other. Implicitly, he does suggest some unelaborated possibilities.

One natural way of interpreting importance in terms of the universe would be as importance to the functioning of the biosphere – taking the biosphere itself as being of moral significance. This would seem to be a very possible interpretation of a reverence-for-life ethic. Insects and bacteria, then, would be important by virtue of their collective significance. This line of thought shifts the moral emphasis away from the individual and toward what appear to be aggregates of individuals – which raises problems. Suppose, for example, that a particular species of insect is important in terms of the proper functioning of the biosphere. How important is one individual insect? One umpteen-billionth part of the importance of the whole species? Or, given the effective continuance of the species, is a single insect of no importance at all? Schweitzer certainly did value individual lives, including those of individual insects, doing so more than could possibly be supported by an appeal to the effective functioning of the biosphere or the universe at large. Indeed, he seems to reserve his sympathy for individuals, attaching no value to nature as a whole. He writes (1969, 120):

> Reverence for life and sympathy with other lives is of supreme importance for this world of ours. Nature knows no similar reverence for life. It produces life a thousandfold in the most meaningful way and destroys it a thousandfold in the most

meaningless way. In every stage of life, right up to the level of man, terrible ignorance lies over all creatures. They can't feel what happens inside others. They suffer but have no compassion. The great struggle for survival by which nature is maintained is a strange contradiction within itself. Creatures live at the expense of other creatures. Nature permits the most horrible cruelties to be committed. . . . Nature lets ants band together to attack poor little creatures and hound them to death. Look at the spider. How gruesome. . . . Nature looks beautiful and marvelous when you view it from the outside. But when you read its pages like a book, it is horrible. And its cruelty is so senseless!

Schweitzer's reverence for life is for lives individually. For the web of life as a whole, he seems to have had only abhorrence. Although individual organisms may – in some sense – have importance in terms of the universe, they do not, in Schweitzer's scheme of things, have moral importance in terms of the functioning of the biosphere. What Aldo Leopold (1949, 129–33) saw in the eyes of the dying wolf Schweitzer never saw. It is quite impossible to attribute to Schweitzer any sort of holistic environmentalism, and his reverence for life is not reverence for what Leopold called "the land." Along with Leopold, I believe that there is something of importance to life that goes beyond the individual organism.

Another way for a thing to be important in the eyes of the universe would be for it to have genuine, or objective, value, even though we might be in a position only to make subjective judgments. Although each life is morally important, this importance, from human to amoeba, would have to be a matter of degree. Indeed, Schweitzer's difficulty in knowing "what importance other beings have in themselves" suggests that there is something important there and that it is a matter of degree. What is there in a life that is morally important in the eyes of the universe, and such that one life might be intrinsically more valuable than another? Schweitzer calls upon us to extend our sympathetic insight

beyond human bounds and recognize in all life what we prize
in our own (1936):

> we find sympathy to be natural for any type of life, without
> restrictions, so long as we are capable of imagining in such
> life the characteristics we find in our own. That is, dread of
> extinction, fear of pain and the desire for happiness. In short,
> the adequate explanation of sympathy is to be found rooted
> back in the reverence for life.

Certainly these sympathy-inspiring characteristics are variable. Still, whether or not sympathy is rooted back in reverence for life, I doubt whether reverence for life can be
founded entirely on sympathy. While Schweitzer calls on us
to extend sympathy to nonhumans, he sees them in terms
that are much too human. Recall his revulsion at the way in
which insects act. Some nonhumans are quite inhuman. If
we are to value them at all, we must value them in their
difference. Insects do not dread, fear, or desire anything.
Even beings more nearly similar to ourselves are little apt to
have such abstract concepts as those of death or happiness,
and are therefore unlikely to have the motivations with which
we are called upon by Schweitzer to sympathize. If we are
to seek an ethic of appropriate reverence for all life, then we
must go beyond mere sympathy, a "feeling with" others that
presupposes a great measure of similarity. Sympathy is an
excellent beginning, so far as it carries us, but to respect other
beings appropriately, we must learn to do so on terms that
are appropriate to *them* rather than merely on our own terms.

It does seem to me that Schweitzer offers us a worthwhile
though very vague suggestion when he refers to the "importance which other beings have in themselves." Other
beings may not conceptualize things as we do, if they conceptualize at all, and they may have different emotional attitudes toward things, those beings that do have emotions;
however, they all at least have certain inherent imperatives,
together with a variety of means for satisfying those imperatives. These imperatives, be they a chimpanzee's social

139

needs or a dandelion's need for water, define that being's interests. We can now broaden the moral focus to encompass not just those interests with which we can sympathize but to encompass those interests that are important to a being in terms of its own life. These values are to be understood as being valuable not because they are like our values, or because the being that has them is like us, both of which may be untrue, but because they are the values of that being. To respect another and different life is to respect the other and different values of *that* life. The wolf must be respected as a wolf. If we take this line – which Schweitzer did not – the basis is shifted from our own subjective feelings to a more objective respect for the differing interests of others. If we go in this direction, it might be possible to develop an account not only of how lives are morally significant, but also of how lives vary in moral significance accordingly as their wellbeing structure varies.

It is a strength of Schweitzer's reverence-for-life ethic that it carries us beyond hedonism's narrow concern with pleasure and pain, and also that it goes beyond a preoccupation with desires (conscious or would-be, linguistically conceived or otherwise), seeking a moral foundation in life itself. It is a weakness that it gives us no means of making distinctions that need to be made, and no way of assigning priorities. We are given no principle by means of which we can even start to decide how much we are to revere humans, insects, mice, or trees. We are told only that we must cultivate sympathy, which is much too inadequate and much too human-centered. (We can go considerably further, I shall suggest, with the principle that we ought to value lives in *proportion* to the interests that are inherent within them.) Neither is there the least recognition on Schweitzer's part of any moral significance in species, ecosystems, or other life systems or holistic entities. Rather, we must recognize that life is a matter of differences, a matter of degrees, a matter of cases, and that there is more to it than organisms taken individually. The Schweitzerian approach is inherently too much a matter of all or nothing. In order to develop a more adequate morality we need to shift the emphasis from life per se – as if there were a per se – to those interests that make up the fabric of life. By focusing on wellbeing interests, in their variety and varying degrees, we are able to draw finer and, I would say, more accurate distinctions. By adopting an ethic based on respect for wellbeing interests we are able to get closer to what it is that gives a life, any life, its particular call on us for reverence or respect.[4]

WELLBEING

According to the account of interests toward which I have been working, interests are a function of our wellbeing needs. Nutrition, for example, is in our interests because it facilitates our life process. It is absurdly superficial to say that we have an interest in nutrition because we have an interest in, or preference for, avoiding the pangs of hunger. Rather, we are organized in such a way as to feel the pangs of hunger because we have an interest in nutrition. The pangs of hunger or the pleasures of a good meal concern us on only one level. It would be closer to the mark, though still inadequate, to say that nutrition is needed to allow us to live to experience further pleasures or the further satisfaction of preference. Even on a long-term basis, pleasure, pain, and preferences amount to only aspects of our life. While pleasure provides much of the payoff in a good life, it cannot stand alone, and certainly it cannot stand in isolation from the whole being. It is the wellbeing of the whole person/animal/

---

4 At this point I would like to acknowledge a debt to Kenneth E. Goodpaster, whose "On Being Morally Considerable" (1978) argues that all living beings are morally considerable. Neither rationality nor sentience draws the moral boundary. He notes that this conclusion lends itself to a Leopoldean-style land ethic, though he does not discuss the moral considerability of holistic entities. I found Goodpaster's ideas quite thought-provoking, and useful in developing my own. Neither our reasons nor our conclusions, however, are quite the same. For one thing, he does not share my emphasis on interests. Accordingly, although he does not rest his case on sympathy, he seems to have much the same problems as did Schweitzer concerning matters of degree.

life process that counts as one's central good. If we recognize only limited aspects of ourselves, we are very apt to find ourselves in a blind alley. (Indeed, the paradox of hedonism – as John Stuart Mill and many others discovered to their cost – is that by valuing only pleasure, we are likely to have a life that has less even of that.) The prudent-desire account of interests is much more adequate in that it moves beyond the narrow confines of hedonism. It is somewhat to be commended for recognizing that our choices make a difference to our good, and very much to be commended for recognizing that we in some way define or determine our own good. What is good for us, after all, is a matter of us. Still, what is good for us is a matter of *all* of us. The prudent-desire account is defective in that it focuses on our conceptualized desires and preferences, real and would be, taking as the source what is, at least often, only the signpost. We must inquire what it would be good for us to desire.

As I take it, our own life process defines what we are and what is good for us. I take our basic intrinsic good – that which constitutes our wellbeing – to be the general integrated functioning of our life process as a whole. Our life defines our good open-endedly, of course, since our life is open-ended. We are beings with not only a present reality but also an orientation and drive into a future that can take many forms. In our future the effective functioning of our life can also take many forms, and many things can facilitate it. This good, though, in whatever form, is not something which we can *acquire*. A good life (or even an interest in a good life) is not a separable item, not something that one can have in the way in which one has a twenty-dollar bill. Nor is it even a state of being that one achieves. It is an ongoing process, not a state of being. A good life may take many forms, but in any form it is an integrated effective functioning of one's self as a whole. Our life is a complexity spanning several levels, from the primitively biological to the abstractly conceptual, by way of emotions and desires, and quite a lot more. Accordingly, the good life is one that functions well over the various aspects of our whole being (aspects that may perhaps

142

be distinguished, but never separated). If we concentrate on only one aspect of our life – pleasures or desires, for instance – then we concentrate on only one aspect of our good.

The conception of our good I am proposing is obviously somewhat Aristotelean. What I take to be our good, as outlined previously, is something like the "happiness" (in a sense going beyond simple pleasure) or *eudaimonia* proposed as our good by Aristotle (as in the *Nichomachean Ethics*). However, I by no means simply adopt Aristotle's position as is. For one thing, Aristotle takes our highest and most essential good to lie in reason, that which is most uniquely human. As discussed previously, I believe Aristotle goes off the rails on that point. Whether some aspect of our being is unique or not is totally beside the point. What is good for us is a matter of us, not a matter of how we compare with or differ from other beings. Reason would be neither more nor less important for humans if we were only one of hundreds of rational species, some of which were more rational than we. This may well be the case in the wider cosmos. Aristotle has a better argument when he says that reason is of primary importance because it is a "higher" attribute – higher, at least, in our own scheme of things. Reason is very important in our lives. It is central in ordering our means and ends. Beyond that, it is an essential part of many of our activities, whether or not oriented toward some external goal, just because it is part of our way of doing things. Still, I do think that the other aspects of our person are not there merely to serve our reason, and I think that reason itself serves our *other* ends more than Aristotle admits. In any case, I attach importance to our whole being, and not just to the supposed top. Moreover, I by no means accept Aristotle's account of the various aspects of our being – though a detailed criticism of his account would not be useful here.

I am inclined to take our basic good as being *health*, taking the concept of health in a very broad sense. This involves our psychological and our physiological wellbeing, both internally and in relationship with the world around us. Leading a healthy life is a matter of our effective overall integrated functioning, and to live so is to have found our own highest good. In order to function healthily, we must have an environment that meets minimum adequacy conditions. Mostly, though, living healthily is a matter of getting along with the world and with ourself. Physically and mentally, we must keep in balance.

This conception of the good may prompt a charge of circularity. If good is defined in terms of *well*being, and both in terms of something like effective functioning, is that not to presuppose a conception of the good? What counts as effective? What function(s) are we supposed to perform effectively? Can we provide definitions without tacitly resting on a conception of the good? I confess that I cannot provide fully developed definitions, nor can I suggest anyone who can. That does not mean that we have come to a blind alley. It is not definitions we need so much as we need discovery of what is certainly there to be investigated.[5] Consider: There clearly is such a thing as physical good health, which evidently is a matter of effective integrated physical functioning, though biologists and physicians cannot yet adequately tell us what that amounts to. Much less can we adequately characterize what is involved in psychological good health, beyond merely noting that it too is a matter of effective integrated functioning. Even so, there is such a thing as being healthy, mentally or physically, and there is such a thing as being unhealthy. Properly, we should say that there *are* such things, for good health, mental or physical, can take many different forms – these being matters that, while meaningful, are not fully determinate. Physical good health and mental good health are themselves only aspects of our overall wellbeing, which is itself only partially and broadly determinate. A good life could take many forms. Altogether, though, what is good for us, in whatever form that good

5 Goodpaster (1978, 323) says "I fail to see why a criterion of moral considerability must be strictly decidable in order to be tenable. Surely rationality, potential rationality, sentience . . . fare no better here" [than does his "life principle" of moral considerability]. They do not fare any better than interest or wellbeing, either.

might take, is a matter of maintaining an effective integrated functional balance. Therein we have our basic interest. Those things that facilitate or contribute to our wellbeing are instrumentally good for us and are therefore in our interests. The concept of wellbeing does not presuppose a conception of the good, but is an empirical matter, determinable in principle in terms of the nature of the entity concerned.

What particular form a good life might take in an individual case must in some part be determined by chance and by surrounding circumstances – and who has not wondered what their life might have been like had they been born in a different time and place? A person who lived a good life as an Eskimo in Greenland might perhaps have had a good life of a very different sort as a shepherd in New Zealand. Wherever one finds oneself, though, one makes choices (recall Jack Benny). Whatever our choices and whatever the requirements, possibilities, and fortuitous influences of our environmental circumstances, there is no doubt more than one way in which a good life might be lived, when living a good life is possible at all. The criteria that determine whether a being has found a good life – attained a satisfactory balance – are criteria implicit within the being/life process itself. Nutrition, emotional balance, and physical exercise, for example, are good for one because they contribute to one's integrated effective functioning. Cancer and neuroses, on the other hand, are bad for one because they disrupt one's integrated effective functioning. Life turns against itself and becomes less coherent. In extreme cases it disintegrates completely.

A tractor may disintegrate from rust. The relevant difference between a living being with a good of its own and a tractor is that a tractor has no self-identity. A tractor has a function, an identity as a tractor, only insomuch as someone considers it a tractor, assigning it that function. It has needs only with respect to its externally assigned identity. By itself, it is only a lump without needs. In contrast, a living being has a self-identity that, within a broad range, entails its own requirements. Whereas cancer is bad for an organism, rust on a tractor is bad only for the farmer. Were there no tractor-user, rust would only be change. Were there no other being to care about or have a use for a cancer-stricken worm, cancer would still be bad for it. As Spinoza remarks, "The endeavor wherewith a thing endeavors to persist in its being is nothing else than the actual essence of that thing" (*Ethics*, 3.7). This is (at least roughly) what Aristotle called the *Telos*, the inherent nature of a being that defines what it is and what its effective functioning is. Living beings have an intercoherent organic wholeness that is self-defining and defines their particular wellbeing requirements within a broad range. By having a good of their own they are, as Kant should have said, ends-in-themselves. Tractors and other machines do not have this self-definition, do not have a good of their own, and can be ends only for others.

I do not claim that it is impossible that a machine might have a good of its own. Perhaps we are such machines. Perhaps some day some very sophisticated, intricately contrived machine – of which Artoo-Detoo and See-Threepio (of *Star Wars*) are prototypes more imaginative than plausible – might have a good of its own, and so have moral status. As (contrived) machines are now, though, even the most complex computer – let alone a tractor – falls far short of having a good of its own. I am in no way suggesting that life cannot arise from nonliving matter. Having life and having interests are each a matter of degree, and both no doubt arose gradually. Whether the early self-replicating molecules (or whatever) were truly alive and whether they truly had interests, and whether life and interests came about at just the same level of development are questions that need not detain us. They came about more or less together, and at first in very slight degree.

The position I am taking is quite radically at variance with most common views about what is good for us. Certainly I differ diametrically with any of the standard forms of utilitarianism on the issue of what one's life has to do with one's good. Pleasure is the intrinsic good according to classical utilitarianism, with one's life being good only secondarily, as a precondition of pleasure. The satisfaction of prudent desire is the intrinsic good according to prudent-desire utilitarianism, with one's life being an intrinsic good only when it is an object of prudent desire, insofar as it contributes to the satisfaction of prudent desire. I take the contrasting position that a living being's intrinsic good is a good life – good as measured according to the inherent wellbeing requirements of *that* life. Pleasure and the satisfaction of desire are good or bad for us only in terms of our overall life and wellbeing. It is not our life that is of only derivative significance; rather, those other things are significant because they contribute to our life. One's living being is primary and runs deeper than thought, let alone conscious conceptualized thought, deeper than the satisfaction or nonsatisfaction of desire, deeper than pleasure and pain, deeper than any of those relatively superficial things celebrated by utilitarians. I do not deny that those things are good or bad for us, I only insist that they are so by virtue of their role in terms of our life as a whole. Pain, for instance, is not a particular kind of sensation, let alone one that could happen in isolation, but is *our* pain, *our* being distressed. Pain and pleasure both are what they are only in terms of a being as a whole. It would be an utter absurdity, totally back to front, to think that the role of the rest of our being was to make pleasure and pain possible. It would be nearly as absurd to think that the role of our whole being was to make our preferences and their satisfactions possible. What we must recognize is that it is our whole in-depth being that is of primary importance.

Chapter 4

Holism

Sweet is the lore which nature brings;
   Our meddling intellect
Mis-shapes the beauteous forms of things:
   We murder to dissect.
      William Wordsworth, *The Tables Turned*

I shall now argue that various beings other than individual organisms can meaningfully be said to have interests, and that these interests are morally significant. In particular, I shall claim that species and ecosystems have morally significant interests – a claim that has important implications for environmental ethics. Making my claim involves denying that species and ecosystems are just aggregates of individual organisms, and denying that their interests are merely the aggregated interests of individual organisms. At first glance this may seem like a preposterous suggestion, one that leads us into metaphysical jungles – as if there were a Great Rabbit distinguishable from individual rabbits. I do not intend to introduce metaphysical monsters. My claim is only that certain wholes have interests that are morally significant, interests that are not the aggregated interests of component parts. Humanity is such an entity, having morally significant interests that are not the aggregated interests of individual human beings. I shall begin by discussing humanity as an interest-having entity, since even those who have no moral concern beyond the human race usually (those who have any sort of moral concern at all) have concern for humanity. To start with, my argument is that it is intellectually respectable (and true) to take humanity as an interest-bearing entity, and that we cannot properly account for the concern most of us do have for humanity, unless we, at least implicitly, do take humanity as such an entity. (Moreover, by arguing that humanity is such an entity, I remove the most common reason given by those who deny that we have moral obligations to the human race as such.) From there I shall go on to discuss the moral significance of other wholes.[1]

DO WE HAVE DUTIES TO POSTERITY?

I think that most people do recognize that future generations have moral standing of some sort. Immanuel Kant believed that "human nature is such that it cannot be indifferent even to the most remote epoch which may eventually affect our species, so long as this epoch can be expected with certainty."[2] So long as we can expect there to be humans, then, according to Kant, we will care about them. In addition to caring, we have duties to posterity. According to Passmore, on the other hand, we cannot love what we cannot know (1974, 88). Our concern for the future is concern for our children and grandchildren, who will in turn love their own children. In this way a chain of love extends into the future, but we cannot love directly into the indefinite future. No doubt Passmore is correct in pointing out that it is quite difficult to care about people we can never know, and cannot properly imagine. It is difficult enough to care about people in a distant country, let alone people who do not yet exist. But, whether or not we care about them, do we not have obligations concerning them? Whatever my attitude toward foreigners, it would be wrong of me to send one a letter bomb. Would it not also be wrong to send posterity a time bomb? As in the case of people now starving in third-world

1 Much of the following discussion is adapted from my "Humanity, Holism, and Environmental Ethics."
2 Immanuel Kant, "Idea for a Universal History with Cosmopolitan Purpose," proposition 8.

countries, many of us would happily accept an excuse for not being concerned, but reference to the difficulty of feeling concerned is as much of a red herring in the case of temporal distance as it is in the case of spatial distance. Neither can we use the excuse that we cannot know what posterity will need. As Passmore concedes, at least we know that they will need a functional biosphere (1974, 82). The only remaining grounds on which we might base a claim that we have no obligations toward posterity is the principle that a being must be in order to be of moral concern.

Such an argument fails if it can be shown that humanity itself is an entity that is an object of legitimate moral concern. I shall argue that this is indeed the case and I am optimistic enough to believe that it would be a welcome conclusion to most people that the human race does have moral significance. While we have a tendency to want to be relieved of troublesome responsibilities toward distant others, I really do think that most people recognize that other people in distant lands have moral status of some sort. Unless they are in the grip of some theory, most people will also, I believe, be prepared to grant that posterity has moral status of some sort – if that is something we can coherently believe. Whether we act as we ought is a different question.

For the moment, let us leave the interests of nonhumans out of account and consider only what is good for humans. Also, for the moment, let us assume a position that is not only anthropocentric, but atomistic: only *individual* humans count. Taking such a position will affect our environmental policy, the atomistic assumption no less than the anthro-pocentric assumption. It leads to conclusions that, apart from implications for the rest of the world, are grossly objection-able so far as humans are concerned. The fact is, some courses of action may be advantageous for each individual human, yet disadvantageous for humanity as a whole, particularly in later generations. We may each rationally and selfishly overuse a common resource (e.g., the environment) so as ultimately to erode and destroy the resource, such being what Hardin called the "tragedy of the commons" (1968).

Where this happens in the lifetime of the current users, it is in the enlightened self-interest of users to institute universal restraints. However, environmental degradation may be a time bomb that will explode some generations hence. Although future generations will reap the whirlwind, they do not now exist, and thus have no rights or interests to be considered.[3] One might perhaps argue that they will exist, and that what we do now will affect them later. However, future generations are quite indeterminate. Everything we do, like Tristram Shandy's father winding the clock, affects who will constitute future generations. If we overexploit the environment, different individuals will mate at different times, and have different children in different numbers, than if we do not overexploit the environment. We face no choices involving any stable set of future individuals.

Still, a situation in which some indeterminate and currently nonexistent people have a healthy environment seems better than a situation in which some other indeterminate and currently nonexistent people have an unhealthy one. Here we appeal to some situations as being better than some other situations. This is impossible to justify on the basis of an atomistic ethic, however, since there is no one set of individuals for the alternative situations to be better or worse for. In any case, the present generation might decide to alter its reproductive rate, reducing the population (through natural attrition) so as to match the declining viability of the environment. Together they would approach some low asymptote. Both present and future generations would then enjoy the advantages of exploitation – we might even opt not to reproduce at all – and there would be no future persons to suffer any disadvantages. I would applaud the decision to reduce the numbers of the human race, though not to eliminate it, but the rest of the scheme seems singularly unattractive One would hope that we would have grounds for

3   For a discussion, see Bryan G. Norton (1982). This point, sometimes known as Parfit's Paradox, has been discussed by Derek Parfit, without resolution, in 1982, and at much greater length, but also without resolution, in 1984.

finding the proposal immoral, not merely improbable, but there is no evident way of faulting it on the basis of an atomistic anthropocentric ethic (see Norton 1982). Since we are presupposing an anthropocentric ethic, we cannot reject these proposals on the grounds that they conflict with values concerning nonhumans. Since we are presupposing an atomistic ethic, we cannot even object to the poor prospect for the human race, so long as *individuals* are not injured. Atomism and anthropocentrism both, as I shall argue, merit rejection.

There seem to be only two ways out of the problem. One way would be to adopt some sort of a totalistic view advocating maximizing the amount of interests being satisfied. Then, situations in which there were many interests satisfied would be better than other situations wherein other people had fewer interests satisfied, or wherein there were no interests satisfied. As Parfit points out, that leads to a variety of unpalatable results. If we are to maximize interest satisfaction the optimum might be a huge population, even though the people had only a slight balance of interest satisfaction. If we are to maximize the average, then the best way might be to kill people who had less than average interest satisfaction. And so on. In any case, this approach is most unattractive in that it puts the value on the interests satisfied rather than on the people who have the interests, the people being only a means to the interest satisfaction. The better way would be to recognize that there is more of human moral significance than individuals and individual interest satisfaction.

IS A SPECIES AN ENTITY?

If we attached moral significance to the continued flourishing of humanity taken as an entity in its own right, we would have grounds for rejecting the proposals in question. On anthropocentric grounds alone, then, such a finding would be of importance for environmental ethics. But, can humanity be considered to be an entity, rather than a collection of individuals? At least since Aristotle, it has normally been taken for granted that a biological species, human or otherwise, is a collection of individuals sharing a common property. Biological taxonomy at one time relied on such an assumption. In logic texts, the individual–species relationship has long been used as a stock example of set inclusion, being assumed to constitute a simple, straightforward, unproblematic example. Actually this assumption is highly problematic. If we try to identify a property that all members of a given species have in common, we are apt to founder. Attempts to define human beings, for instance, have fared poorly, ranging from early attempts to define us as featherless bipeds (with broad nails) or as rational animals, to more sophisticated scientific attempts. Always we include too much or too little, or take refuge in irrelevancy. While we can find common properties for some species, this becomes difficult when it comes to species that are highly variable or even polymorphous, contain radically different life stages, or are beset with anomalies. A closely related problem is that species terms are highly resistant to acting in the way in which class terms are supposed to act in scientific theories (Hull 1978). They seem more like terms for individuals. This had led many biologists to suspect that the whole idea of species needs rethinking.

Taxonomic biology has long since abandoned the attempt to characterize species in terms of essential properties, instead defining species membership in terms of relevant similarity to a chosen representative (which is *not* to say typical) organism. But what is to count as relevant and what as similar? Theorists now often invoke cluster concepts and family resemblances. Given the difficulty of giving any theoretical account in terms of resemblances, many biological theorists have gone on to a rather startling conclusion.[4] They argue that as species function evolutionarily, a species has to be

4 The first major statement was by M. T. Ghiselin (1974). The idea has since been carried further. For more subsequent discussions, see Hull (1976), Kitts (1984), Bernier, (1984), Ghislin, "Can Aristotle Be Reconciled with Darwin?" (1985), Eldredge (1985), and Flowers (1986).

understood not as a class or collection of individuals, but as itself a spatiotemporally localized *individual*. What, if anything, could define the traits of a species? Genes? It is not genes or sets of genes that persist during the life of a species. Any individual gene or group of genes lasts at most only a single lifetime. Nor do genotypes persist unaltered, at least not as a general rule, since genetic replication does not produce perfect copies. Species evolve. What are central to species are genetic lineages – whether or not they define cluster traits inherent in the species. Unlike essential properties, genetic lineages can be identified. According to David Hull (1978, 340–1),

> Single genes are historical entities existing for short periods of time. The more important notion is that of a *gene lineage*. Gene lineages are also historical entities persisting while changing indefinitely through time. . . . Like genes, organisms form lineages. The relevant organismal units in evolution are not sets of organisms defined in terms of structural similarity, but lineages formed by the imperfect copying processes of reproduction. Organisms can belong to the same lineage even though they are structurally different from other organisms in that lineage. What is more, continued changes in structure can take place indefinitely. . . . Single organisms are historical entities, existing for short periods of time. Organism lineages are also historical entities persisting while changing indefinitely through time.

He says elsewhere (1981, 146):

> I am not sure why, but in the past philosophers have not realized that the characteristics usually attributed to species make no sense when attributed to classes as timeless entities. Species are the sorts of thing which evolve, split, bud off new species, go extinct, etc. Classes are not the sort of things which can do any of the preceding.

What ties a species together then is not a shared property or even a family resemblance, but the link of genetic connection. We can now see a species as an ongoing entity, a homeostatic system, filling an environmental niche, shaped by genetic

factors and by its response to environmental factors influencing genetic selection and restricting divergence (N. Eldridge and Stephen Jay Gould 1972). Like individual
organisms, species entities can profitably be considered to
be ongoing processes as well as things.

Organisms clearly do cluster into species, and most of the
time biologists have little difficulty assigning an organism to
its species. The point is that being a member of a species is
not a matter of having a particular set of properties, but of
being of a particular complex genetic lineage. It must be
confessed that the theoretical battle in biology is not over
though the tide seems definitely to be moving toward the
view that species are entities rather than classes. It must be
born in mind, though, that the question with which we are
dealing is not one of biological taxonomy. Whatever might
turn out to be the most convenient taxonomic scheme in
biology, for purposes at hand there, our question remains
one of whether species, *Homo sapiens* in particular, are entities, life processes, with their own identity, wellbeing needs,
and therefore interests.

DO SPECIES HAVE INTERESTS?

Is a species a thing to an extent that it can have its own
interests? A species, as we now understand species, does
seem to be an entity of sorts – though just what is to count
as an entity is at best a difficult question to answer defini-
tively, and might be answered several ways. A wave moving
horizontally over the water might be taken as an entity. Or
is it a sequential collection of water molecules vertically? Is
a plant an entity, or is it a changing collection of cells, interacting in a certain way? I cannot pretend to offer a definitive universal answer to the question of what is to count as
an entity, but it seems to me evident that a plant, an ongoing
life sequentially embodied in different bits of matter, is a
living entity of some sort. Certainly it fits Kenneth Sayre's
definition of a living system (1976, 91):

> The typifying mark of a living system ... appears to be its persistent state of low entropy, sustained by metabolic processes for accumulating energy, and maintained in equilibrium with its environment by homeostatic feedback processes.

A living system, such as a human or a tree, is not a concrete thing, like a tractor, but is a life process that takes place through concrete things. It is the nature of a living system that it tends to achieve or maintain states that are optimal in terms of the inherent nature of that life process. I shall further elaborate this characterization in the next-to-final chapter. The point, though, is that a living system has wellbeing needs, to whatever extent, in terms of what is necessary to maintain it, and has interests accordingly.

A species, an ongoing genetic lineage sequentially embodied in different organisms, is evidently a living system. A species is not clearly an organism, as is a plant, but it clearly is a living system.[5] Rather than become overly concerned about questions concerning what it is to be an entity, it would be more profitable to inquire into the interests of such a system and the question of how they might be favorably or adversely affected. I shall hereafter use the term *entity* to refer to anything that meets the preceding characterization. There is an obvious and trivial sense in which a species can be said to have interests: One might, uselessly, say that the interests of the species are comprised by the interests of the individual species members. Yet if we do that, we might as well bypass species entirely and just concern ourselves with individuals. This brings us no closer to dealing adequately with the problems we posed about the future of humanity. More to the point is to ask whether a species, *Homo sapiens* in particular, can be said to have interests that are not just the aggregated interests of individual species members. If a species were a class rather than an entity, the answer would clearly have to be in the negative. Classes have properties,

5   To avoid cumbersome language, I continue to reserve the term *individual* for individual organisms, even though species are also individuals of a sort. I shall also refer to individual organisms as being members of a species, though that is not to be taken to indicate class membership.

and often members, but a class does not have any wellbeing to be contributed to or detracted from, and therefore has no interests.

A species, like an individual organism, but unlike a tractor or a rock, is an ongoing coherent organic whole, a thing process, with past, present, and orientation and drive toward the future. Such is *Homo sapiens*. Humanity is not just a collection of persons with interests but is itself a living system.[6] But can *Homo sapiens* flourish or suffer other than in the aggregated flourishing or suffering of its members? Yes, because a species has complex properties and engages in complex activities that are not just the aggregate of those of the individual species members. This need not involve emergent properties. These properties and activities may or may not be analyzable in terms of the component units. In either case they remain properties and activities of the species itself. (What a plant or person does is not just the summation of what its individual cells do, nor are its interests the summed interests of those cells. Accepting this clearly true point need not lead us into a metaphysical morass.) *Homo sapiens*, for instance, has cultures, and a host of sociocultural pursuits.

---

6   To forestall possible misunderstanding, it would be well to state explicitly that at no place in this book do I advocate a holism that denies that wholes can be "reduced to" or analyzed in terms of simpler elements, nor do I claim that there are any "emergent properties" that cannot be analyzed in terms of simpler elements and their properties. I remain agnostic on those issues, so far as they have been defined. I do claim that many wholes, quite unmysteriously, have properties their elements lack. Tractors, for instance, have certain properties, such as that of being able to pull a plow, that their component wheels or ignition points lack. Such a claim is neither surprising nor controversial. Moreover, some entities, such as human beings, are wholes with enough unity and self-identity to have morally significant interests. To say this is not to deny the possibility that humans might be reductively analyzable in terms of organs, molecules, quarks, or whatever. I claim, too, or shall claim, that species and certain other things or life processes have enough unity, self-identity, and so forth to be entities with morally significant interests. If such claims are surprising or controversial, it is not because I am making surprising or controversial claims about emergent entities, but because I am saying something else surprising or controversial.

These are not the summation of what individuals are doing, but involve (among other things) complex interactions between people. These activities can serve human needs at the level of individual interests, but they can also develop in a way that transcends individuals. They are characteristic activities of the human race. The first lunar landing was indeed a small step for a man but a great step for mankind. From a more biological point of view, a species has an interest in maintaining itself in functional equilibrium with its environment as a matter of its continuing viability.

Let us now consider the proposal that puzzled us earlier, that the human race might exploit the environment while reducing its numbers accordingly. We now see how this would not be in the interests of humanity as a whole. Acting on such a decision, humanity would be in disequilibrium with its environment. Whereas it would be quite in the interests of the human race to have a smaller population in balance with the environment, being out of balance with the environment would not be in its interests, no matter how we juggled the numbers. Moreover, a species entity like an individual organism has an interest in continuing to exist. Indeed, we might say that the species has more of an interest in continued existence than does the species member, since, unlike the latter, the species does not have an inherent mortality. (Though many species do become extinct, they do not inevitably do so.) Thus, the termination of the human race would be contrary to its interests, even if it were to happen in such a way as not to infringe the interests of individual humans.

ARE THE INTERESTS OF HUMANITY MORALLY SIGNIFICANT?

Granted that humanity has interests in its own right, are those morally significant? This may seem one of those things that are beyond being argued for. Even so, one might conceivably agree that humanity as a whole has interests, yet hold that those interests are not morally significant in their

own right, apart from the interests of individual persons –
just as we might conceivably agree that a business corpo-
ration has interests and yet deny that they are morally significant, though the interests of stockholders, employees,
consumers, and other persons are morally significant. The
idea that the interests of humanity as a whole are morally
significant is not a direct corollary of our presupposed
anthropocentrism.

I argue that the interests of humanity as a whole are morally significant. As I am (for the moment) presupposing anthropocentrism, I must rely on whatever factors are supposed
to make the interests of individual humans morally significant. So far as I am concerned, any interests are morally
significant, but I must here restrict myself to more widely
accepted principles. The commonly given reasons are that
humans are rational, autonomous, capable of moral agency,
sentient, or are beings with which we have interpersonal
relations. Humanity as an entity has at least some of these
properties. Individual humans are typically rational, but so
is humanity as a whole rational, with a rationality that is not
just the aggregation of that possessed by individual rational
beings. Our cultural histories, our science, philosophy, arts,
laws, and the languages that serve as their vehicle, are all
complex activities that are more than aggregations of individual activities. In engaging in them, humanity acts as a
rational being. Moreover, it acts as a moral agent, doing or
not doing things for morally relevant reasons. To be sure,
human activities and institutions are tools by means of which
individuals achieve their ends, but sometimes we are their
instruments. They function and achieve effects that are not
just the summation of what individuals do or intend, and
they do so, in considerable part, for morally significant reasons inherent within them. What the Magna Carta means
now is not what was conceived by its framers, and all that
it means now is not entirely grasped by any individual. Nor
is it just the summation of individual intentions. In a metaphorical but nevertheless real sense, our institutions and
systems develop a "life" of their own. Humanity is auton-

159

omous in at least as strong a sense. Both individual and species are limited in their possible courses of development by their environment, but both very often follow their own rationale. Again, individuals do have interpersonal relations; individuals also have reciprocal relations with humanity as a whole. We gain benefits from the human race and contribute to its interests, or each may fail the other, just as we may fail with regard to other individuals. Because rationality, autonomy, moral agency, and significant relationships characterize humanity as a whole as much as they do human individuals, they provide equally good reasons for considering the interests of the human species as a whole to be morally significant.

There remains the question of sentience. *Homo sapiens* the species certainly is not sentient in any straightforward sense. The species as a whole might properly be said to respond to its environment in many ways, and we might conceivably hold that it has awareness, but so far as we have any reason to believe, we are sentient – have feelings – only on the level of the individual organism. Why and in what way is sentience thought to be necessary for moral considerability? The most plausible reason why sentience should be necessary in order for interests to be morally significant is that it should make a *felt* difference to the interest haver, whether its interests are satisfied. It is not interests as such but the felt satisfaction (or felt nonsatisfaction) of them which, on this line, is taken as the key factor. If we adopt this approach, then the extinction of the human race would have to be accounted as morally unimportant so long as no one felt bad about it.

We might perhaps argue in the opposite direction. We might argue against the sentience requirement on the grounds that the wellbeing of the human race *is* of direct moral significance – however individuals might feel about it – and that this direct significance is incompatible with the sentience requirement. There are other, independent, reasons for rejecting the sentience requirement. In connection with Nozick's fanciful "experience machine" we argued that feeling (experiencing the mental state appropriate to) the satisfaction of a morally significant interest is not always a necessary and sufficient condition for the morally significant interest to be satisfied. Sometimes it is necessary and sufficient, these being the cases wherein it is the experience itself in which we have the interest. However, it is not always sufficient, in that one might conceivably have the experience of the satisfaction of an interest, though not the actuality of its being satisfied, in a case where the experience on its own is not all that is of significance. I earlier suggested a few examples. Again, cases indicated that the experience is not always necessary. To be sure, it is very nice to experience the satisfaction of one's interests. Even so, sometimes the actuality is morally significant in its own right, whether or not we experience the satisfaction. If the sentience criterion is not always applicable in the case of individual humans, we can hardly demand that it must necessarily be applied in the case of the human species. Unlike the species, we human individuals are geared to feel about our interests, so it is hardly surprising that our interests are commonly tied to our feelings. Species, however, our own included, are not organized in such a fashion. In the case of species, therefore, there is even less plausibility to the sentience criterion as an *a priori* requirement for moral significance.

Because *Homo sapiens* does have interests in its own right, and because those interests are morally significant by any plausible criterion – the sentience criterion not being plausible for universal application – and because there is an initial presumption in favor of the human race as being morally significant, a presumption that can be met only if the species is an entity/living system with morally significant interests in its own right, we should proceed to draw the intuitively plausible and logically indicated conclusion: that the interests of *Homo sapiens* as such indeed are morally significant.

That the human race is an entity or life system with morally significant interests clearly has implications for environmental ethics. In common with many other ongoing wholes, as well as individual organisms, humanity has an interest in continuing in a healthy equilibrium with its environment.

Preserving (or, perhaps more accurately, establishing) the wellbeing or health of our species will clearly require choices affecting the environment and our relationship with it, and those things that we do affecting the environment will often, if not always, affect our species. Even from an anthropocentric point of view, the interests of individual humans are not the only interests that require moral consideration. There is humanity itself to consider. There are many problems of the "tragedy of the commons" type arising in matters regarding reproductive policy, environmental utilization, and general life-style. In such matters we are obliged to try to give due consideration to *all* relevant interests.

That species in general have interests will be of even more importance for environmental ethics if we accept, as I have already argued, that nonhuman interests are also morally significant. This opens the door to a vast range of possibilities. By way of example, that a species has morally significant interests certainly tends to support our common intuition that there is something particularly wrong with causing (or allowing) the extinction of a species. A general condemnation of causing (or allowing) extinction would be very hard to support unless we appealed to something more than the interests of individuals, human or otherwise. Apart from both the question of whether the snail darter, for instance, is of benefit to humans, and the question of whether individual snail darters have morally relevant interests, there is the matter of the interests of the snail darter species itself to be considered. I believe that those interests are morally significant, sufficiently so as to provide good reason for not driving that species of fish to extinction. The interests and moral status of species are matters we will have to go into more thoroughly.

Species may not be the only wholes that have morally significant interests. It may be that wildernesses and ecosystems also have morally considerable interests. Does it seem too farfetched that a wilderness or ecosystem should be enough of a thing to have interests? Let us ask first whether a lichen has interests. A lichen is a symbiotic association of algae and fungi combined with mutual benefit as a result. Individual algae and fungi, and their respective species, all have interests. Does the individual lichen, which is really something like a small closely knit ecosystem, have interests? It is an organic ongoing whole, a continuing life process that can flourish or languish, and which clearly has a wellbeing. I believe, then, that a lichen does have interests. For parallel reasons I hold that a wilderness or an ecosystem is an entity/life process that has interests. To respect the integrity of a wilderness or ecosystem would include permitting it to function spontanteously in accordance with its own nature. The interests and moral status of such holistic entities as these are something we will go into more thoroughly in the following.

ON THE ETHICS OF EXTINCTION AND SURVIVAL

It is not only among humans that the interests of the species are not just the aggregated interests of individuals. There are moral reasons against causing or allowing the extinction of species, and we cannot give adequate recognition to the interests of species merely on the basis of a respect for the interests of individuals. I shall argue these points, and argue further that interests of species encompass more than simple survival. The interest in survival is only one aspect of a complex of interrelated interests, interests that largely center on the relationship of the species with its environment. When, for instance, the mountain lions were removed from the Kaibab Plateau of northern Arizona, the resulting population explosion of the Kaibab deer, the attendant environmental degradation, and the subsequent crash of the deer population weakened the species in numbers, health, and environmental stability. The interests of the species had suffered – even though the species itself was not actually threatened with extinction. The species, unlike individual deer, had an interest in being preyed upon. (For a more than usually thorough discussion, see john P. Russo [1964]. There was, of course, more to it than just the deer–mountain lion balance.)

I do not wish to prejudge the issues of extinction by claiming that extinction is always and inevitably bad. We might
say "good riddance" in the case of the smallpox organism,
and perhaps, in the distant past, it was time for the trilobite
or Neanderthal man to take its leave. Neither shall I condemn
as moral monsters all who were willing to condemn the snail
darter. One can at least raise questions of costs and benefits.
Still, the enormousness of extinction, whatever we decide
about its enormity, makes it something that requires considerable justification so far as moral agents have any choice in
the matter. Let us consider some of the reasons commonly
suggested why, at least normally, we ought to protect other
species rather than cause or permit their extinction. Reasons
often given are concern for individual members of other species, and preservation of the ecosystem (or the beings in it)
for the benefit of present or future humans as an economic,
recreational, aesthetic, scientific, or genetic resource. Some
of these reasons have considerable merit, so far as they go.
As we become more sophisticated we become progressively
more aware of how tampering with the natural world can
rebound against us humans in previously unforeseen ways.
Too, increased concern for nonhuman individuals may lead
us to deplore their wholesale slaughter. Yet such reasons
only go so far. I shall argue, first, that anthropocentric reasons cannot provide us with a basis that is in general adequate for assessing the significance of species survival and
extinction. We must take nonanthropocentric considerations
into account. I shall go on to argue that even on a nonanthropocentric basis we must go beyond the consideration of
individual interests, and take into account the interests of
wholes. I have already argued that interests are significant
and that wholes have interests. Now I am arguing that we
must actually have recourse to nonhuman and nonindividual
interests in order to deal with this question. We can get by
with nothing less.

For tactical reasons, when dealing with politicians and the
general public, environmentalists often find it convenient to
propose anthropocentric reasons in favor of their conclu-

sions. Such reasons are more widely accepted. There are a number of anthropocentric reasons why we might want to preserve another species, reasons that are quite independent of any concern we might feel for nonhumans. Many of these reasons are economic. Whatever his attitude toward whales, a whaler might well wish to avoid the extinction of his source of livelihood. The plain fact is, though, that many species, including endangered species, are of no economic benefit. Aldo Leopold (1949, 210) was quite right in pointing out that:

> One basic weakness in a conservation ethic based wholly on economic motives is that most members of the land community have no economic value. Wildflowers and songbirds are examples. . . . When one of these non-economic categories is threatened, and if we happen to love it, we invent subterfuges to give it economic importance. At the beginning of the century songbirds were supposed to be disappearing. Ornithologists jumped to the rescue with some distinctly shaky evidence to the effect that insects would eat us up if birds failed to control them. The evidence had to be economic in order to be valid.

Not only are many species of no economic value; some of them would be expensive to maintain. Much has been made of the snail darter and Furbish lousewort cases in the United States. Neither of these endangered species could plausibly be considered to be a useful economic resource, and both have gotten in the way of economic development. There are many other such cases in various countries. If there are reasons for preserving such species, the reasons will have to go beyond their simple economic value.

Not all anthropocentric reasons for species preservation are straightforward economic ones, however. Because we depend on the biosphere for our very lives, we prudently should see to it for our own sake that it continues to function adequately. Some species are of considerable but indirect benefit to us, something we all too often discover to our cost, finding out only when something happens to the species. Rachel Carson's *Silent Spring* drew this point to public attention quite forcefully, and now there seems to be a high degree of public awareness of it. Accordingly, environmentalists often appeal to this point when attempting to rally public support for species protection. After all, it might be pointed out, the value of the mountain lions of the Kaibab Plateau was not known until their extermination demonstrated it. Again, to take a mere one of Carson's examples (1965, 22), no one attached much importance to those insignificant-seeming insects that preyed on the red-banded leaf roller, until they were killed off by spraying programs. Then, the DDT-resistant leaf roller went on to annihilate great numbers of apple orchards. Numerous other cases can be cited where we did not know of the potential danger until we disrupted the natural balance in particular ecosystems. We can thus argue that the extermination of species might yield dire consequences that would not be discovered until too late, consequences that perhaps threatened not just our bank balances, but our very life-support system. Once the species were gone, we could not repair the damage.

The fact remains that some species are not at all important to the functioning of the biosphere. For instance, some species occur only in very restricted areas. When the Tasmanian Hydro-Electric Commission flooded beautiful Lake Pedder in South-West Tasmania (in 1972), they exterminated seventeen species of plants and animals. Their absence caused no material harm to any human. Perhaps they were vital to their own tiny ecosystem, but that ecosystem as a whole was destroyed without material injury to human interests. Materially, the case is the same as if the region had been under water from the start, for natural reasons. Morally, though, we have done injury, and have morally diminished ourselves. We can fall back on yet other reasons for preserving endangered species. Perhaps the organisms are of scientific interest. It might even be that the creatures have some currently unknown property that would benefit humankind greatly. Seemingly insignificant and unlikely species have proved very valuable in the past. Penicillin was among the most unexpected of discoveries. As it happens, many of our pharmaceuticals are derived from uncommon plants. (There are others that are now human-made but which were discovered only because of their natural occurrence.) More such pharmaceuticals are being discovered every year. Human lives are being saved that could not have been saved before. Yet all too often the race to find them is a race against extinction. On almost a daily basis, barely known species of plants, particularly in tropical rainforests, become extinct. No doubt some become extinct without our being aware of them at all. In all probability, some of those extinguished species would, if understood, have been of considerable benefit to humanity. By causing (or, much less commonly, merely allowing) those species to become extinct, we thereby forever lose any possibility of reaping those benefits.

It is not just a matter of strange plants with weird and wonderful pharmacological properties. It frequently happens that rare species of animals are found to have a scientific value that is both considerable and unexpected. Numerous examples may be cited. The primitive Australian ant *Nothomyrmnecia macrops* is an instance of a rare species achieving unexpected scientific prominence (Hölldobler 1984). The insect is of no economic or medical value. One would hardly expect that one kind of ant more or less – an extremely rare one, at that – would have any particular significance. Besides, if scientists wanted to know more about them, there were preserved specimens that could be inspected. Recently, however, this ancient species has attracted attention for the light it sheds on the early evolution of social behavior. It represents an early developmental stage in the rise of insect social life. The colonies are smaller, and organized differently from less primitive species. By investigating *N. macrops* we may find out more about how insect societies came about. By investigating many social species we may eventually come to a better understanding of the evolutionary background of human society. Scientists are very hopeful. To gain the information they want about *N. macrops*, they will have to study the species not as dead specimens, but as living societies functioning in their native environment. Scientists are asking questions here that not only were not asked before, but could not have been asked before, as no one knew how to ask them. Indeed, they are still progressively working out what questions they need to ask. Sociobiology is still a new science, in a formative stage. More generally, we obviously cannot know now what the questions are that the various sciences do not yet know how to ask. Nor can we yet know what species we will want to ask about. We can only hope that the species will still be there when we are able to raise the right questions.

These reasons for not exterminating species have a great deal of cogency and are usually decisive (which is not to say that they will effectively persuade politicians). They are reasons to be weighed in any case of an endangered species, and they provide particularly compelling arguments against the mass extermination of little-understood species, as in the case of the large-scale clearances of tropical rainforests. Even so, such anthropocentric reasons are not always decisive. Let us suppose a worst case – worst for the interests of an endangered species. Let us suppose that we have a single species that occupies a very restricted area, and let us suppose that there would be considerable human benefit derived from destroying that habitat, thereby exterminating the species. We assume that the species cannot be transplanted. Neither the dam that flooded Lake Pedder nor the dam that destroyed the snail darter provides a case in point, since neither dam was needed. Let us imagine some case where the development actually would be of significant benefit to humans. As a hypothetical case, imagined on the basis of actual cases, let us suppose that considerable human benefit could be derived from utilizing a remote and not particularly attractive valley in Australia. For some reason, no other valley will do. No wilderness will be despoiled, no scenic spot marred, no person harmed. The only conceivable reason for not proceeding with the project is that the valley is the sole habitat of a single one among the many species of Australian possum. The project would doom that particular species of possum.

Are we offered adequate reason for sparing the possum

species by the bare possibility that the little creature might be of some scientific interest, or that it might have some currently unknown property that would benefit humankind greatly? Suppose that we bring in a team of top-flight possum specialists to study the species. These scientists conduct as thorough an investigation as other species of possum (and there are very many others) are likely to receive in a great many years. The committee of inquiry unanimously reports that this possum, though undoubtedly a distinct species, does not offer us properties strikingly different from those of many of the other species that are quite common. It seems highly unlikely that the particular array of characteristics that this species embodies would turn out to have unusual, let alone unique, significance. Extinction, then, would represent little loss of genetic resource. If anyone ever needed a possum for anything, there would still be plenty to choose from, with not much to choose between them from our point of view. Aesthetically, the possum provides only a marginal resource. It is moderately cute, but no more so than other possums. Very few people could tell them from other possums, and many more people would benefit from the project. In short, the species would never be missed – as many species have not been missed. Of course, there is always a *very* slight possibility that this particular species could turn out to be beneficial. Still, if we capitulate to long odds like that, we could never do anything. What is much more certain is that humans would benefit from its demise.

I would wish to spare an endangered species such as that. Even if the species were of no earthly use to us, or to the rest of the biosphere on which we rely, and even if there were substantial economic or other benefit from forcing its extinction, I would still believe that we ought to preserve the species. *That* living entity has moral significance in its own right. That other species are largely similar or that they can equally well serve human purposes is beside the point. Perhaps if the stakes were high enough, causing extinction would be allowable, but they would need to be very high. I have already presented my nonanthropocentric reasons for reaching such a conclusion. My point here is that, in general, we cannot reach such conclusions by arguing on anthropocentric grounds alone. Substitutes are inadequate.

An ethic that deals adequately with the issues of extinction must not only avoid being anthropocentric, it must avoid being atomistic. We must recognize that species *as such* have morally significant interests as living entities in their own right. A concern for nonhuman individuals does not by itself entail a concern for species protection. If we adopt the moral principle of giving equal consideration to the equivalent interests of all beings, that is a reason for considering individuals, but by itself it is not a reason for preserving species. Why should we preserve the habitat of about a hundred or so whooping cranes, and otherwise protect them, when the same amount of time and money might aid many more members of other species? A hundred starlings have interests at least roughly comparable. A similar expenditure would feed some number of starving humans elsewhere in the world. Is it not speciesist to differentially cater to the interests of members of one species, for example the whooping crane species, just because they are members of that rather than some other species? Of course it may well be maintained that members of some species have more interests, or have properties that make them inherently more worthy of moral consideration. Whales, for instance, arguably are quite intelligent. Whooping cranes, however, and members of many or most other endangered species appear not to have extraordinary levels of intelligence, nor any other property that could plausibly qualify those individuals for preferential treatment. While sentient, whooping cranes are hardly exceptional in this regard. Still, they are rare. Unlike intelligence or sentience, however, rarity is not a property of individual candidates for moral concern. Although whooping cranes are an endangered species, an individual whooping crane is neither more nor less endangered than any other individual in an equivalent physical situation. Given that neither rarity nor endangered-species status could possibly be a property of an individual animal at all, let alone a morally significant one, why would it not be speciesistic, if indeed it is not, to give preferential treatment to whooping cranes? This is not a difficulty the preservationist can avoid by positing a problematic interest on the part of individual whooping cranes in having descendants. An individual whooping crane has no more of a procreative interest than does an individual starling. On the criterion of individual interests, then, it seems to follow that we have no reason not to let a species go quietly extinct if its individual members make no outstanding call on us, or if the interests of those individuals are less important than those of other individuals. If we are to take species preservation as a moral priority, we need a better justification than just a concern for individual species members. We need to recognize the moral standing of species as wholes.

Not all who base their ethics exclusively on the interests (or rights) of individual organisms would accept this imperative. According to Tom Regan (1983, 360):

> On the [individual] rights view, the reason we ought to save the members of endangered species of animals is not because the species is endangered but because the individual animals have valid claims and thus rights against those who would destroy their natural habitat, for example, or who would make a living off their dead carcasses. . . . But though the rights view must look with favor on any attempt to protect the rights of any animal, and so supports efforts to protect the members of endangered species, these very efforts . . . can foster a mentality that is antagonistic to the implications of the rights view. If people are encouraged to believe that the harm done to animals matters morally *only when* these animals belong to endangered species, then these same people will be encouraged to regard the harm done to *other* animals as morally acceptable. In this way people may be encouraged to believe that, for example, the trapping of plentiful animals raises no serious moral question, . . . [however] the mere size of the relative population of the species . . . makes no moral difference. . . . Since [members of endangered species] are not

171

mere receptacles of interests or renewable resources placed
here for our use, the harm done to them as individuals cannot
be justified merely by aggregating the disparate benefits derived. . . . That is what makes the commercial exploitation of
endangered species wrong, not that the species are endangered.

Regan is quite right in pointing out that we should not
be misled into thinking that we may treat members of a
well-populated species just as we please, merely because
there is no shortage of them. He also has a strong point
when he notes that species would not be likely to be endangered if we did not injure individuals or deprive them
of their habitat. When we exterminate species, we frequently do so not by murder but by starvation: We deprive species of a viable habitat. Still, this point will only
carry us so far, and not far enough. Regan's focus on sentient animals for one thing leaves open the question of
insentient animals and plants. What do we do about endangered plant species, such as the Furbish lousewort?
On my account, a plant species has morally significant interests and by virtue of those interests ought, at least normally, to be protected from extinction. I also recognize
that individual plants have morally significant interests,
though I consider their interests in not being eaten to be
very slight, much slighter than my interests in eating them.
Even on the plant's own terms, life is relatively unimportant compared with reproduction and the flourishing of its
species. The plant species, however, has a further set of
interests, with survival at the top of the list. The interests
of individual plants are slight, whereas the interests of the
species are considerably more important and we ought not
to allow lightly the extinction of any species. Perhaps others will assess the moral significance of individual plants
differently than I do. The fact remains that whatever
moral status we assign plants, if we are willing to sanction
plant killing, then any moral principle opposed to causing/
allowing the extinction of plant species must be based on
something other than a concern for individual plants. Any

such principle must be based either on a concern for other individuals who or which might be affected, or on a concern for the species itself (or for the ecosystem of which it is a part). I maintain that we cannot do justice to the ethics of plant extinction unless we take the interests of plant species into account.

The point I made in connection with plants really extends to sentient forms of life as well, whatever the basis on which we assess the moral status of individuals. If our concern is solely with individuals, then, we must concede the possibility of acquiescing in extinction without further consideration if the rights or interests of individuals so dictated. Regan accepts this conclusion. As we noted before, he says (1983, 359):

> If, in a prevention situation, we had to choose between saving the last two members of an endangered species or saving another individual who belonged to a species that was plentiful but whose death would be a greater prima facie harm to that individual than the harm that death would be to the two, then the rights view requires that we save the individual.

There is room for dispute about how we are to assess and assign priorities between individual interests, but Regan's conclusion is inescapable. If our ethics is to be based on respect for individual interests, then considerations of individual interests must prevail. Hence, I conclude, the interests of species are not adequately protected by a concern for individuals. Not only are the interests of species morally significant, but a consideration of their interests is not redundant.

This does not mean that we ought to shed tears for the extinction of the smallpox organism. The smallpox species and even its individual organisms have an interest in survival. Yet individual humans and the human race as a whole have an interest in avoiding the depredations of smallpox, and these are interests that appear to me to be more, and more significant, then any smallpox interests. Even so, there is cost as well as benefit in the eradication of smallpox. Although I would not put an absolute ban on causing extinction, I certainly would not draw my lines in the same places that Regan draws his. I would agree to causing very considerable inconvenience to humans or other sentient individuals in order to preserve the Furbish lousewort, though this is a matter of degree and limits. (I could not agree to half the population of North America being tortured to death in exchange for the lousewort – a choice we are unlikely to be faced with.) Moreover, I advocate interfering with – if necessary, shooting – feral cats, Grand Canyon burros, rabbits in Australia, or other environmentally disruptive sentient individuals in order to preserve plant or animal species, or to preserve the integrity of an ecosystem. I would so do even where the balance of individual interests was to the contrary. Just where we draw the lines will be a matter of cases, and a matter for disagreement, but if our moral lines are to be morally defensible, we must recognize the interests of species and, I believe, ecosystems.

Regan tells us (1983, 362):

> The [individual] rights view does not deny the possibility that collections or systems of natural objects might have inherent value – that is, might have a kind of value that is not the same as, is not reducible to, and is incommensurate with any one individual's pleasures, preference-satisfactions, and the like, or with the sum of such goods for any number of individuals. The beauty of an undisturbed, ecologically balanced forest, for example, might be conceived to have value of this kind. The point is certainly arguable. What is far from certain is how moral rights could be meaningfully attributed to the *collection* of trees or the ecosystem. Since neither is an individual, it is unclear how the notion of moral rights can be meaningfully applied.

The emphasis is Regan's. If we see species and ecosystems as *collections*, rather than as wholes, then the problem truly is unsolvable, for the interests of a collection would have to boil down to the interests of the members of the collection. The key issue is not whether species and ecosystems are collections that somehow have distinctive interests, but whether they are collections to start with. They are not.

ENVIRONMENTAL FASCISM

Regan makes another point here as well, a point that does have considerable merit. He is concerned that the rights of the individual might be sacrificed for the sake of some overarching environmental whole (1983, 361–2, quoting Leopold 1949, 205 and 224–5):

> It is difficult to see how the notion of the rights of the individual could find a home within a view that, emotive connotations to one side, might be fairly dubbed "environmental fascism." To use Leopold's telling phrase, man is "*only* a member of the biotic team," and as such has the same moral standing as any other "member" of "the team." If, to take an extreme, fanciful, but, it is hoped, not unfair example, the situation we faced was either to kill a rare wildflower or a (plentiful) human being, and if the wildflower, as a "team member" would contribute more to "the integrity, stability, and beauty of the biotic community" than the human, then presumably we would not be doing wrong if we killed the human and saved the wildflower. The rights view cannot abide this position, . . . because it denies the propriety of deciding what should be done to individuals who have rights by appeal to aggregative considerations, including, therefore, computations about what will or will not maximally "contribute to the integrity, stability, and beauty of the biotic community." Individual rights are not to be outweighed by such considerations (which is not to say they are never to be outweighed). Environmental fascism and the rights view are like oil and water: they don't mix.

There is quite a lot to be said about this. First, we must recognize that Regan does have a very valid point in the midst of the above. History is full of bad excuses for the repression of individuals, tyrants and demagogues always having some high-sounding claptrap about the greater good. People have been called upon, or forced, to sacrifice themselves for the country, the race, the working class, the true faith, future generations, or whatever. Calls for personal sacrifice for the greater good have come to have quite a bad reputation – particularly when it is someone else doing the calling. Regan is right to object to that sort of thing. Yet we should not overreact and go to another extreme, finding moral importance *only* in the concerns of individuals. Just as interests are interests, whether they are had by humans or nonhumans, interests are interests, whether they are had by individual organisms or by wholes. Although it is difficult to compare the interests of different beings, and even more difficult, in both theory and practice, to compare the interests of different sorts of beings, that is no excuse for simplifying matters by dropping some of the variables out of the problem.

Regan evidently does allow that sometimes an interest of one individual ought to give way to that of another individual as when we are called upon to respect the rights of another. Why, then, may it not sometimes be that an interest of an individual ought to give way to that of a whole? Because the whole is thought to be only some sort of collection, with aggregated interests? Regan, no utilitarian, holds that some rights take precedence over the aggregated interests of others, with mere numbers not making a critical difference. To illustrate Regan's point, we can use one of the stock antiutilitarian examples: It is not right to torture a person to death, even if the agony of the victim is less than the combined ecstasy of the participating sadists. This seems to me to be fairly persuasive. Even if we agree that some rights or interests are not to be overridden by aggregated lesser interests, however, we need not presuppose that the interests of wholes are aggregates. Neither need we presuppose that wholes cannot have rights that take precedence over many of the interests of individuals. Perhaps a wilderness, a nonhuman species, or future generations (the human species) have interests that ought not to be sacrificed in favor of the interests of bureaucrats or contractors in building a dam. This might be, even if it were the case that bureaucrats and contractors had more to lose by not building the dam than any individual had to lose by its being built. If some rights or interests are not subject to simple utilitarian considerations, it may be that wholes as well as individuals have such privileged rights or interests.

There is still more to be said here. The term *environmental fascism*, introduced by Regan with scare quotes and subsequently used without the quotes, together with the hypothetical example about killing a person to save a rare wildflower, conjures up a picture of fanatic environmentalist monomania. Similarly, animal rightists such as Regan himself have been lampooned by suggestions that they would shoot a hunter to save a duck, or that they would allow a baby to die of leukemia rather than perform medical research on a mouse. Narrow criticisms contribute no more to the discussion than do narrow ethical theories. Environmentally oriented philosophers do not claim that ecosystems (or other environmental wholes) are the only things that count, any more than animal rightists claim that (nonhuman) animals are the only things that count. Leopold was saying something rather novel, and to many people incomprehensible, when he claimed that the biotic community has moral standing and great moral significance in its own right, but his claim that acts are right or wrong accordingly as they contribute to or detract from the wellbeing of the biotic community was by no means intended to serve as an exhaustive definition of right and wrong. To say that things that affect the biotic community are thereby morally significant is not to say that this is the only dimension of moral significance. Nor is it to say that in all instances, environmental interests must take precedence over any other interests, without any further consideration of relative importance. Even if such an absurd position could properly be attributed to Leopold, we would then have only a reason for rejecting that position, and not for rejecting a position holding that environmental wholes are included among the various centers of value. In this connection, I was rather surprised that Regan finds it objectionable that Leopold holds that a human is "*only* a member of the biotic team" (again, Regan's emphasis). I suppose that

Regan interprets this to mean that a person has value only as a functional component of the biosphere. Such a view certainly would be objectionable. For my part, I interpret Leopold as meaning that we do not occupy an automatically privileged position, that our claims have to stand on their own merits. This is not to say that a person has no stronger claim than does a dandelion. It is to say that our claims are to be assessed for what they are, not for the special position we arrogate to ourselves. With that I am sure Regan would agree. What we must not do is fall into the trap of thinking that we must choose between accepting individual values or accepting holistic values. Not only can we have it both ways, we *must* have it both ways. As Leopold rightly tells us, "In short, a land ethic changes the role of *Homo sapiens* from conqueror of the land-community to plain member and citizen of it. It implies respect for his fellow-members, and also respect for the community as such."[7]

THE WELLBEING OF SPECIES

Survival is one interest of a species, one that is presupposed by other interests. Yet we must keep sight of the fact that species do have other interests. Just as an individual has an interest in living well, which is more than merely living, so species have an interest in surviving well. Both species and individuals need to fulfill their nature in an appropriate environment. A species has an interest in continuing in equilibrium with its environment, in fulfilling its nature as a species, and in fulfilling its nature in its individual species members. These other interests normally go hand in hand with the survival interests, but this is not necessarily the case.

---

7 (1949, 204). While Leopold's fields were forestry and land management rather than philosophy, his holistic views have had an immeasureable influence on environmental philosophy. Directly or indirectly, they have had an impact on nearly everyone concerned in any way with environmental affairs. For some of many discussions of his views, see Callicott (1979) and (1982), and Heffernan (1982). For background on Leopold and the development of his thought, see Flader (1974).

Consider a species that survives only in captivity – in zoos, or perhaps in a few inadequate reserves. The species has been preserved, and is no longer threatened by extinction. I am delighted when any such species has been rescued, but such a species has still suffered a loss – and not just a loss in numbers. The species loses contact with the rhythms and priorities of its natural environment, and thereby loses some of its coherence and integrity. It survives, but it is diminished. An example is Przewalski's horse, which has (apparently) become extinct in the wild (Ehrlich and Ehrlich 1981, 209–10). *Equus przewalskii* has a noble history, and it is thought by some that it was a version of this horse that the Mongol warriors rode. This horse survives only in zoos and similar institutions. In well-run places like the San Diego Zoo an individual is hardly likely to experience the hardships to which animals have sometimes been subjected in less enlightened establishments. Even so, not all is well with that species. Part of the problem is its depleted gene pool. Breeding from a base of too few individuals, the species now has a less than an optimum amount of genetic variation. This, of course, is a problem of limited numbers, and it would be a problem whether the species were in the wild or not. A related problem, specific to captivity, is that outside of its native habitat, Przewalski's horse is being transformed. Species are shaped by their environment, and it is part of the self-identity of a species that it interacts with a particular sort of environment. In a different environment a species starts to acquire different characteristics. Przewalski's horse now looks somewhat different than it did before, and it is changing its life patterns. For instance, many of its foals are born outside of the only time of year that would allow their survival under natural conditions. The species is losing its self-identity and is acquiring a much less coherent identity as a zoo inmate. In short, the species is disintegrating.

Even so, a species may survive indefinitely in captivity. Père David's deer, *Elaphurus davidianus*, has survived in captivity for around three thousand years since it became extinct in the wild (Ehrlich and Ehrlich 1981, also Kohl 1982). Its original habitat, presumed to have been swampy areas of the plains of northeastern China, was preempted by human beings. Père David's deer, as it eventually came to be called, survived as wards on the estates of the emperors of China or, more recently, on those of the dukes of Bedford. To what extent the species has changed in three millennia in captivity is not known, nor is it known whether the species could now survive in its native habitat. Attempts are currently being made to reestablish it in northeastern China in something approaching the original environment, but we cannot now assess their success. Assuming that we could successfully reintroduce a species into its native environment, would it be in the interests of the species for us to do so? If its chances of survival were just as good in captivity, and if survival were the only interest a species had, then it would be a matter of indifference, so far as the interests of the species were concerned, whether or not it were reintroduced into the wild. My conclusion, however, is that being reestablished in its proper environment would be a boon to the species. I come to this conclusion on the basis of my general account of interests. A species, like any other thing with interests, has an interest in maintaining itself as a coherent, integrated, functional ongoing whole with a particular self-identity. This requires more than just survival. It is a matter of what survives. Relating to a particular sort of environment is part of the self-identity of a species – and pressure from the environment helps a species to maintain its self-identity. What does a species profit if it gains survival and loses its soul?

Let us take it that survival alone is not enough, that a species belongs in an appropriate environment. As well, I argue, it is meaningful and correct to say that an ecosystem has an interest in retaining its appropriate species. Also, it is at least normally in the interests of an individual to live its life in an appropriate environment. Let us briefly consider this latter point before we go on to consider the complicated question of the interests of ecosystems. In claiming that an animal needs a suitable environment, I am certainly not claiming that it needs a wilderness environment, or that it needs to be in the ecosystem of its ancestors. Moreover, I quite recognize that individuals do not have the need that species have for an environment that helps to maintain its genetic self-identity. For some species, a very wide range of environments will be suitable. Cockroaches and sparrows seem to thrive everywhere. For individuals of many species, zoos provide an adequate environment. Why else would free-loading wild ducks, for instance, so frequently drop into the zoo for the winter? As a minimum, an environment must be adequate to provide for the being's sustenance. Still, an animal lives not by bread alone. As we are all too aware from horrible examples, animals in captivity may have adequate food and water, and protection from the elements, yet lead thoroughly miserable lives with their psychological needs unmet and their instincts frustrated. A being does not have to be miserable to be not living the sort of life that, according to its self-identity, it ought to live. The pointless and empty human life in *Brave New World* was not miserable – though it was a miserable excuse for a life. We do animals an injustice if we claim that only humans are capable of lives that go deeper than the superficialities. To be sure, it is doubtlessly true that individuals of many species are well enough off in some of the better zoos, and they are often safer and live longer in custody. This is a matter of cases. Caring for dolphins or chimpanzees, for example, is much more problematic than caring for mice, and there is more to it than merely providing food, shelter, and mates. In general, the more complex a being and the richer the life natural to that being, the richer the environment that is needed for the being to have a good life – and the harder for a zoo to supply it. I wonder: Although a lion in a zoo may be adequately well-off as it naps under a real tree and waits for the keeper to bring it meat, would it have a more fulfilling life in Africa? Perhaps it would live neither so comfortably nor so long, but would it not have a *better* life making its living as a lion? Too, I wonder about us.

When I see chimpanzees attired in suits or dresses and having a tea party, or sea lions balancing balls and waving flags, I feel that something is being perverted, that here are creatures that are smaller than life. I try not to be a killjoy. I enjoy a seal show once in a while, and I take the kids. Still, I think it highly unlikely that the performers are living full lives. With an artificial life in an artificial environment, they are alienated from their self-identity. In a sense, they are not real sea lions. Once I was snorkeling in the Galapagos Islands, not far from a number of sea lions. Admiringly I watched them move through the water with fluent grace, gliding and turning with seemingly effortless agility. I could only guess whether they were enjoying themselves, but certainly I believe that they were. From time to time one would swim over and stare at me through my face mask, or even experimentally touch one of my flippers, then go on about its business of being a sea lion. Mostly they ignored me. Still, when I got a little too close to a group congregated on the shore, a large male came splashing through the water at me, barking and making a great commotion. Obviously, he was telling me to get lost – or else. I got lost, spending the afternoon elsewhere, in search of marine iguanas. I had been in contact with *real* sea lions.

I have suggested that another reason why the extinction of a species is to be avoided is that the loss of the species would detract from the wellbeing of those ecosystems to which the species is *indigenous*. (Of course, I do not claim that the loss of exotic species would harm an ecosystem. Often the reverse is true. Removal of the feral burros may well have been the best thing ever to happen to the Grand Canyon's beleaguered ecosystem. Certainly I wish we could find a way to get rid of the rabbits and feral cats, plus a few other intruding species, here in Australia.) However, claims that ecosystems would be injured by the loss of indigenous species (and benefited by the removal of exotic species) presupposes that ecosystems do have interests. Whether that is so, obviously, is a matter of critical importance. In the next chapter we shall go on to consider whether ecosystems and other holistic entities do have morally significant interests. That will open the way for the discussion of further issues.

Later, we shall briefly return to the question of extinction and the interests of ecosystems in maintaining their species.

Paul W. Taylor (1986, 69–70n) maintains that a holistic approach to species is incorrect, as species are only classes, being composed at any given time of a species population. He maintains that I (in my "Humanity, Holism, and Environmental Ethics") "confuse the preserving and furthering of the well-being of an entity [viz., a genetic lineage] with the continued occurrence of instances of the entity." That might be so if I took a genetic lineage to be something that *had* instances, presumably a class of some sort, but I construe the genetic lineage to be a life process, a living system. Like any living system, its wellbeing is served not by having instances but by continuing – that is, continuing to live, and continuing healthily. As I note, a species can suffer without becoming extinct, as when its genetic integrity deteriorates. Taylor does not address himself to any of the reasons for believing that species are not classes.[8] Thus, although he argues for an ethic based on respect for the inherent worth of environmental entities, which is commendable, his approach does not allow us to recognize inherent worth in enough entities to ground an environmental ethic adequately.

8 Another otherwise valuable book that is marred in this respect is *The Preservation of Species*, ed. Bryan G. Norton. Although it offers much of value concerning the problems of extinction and survival, and is very well worth reading, it dismisses the idea of species entities with only the most superficial consideration.

Chapter 5

On the limitations of moral theory

> Our discussion will be adequate if it has as much
> clearness as the subject-matter admits of, for precision
> is not to be sought for alike in all discussions, any
> more than in all the products of the crafts. . . . goods
> also give rise to a similar fluctuation. . . . We must be
> content, then, in speaking of such subjects and with
> such premises to indicate the truth roughly and in
> outline, and in speaking about things which are only
> for the most part true and with premises of the same
> kind to reach conclusions which are no better. In the
> same spirit, therefore, should each type of statement
> be received; for it is the mark of an educated man to
> look for precision in each class of things just as far as
> the nature of the subject admits.
>
> Aristotle, *Nichomachean Ethics*, 1094b

I have argued that species as well as individuals have interests, and that their interests are morally significant. As suggested, I have also been building toward the conclusion that
ecosystems (and the like) have morally significant interests.
That such interests are morally significant puts us under
some sort of obligation, at least on occasion. Before I continue
on to argue that ecosystems do have interests and moral
status, however, I shall here interpose some remarks about
what I can and cannot offer by way of an articulated ethical
system.

184

On the limitations of moral theory

I must say right now that I cannot offer an adequate formula for determining the nature and scope of our moral obligations. I cannot do so even in the case of humans, and certainly I cannot pretend to do so with regard to the nonhuman world. I do not believe the lack to be catastrophic, however. In any case, no one else has ever been able to offer a satisfactory formula, either, not even in the similar case of humans only – whether or not this is admitted in all quarters. Now, my fundamental claim is that the interests of all interest-having beings are morally significant. Very broadly I have offered as a principle:

> Give due respect to all the interests of all beings that have interests, in proportion to their interests.

I accept this principle as far as it goes, and I recommend it to others, but it does not amount to a fully articulated ethical system. It does not tell us how to determine what consideration is due to particular interests under particular circumstances. There are various questions we can raise here, and various lines of approach we can take toward fleshing out the principle enough to provide a guide to practical action. Further problems seem to emerge with each approach.

Naively, it is tempting to propose an interest utilitarianism, perhaps advocating that we should

> Act so as to maximize the satisfaction of interests, with all the interests of all beings that have interests to be taken into account.

Such a formulation gets us scarcely any further – if it gets us anywhere at all. To start with, it is subject, in fairly extreme form, to many of the traditional problems of utilitarianism. One of those problems is that of weighing interests. This problem is not unique to utilitarianism, to be sure, but the problem becomes absolutely critical where all answers are to be based on utilitarian calculation. Even in the relatively simple case of that hedonistic utilitarianism that is concerned with humans, it is notoriously difficult to weigh the comparative pleasures and pains of different people, or even the different pleasures and pains of the same person.

Preference utilitarianism can partially get around that problem, since it is theoretically possible to determine the order and relative weights of our preferences. Then (crypto-Kantianism?) we can proceed on the assumption that every person's package of preferences has equal weight, thus allowing us to develop an interpersonal assignment of weights. That may be a fatuous assumption, however. To me it appears problematic. It seems quite plausible, I should think, that of two people, one might live life much more vitally than the other, having more intense desires and aversions, more intense pleasures and pains, more intense satisfactions and disappointments. It may be that each has a desire for some benefit, giving it the same relative weight within his or her own value system. Still, it may be that the one would experience greater gain in receiving the benefit, while the duller one would experience less loss in being deprived of it. We might compare the duller one to a circuit that operates on a lower voltage, his or her total package of values having less overall value. *Voltage* and *weight* are each metaphorical, of course, but it does not seem to me to be inconceivable that sense could be made of the claim that one individual's bundle of less intense interests might have less moral importance or significance than those of another individual. This is very often said of animals. Having a lower level of awareness, their interests, while significant, are held to be of less importance. That there might be differences in moral importance between the value packages of individuals can be ruled out by the arbitrary expedient of defining the possibility out of existence. There are considerations of egalitarianism and theoretical convenience to recommend this expedient. Still, it is arbitrary. I could as well proclaim that the value packages of all preference-having beings, human or otherwise, are on a par. Or, if that is inconvenient, I might define the interests of members of my own race as being on a par and having precedence over all others. Or, perhaps we might avoid that by giving moral priority to beings that use language. That makes it easier for us to learn of their interests, but it is strange that interests should be more or less morally significant according to the ease with which we learn of them. And then, of course, there are infants. And how much importance *are* we to give to the lesser interests of those beings not on a par with us? Surely they are due *some* consideration.

How we are to assess the interests of different beings is a difficult problem, then, even if all the beings in question are human, and certainly I am not prepared to concede that anyone has solved it. Rather than solve it, the usual move in the case of humans has been to dissolve it by fiat, declaring that the interests of all are to count equally. In practical terms, that is undoubtedly a good thing, since recognizing that the interests of some people count more than do those of others would open the way – has opened the way – to incomparably more horrors than could conceivably be offset by any possible benefit. We have seen far too much of that already. That is a shortcoming not of truth but of humanity. Even so, if, in one of those extreme and highly improbable cases beloved of philosophers, I were forced to make a choice between granting exactly five years of life, with 90 percent preference satisfaction, to a bright and lively ten-year-old or to a dull ninety-year-old, I would favor the ten-year-old. I would do this partly because the older person had already had his or her chance, and maybe because society might get more out of the younger person – but mostly because the younger person would get more out of the satisfaction of his or her preferences. (Still, I am not sure that I would want to subscribe to the rule that benefits are always to go to those who could gain the most from them. Perhaps that would be unfair to those with more modest needs.)

If it is difficult to assess the interests of humans, and assign priorities, it is all the more difficult when we try to take nonhumans, with their bewildering diversity, into account. As I have said, I cannot pretend to give an adequate formula for doing so. If we are to try to compare the moral significance of different lives or living systems, however, it seems clear that we must go beyond the comparison of preferences to a consideration of different forms of wellbeing. I believe that any even moderately viable means of morally assessing a life or a life system would, at the very least, have to take into consideration the degree of complexity of the life system in question and its degree of coherent, integrated, functional organic unity. Now a human, presumably, having much more complexity than does a dandelion, would also, thereby, have a greater interest in life and a higher moral status. But how might we compare the life of a rat with that of a redwood? More practically, how might we balance the interests of feral horses against those of native vegetation? How are we to evaluate the economic and diverse other interests of humans in comparison with the interests of endangered species and vulnerable ecosystems? I shall have more to say in the chapter after next about the interests of ecosystems and the like, but I can suggest no system for assigning priorities that is even remotely adequate. There may be a number of different ways to assign priorities, none of which is uniquely correct or without disadvantage. Still, I think it wrong to turn my eyes away from what I cannot reduce to a formula, facilely dismissing it as unimportant.

Although we must recognize moral significance in widely varied lives and life systems, it may perhaps be that the moral answers do not lie in weighing-up interests and satisfactions, and performing cost–benefit analyses. This is one of the standard objections against utilitarianisms of every sort. It is arguable that people (at least) have some rights that ought not to be violated, even when the benefits to others of violating a right would be much greater than the loss to the rightholder. Or perhaps the presumptive right becomes morally inoperative if the benefits to others are *very* much greater. Or perhaps this happens only if the greater benefit is of a particular sort. Or perhaps we might be allowed to infringe on a right in order to prevent great loss, but not to achieve even great gains. Again, perhaps distribution of benefits must in some way (what way?) be balanced against maximization of utility. (It leaves considerable to be desired if we gain great benefits but concentrate them in a very few hands – another point that has frequently been urged against utilitarianism.) By taking a nonutilitarian line we come no closer to avoiding our difficulties. Indeed, we incur new ones. We still have all the problems of comparing the interests of different beings, but now we add to them the no less intractable problem of finding a justifiable way to balance rights and distribution against utility. This too is a matter of assigning priorities between values of different sorts. Here again, it may be that we cannot develop any adequate formula, or it may be that several formulas are (largely) adequate, but none uniquely. We cannot escape such problems by taking morality as being concerned only with rights and procedural moral rules, leaving utility and distribution out of account. As we noted previously in connection with Kant, we can develop a scheme of rights and procedural rules only on the basis of some conception of interests, and of some interests taking precedence over other interests. This has never been done adequately.

One likes to think that there is some highest good, some *summum bonum*, that reconciles all moral differences, the possession and skilled use of the knowledge of which resolves all moral problems. Still, perhaps not even in principle are all desirable things simultaneously attainable in each case. Perhaps there is no pure good unmarred, or universal principle without shortcoming. One should beware of pat theories that claim to wrap it all up. Indeed, I believe there is application not only in ethics for what I nominate as Thinking Person's Axiom One:

If you think you have *the* answer – you are wrong.

So, how are we to act toward those, human and nonhuman, around us?

BUT NOT THAT BAD

We are part of the world and it is not only desirable but unavoidable that we should interact with it in some way. We must deal with our fellow humans, and also with the wider nonhuman world. We cannot opt out. How, then, are we to conduct ourselves properly? It would be quite handy if we had an adequate set of moral principles – a philosopher's stone – by means of which we could, at least in principle, decide what we ought to do in a given case. However, quite apart from considerations having to do with nonhumans, we humans just have not worked out any completely satisfactory set of principles for getting along with one another. That is not a reason to conclude that it makes no moral difference how we treat other people. It makes a very great difference. Nor should we think that we can never tell what is the right thing to do. Quite often we can. When we treat other people wrongly, this is very often because we do not care about acting morally, or because we do not recognize the others affected as having moral standing, or because we are ignorant of the effects of our actions on them. Once we recognize that other people do have moral standing, then we are well under way toward treating them decently. The same applies with respect to nonhumans, which is my primary point, but for the time being I shall center my remarks on ethics concerned with humans.

I am not at all trying to deny that there is much more to treating other people decently than just recognizing that they have some sort of moral standing. There is still the point that, on the practical level, we need to work toward an understanding of other people, and of what their interests are and how we are affecting them, realizing that their interests may differ quite markedly from our own. Beyond that, there are all the theoretical questions about just what morality calls for, and what the rules of procedure are to be. My claim is that the critically important step in human morality is to recognize that other people really do count morally, and count fully. Once we truly and genuinely accept that, if we cannot get along with one another in the very best way, we can at least get along with one another.

That other people do count morally is a point that did not win acceptance all at once. Indeed, it has still not been entirely accepted in all quarters. To be sure, most people these days do hold – at least in lip service – that all people count morally, but this has not always been the case, nor is it now always the case that others are accorded the moral signifi-cance they ought to be accorded. I shall here briefly review some aspects of what is involved in recognizing the moral significance of other people, as background to questions of the moral significance of nonhumans. Now, at various times it has been held that certain categories of people had a lower moral status, though this was not always distinguished from the different claim that such people had fewer interests, or that they had interests only in a lesser degree. For instance, such coarse-grained individuals as slaves were often thought to feel pain much less intensely than did the refined slave holders. They were also thought to be incapable of exercising autonomy, and therefore not in need of it. In general, they were held to have fewer and simpler needs. Such rationali-zations obscured the issue of whether the interests that such people did have morally required equal consideration. When the issue was raised, various excuses were offered why their interests were less important: They are not members of our group, they have less noble characteristics, God decreed their lower status, it serves the greater good. Similar arguments are still being used by the closet racists and speciesists. When moral progress occurred, it was on two major fronts. For one thing, it was slowly recognized that the others were suscep-tible to a great many forms of injury and benefit, and that injuries and benefits made just as much difference to them. Also, in supplement, it came to be recognized that the rea-sons contrived for not giving full moral status to others were grossly inadequate. However, this moral progress was not contingent upon there being general agreement as to why people should have full moral status. There is much disa-greement about the why. Neither was moral progress con-tingent upon there being general agreement about exactly how we ought to act toward others. There is still no such agreement. It was not agreement on theoretical principle that fueled moral progress, but simple recognition that other people can be injured and suffer deprivation, that they can benefit from better conditions, and that this truly does have moral relevance. Once we accept that, we are at least started in the direction of recognizing that all people are morally significant on an equivalent basis – whether or not we actually go that far in our thinking.

Often we have not gone that far in our moral thinking, as our history has been one of slow and too-often incomplete moral progress. Frequently we have admitted others to the moral community without admitting them on an equivalent basis. Blacks are recognized, to a point, as being members of the South African moral community. Even when the same rules apply to everyone, it is not necessarily the case that everyone is treated with equal justice. Equal law too often has unequal burdens and benefits. Differential treatment may be more subtle than in South Africa, as when a millionaire and a poor student are each fined twenty dollars for the same parking offense. Progress is made when we recognize that our codes, moral and legal, are better, other things being equal, when we given equitable consideration to the differing interests of differing people.

TOWARD SOMETHING BETTER

As we have already remarked, utilitarian and nonutilitarian ethics all have their problems, and partisans of one approach or another have been quite successful in drawing attention to the various motes in the other's eyes. Undeniably the motes are there. The motes, however, should not obscure from our own eyes those things of value. Utilitarianism and nonutilitarian ethical theories – of the latter I shall discuss Kantianism in particular – offer us valuable insights we can apply to our dealings with other humans, and with nonhumans. I have just suggested that there is considerable moral progress when we recognize that other people do have interests and that the various excuses contrived for excluding others from moral consideration, partially or wholly, do not withstand scrutiny. In quite different ways, both utilitarian-

192

ism and Kantianism help us to focus our awareness that the interests of others count morally, and help us to understand better how they count.

We gain a most valuable perspective when we come to appreciate sympathetically the fact that different people in different circumstances fulfill their needs in different ways. It is one of the better features of utilitarianism, even in its primitive, Benthamite form, that it sees and allows for this relativity. Although pleasure and pain, or whatever, may come to us in any number of quite diverse ways, we are called upon to give equal consideration to the equal fundamental interest we all share in maximizing our own interest satisfaction. In theory, and in the actual practice of nineteenth-century social reform, this had the effect of deemphasizing rules as such, and of putting increased emphasis on the consequences of our actions for individuals. One might still formulate and act on rules, but the rules were to be assessed in terms of the effect of their implementation on human interests. I find moral progress not only in the deemphasizing of rules as such, but in the conception that a morally significant interest may take different forms and be pursued different ways.

We have made moral progress when we supply left-handed desks for left-handed children to use at school, thereby treating them more fairly than if we required them to use right-handed desks like the majority of their classmates. Although they are accorded different treatment, this is truly justified by the fact that they have relevant interests that differ. To be sure, we can formulate a rule that does apply to all students without exception, calling for them to be permitted the use of desks appropriate to their handedness. It is a matter of choice whether we describe ourselves as applying different rules to left- and right-handed students, or as applying the same more general rule. As we progress morally, though, we find that we can use the same overall rule structure for different people only if we progressively generalize our rules. This is moral progress away from recognizing only a particular body of interests (presumably those interests most significant to the rulemakers). After we rec-

193

ognize that left-handed students ought to have their handedness interests provided for, we come to see that we ought to consider the needs of paraplegic students and blind students. These students, too, have an interest in the means by which they may be students. And then there are those children who are too retarded to be students. Eventually we come to see that people can be said to have the same interests only if we go to some extremely high level of generality. Really, about the only interest we all have in common is our interest in having our interests satisfied. It is a merit of preference utilitarianism that it recognizes this point and gives it moral recognition. It goes well beyond hedonistic utilitarianism, although it still has a too shallow view about what makes an interest an interest. The great progress we have made here, then, is respect for the interests of others, even when they and their interests are very different from us and ours. Accordingly, our moral and legal codes are better when we adjust the rules to conform to interests, rather than when we demand that our interests conform to the rules. Much of our contemporary moral and legal thought is concerned with trying to work out the practical applications of just this point. This has been particularly true, in recent years, with regard to various minority groups, where I believe we have made substantial progress.

Unlike utilitarians, Kantians are not, on the most fundamental level, concerned with consequences – neither with consequences for the individual, nor with any other sort of consequences. Instead, Kantians put much greater weight on moral rules, calling upon us to accept universally binding categorical imperatives. Whereas utilitarians would sanction a useful act of injustice in order to prevent the heavens from falling, or to forestall much lesser ills, Kantians call upon us to obey the moral law no matter what. There is considerable merit in the idea that we ought not to infringe a person's rights in the name of utility. Still, historically, one of the key objections has been that it seems so implausible that the categorical imperatives must be obeyed even in those extreme cases where doing so leads to catastrophic consequences. It can get to the point where others are victimized when rights are inopportunely respected. We can even imagine cases where the only way to prevent World War III would be to kill one innocent person. Of course no sane person, Kantian or otherwise, would maintain absolute rights at such a cost. Somehow, we must make trade-offs between utility, rights, and equity of distribution. Neither Kantians nor utilitarians, I am inclined to think, have it quite right on this score. Nor has anyone else been able to present a convincing account.

Another objection to Kantian ethics, less frequently urged but equally serious, I of course believe, is that it incorrectly takes only rational beings as having moral significance. Even so, I see Kantian ethics as making a great moral advance, though an advance of quite a different sort than that made by utilitarian ethics. Kant calls upon us to treat others as ends-in-themselves, and never as means only. There is a strength latent in this conception that is lacking in utilitarianism. One of the strongest objections against utilitarianism is that it takes pleasure (or the objects of preference or prudent desire, or whatever) to be that which is ultimately valuable, rather than those beings that feel the pleasure or have the preferences, or whatever. Singer, recall, even went so far as to suggest that there would be no moral harm in killing a being, even though it was a proper object of moral concern, if we were to replace it in due course by another being that experienced equal satisfaction of its interests. In effect, we seem to be taking a being as a means to an end, the end being interest satisfaction. (That is one reason why I argued against taking interests as if they were separable from the beings having them.) Kant's call for us to recognize others as ends-in-themselves has at least the merit of taking the *person* as being of primary significance.

Kantianism, I believe, has an inadequacy in that while it tells us to treat persons as ends-in-themselves, it does not tell us what doing so amounts to in practice. Kant's universalization principle cannot tell us, because to make that principle work, we must already have some conception of what a person's (morally significant) interests are. Still, the conception of treating people as ends-in-themselves seems to me to carry us in the direction of recognizing the good of the individual as being defined by the self-identity of that individual. Respecting a person as an end-in-himself means that rather than take the person as a means to some good, even if the good is interest satisfaction, we instead take what is good for that person as morally significant because of the moral significance for *that* person. What is good for that person, in his or her own right, must be determined by that particular person's own nature – his or her own self-identity. If Kant had carried on in this direction, it would have taken him beyond identifying only rational beings as objects of moral concern. Certainly I think this would have been the right direction. In any case, Kantianism did take us in the direction of defining the good in terms of the particular individual. In its own way, utilitarianism has also been tending in a similar direction, though not going far enough. Identifying one's good in terms of one's preferences or prudent desires, whatever they may be, is a salutary step toward recognizing that different individuals have their own distinct goods. This is a great advance on simple hedonism, which took just pleasure as the be-all and end-all, the meaning of everyone's life. Even so, preference utilitarianism still tends to separate the good from the individual. And, as I have argued, it entirely loses track of the wellbeing factor, and so loses sight of *why* we normally prefer our good.

Ultimately, we must come to the conclusion that the morally significant good of the individual varies with the individual according to the nature of that individual. It seems to me that utilitarianism has tended to evolve in this direction, and that, arguably, such a conclusion is implicit in Kantianism as well. Still, another conclusion we must come to is that the good of the individual truly is of the individual, and is inseparable from that individual. The individual is not just a container for some amount of good, of importance only instrumentally for the good he, she, or it makes possible. Kant was well aware of this, but utilitarians often seem not to be. As well, we must come to the realization that the good of the nonhuman individual is morally significant. Utilitarians have a better record on that score but, I suggest, they have thus far not been able to do full justice to nonhumans. Still, in sum, I believe that the best insights of these major schools of ethics do tend to lead us in the right direction.

ANTHROPOCENTRISM AND BEYOND

One could develop either a utilitarian or a nonutilitarian ethic that was not anthropocentric, but the fact remains that utilitarianism, in its usual forms, and nonutilitarian ethics, in their usual Kantian forms, are all biased in favor of beings with humanlike qualities. Kant focuses explicitly on rational beings. Preference utilitarianism also, though more subtly, favors rational beings. By defining the good in terms of preferences or prudent desires, it puts a premium on the wellbeing of those who can conceptualize their wellbeing needs (or who can, at least, form preferences). Forming preferences, *pace* Frey, does not require human levels of rationality. Even so, it is biased toward beings that can form preferences about their wellbeing needs. Their wellbeing needs are counted morally only to the extent that the being can form preferences about them, and this unjustifiably favors beings who are like normal humans. Preference utilitarianism, then, recognizes the moral status of some interests while discounting others. Hedonistic utilitarianism, apart from its other deficiencies, is also biased, though somewhat differently. Whereas the one is biased toward those whose preferences reflect their wellbeing interests, the other is biased toward those whose pleasures and pains reflect their wellbeing interests. Ethics of the latter sort evidently would give greater than usual recognition to sentient beings with lower levels of rationality, which is all to the good, but it distorts our moral perception of beings whose wellbeing is less closely tied to pleasure and pain. The latter group includes beings ranging from plants to intellectuals. (Even here we contrive to favor humans, by giving a higher level of recognition to those pleasures and pains that do presuppose human intellect.) It would be silly of me, however, to attempt to map out just what beings are most unfairly favored or discriminated against, and by how much, by which ethical system. My point is that the major systems have all had biases that led them to favor unduly certain interests, that the favored interests tend to be characteristically human, and that the grounds for discrimination are inadequate.

Certainly rational beings have interests involving their rationality, interests that nonrational beings lack, and these interests are morally significant. Preference-having beings have interests involving preferences, interests that beings that do not have preferences lack, and these interests are morally significant. Sentient beings have interests involving their sentience, interests that nonsentient beings lack, and these interests are morally significant. As these interests of different sorts are all morally significant, we must try to give them all their due weight – whatever that is. We need not concern ourselves with such interests in the case of beings that could not conceivably have such interests. Still, we cannot end our ethical considerations with just that, for to do so would be to ignore *other* interests, interests that ought not to be ignored. We would wrongly be taking sufficient conditions for moral significance as being necessary conditions. With one degree of blatancy or another, we would be rigging the moral rules to serve special interests – interests quite like our own. Unfairly, beings sharply divergent from us would have some or all of their interests ignored or minimized. It is only when we focus on the underlying factor, wellbeing needs, that we focus on that which could serve as the basis of a general theory of ethics, and which does serve to give interests of differing sorts their due moral significance. The conclusion I return to is, as stated, that we should adopt as a principle:

> Give due respect to all the interests of all beings that have interests, in proportion to their interests.

This, as previously noted, leaves us to deal with the problems of relative moral significance, distribution, and procedural moral rules, problems that have never been adequately solved. We might attempt to solve these problems on a utilitarian or a nonutilitarian basis. Perhaps these problems will prove intractable. Even so, we must not just ignore morally significant interests, human or otherwise, even though we may not fully know how to deal with them.

In dealing with our fellow humans we do not entirely know how to proceed, though if we are at all interested in acting morally toward them, we understand that we ought to act toward them with at least minimal goodwill. We act on the presumption that we ought not to kill them, interfere (greatly) with their vital interests, or treat them merely as means to ends, things to use for our own convenience. Arguably we can do any of those things under sufficiently grave circumstances. Obviously, there is no end of difficulties in working out rules of procedure, and settling boundary-line questions. I suspect that some gray areas will remain permanently and incorrigibly gray. Even so, if we act with merely minimal goodwill toward others, we will avoid by far the worse crimes. The worst excesses of human immorality do not stem from inadequate ethical systems. They stem from people not being concerned to act morally toward (some) others, from people not having goodwill toward them. The inmates of Dachau and the Gulag Archipelago were not treated with moral consideration. The problem was not that Hitler and Stalin wanted to act morally toward others, but could not figure out how to do it. Drug companies dump dangerous drugs on third world countries because they are concerned with profits, not because they are ignorant of the consequences. From international terrorism, to mass murder, to the episodes of petty nastiness or simple inconsideration of day-to-day life, we so often fail morally because we lack goodwill toward some or all others. If we were morally aware of other people and acted toward them with goodwill, and attempted sensibly to arrange our institutions accordingly, we would still not do perfectly, but we would do very well.

Much the same could be said with regard to our dealings with nonhumans. If we were morally aware of nonhumans and acted with goodwill toward them, and if we sensibly attempted to arrange our affairs accordingly, we would probably, after a time, come to do quite well. Certainly we would do far better. The basic policy of not (greatly) interfering with the vital interests of others, and not using them as mere means to our own ends, will require some adaptations if we are to apply it to nonhumans. Still, it can very properly be adopted as a basic policy, and I suggest that morally we ought to act with goodwill toward nonhuman individuals and toward organic wholes as well. Now, it seems to me very reasonable to think that toward the bottom end of the scale there is less moral weight to individuals than there is to an organic whole. Thus, while killing a few insects would count for next to nothing (though still something – a point we must not forget), species, ecosystems, and certain other organic wholes would count for a great deal. We should not destroy them or greatly interfere with them without very good cause. Often, we ought not to do so at all, and when we do so, we ought to proceed only with moral consciousness, and with caution and restraint. Always we should act with goodwill, remembering that we are acting within the moral sphere. These things too have intrinsic value and are ends-in-themselves. This holds true of individuals as well, though individuals toward the lower end of the scale have much less of a wellbeing to be enhanced or infringed. Still, although the interests of the lowest beings may be overridden for nearly any worthwhile reason, we should bear in mind that we are overriding something that is not just nothing. We ought not to step on ants just for the fun of it. Individuals higher up the scale merit more individual consideration. Sentience, preferences, and rationality would give us indications of greater moral significance, though I should think that they would be only rough indications of the moral significance of the underlying wellbeing needs. Here, as elsewhere, I doubt that we shall ever find any entirely adequate formula for determining moral priorities. Even so, we can go a long way

200

with goodwill together with moral awareness of nonhuman entities.

In mentioning the interests of ecosystems and other organic wholes I have gotten somewhat ahead of the game. A discussion of those interests, and of their moral significance, will be the subject matter of the next chapter.

Chapter 6

Eco-interests

Sweet is the lore which nature brings;
  Our meddling intellect
Mis-shapes the beauteous forms of things:
We murder to dissect.
    William Wordsworth, *The Tables Turned*

I claim that an ecosystem is the sort of thing that can have interests, that ecosystems do have interests, and that their interests are morally significant. In claiming that the woods as well as the individual trees are morally significant, I claim that an ecosystem is more than a collection of various living beings that have their own interests. Individual organisms are certainly involved, and their interests do count, but ecosystems have morally significant interests that are not just the aggregated interests of individual organisms. Ecosystems have, in a legitimate sense, a life of their own. These are claims I shall now try to make good. This discussion leads on to further issues among which, obviously, is that of how we ought to act concerning such entities.

LIFE

I shall begin by reconsidering the question of what it is to be alive – being concerned not only with individual living organisms but, particularly, with living systems that have an organic wholeness. As J. E. Lovelock points out in his *Gaia: A New Look at Life on Earth* (1979, 3), we are all quite good in practice at recognizing (individual) living beings and telling them from nonliving things, yet we cannot properly account for how we do it. It is clear though that life involves a high degree of order and some systematic means of maintaining it. Life is a matter of a system having reduced entropy – that is, with a high degree of order – maintained by a flow of energy that is passed on in degraded form. This characterization is true of viruses, bacteria, mushrooms, fish, trees, humans, and all those other things we recognize as living beings. By photosynthesis, eating, or something of the sort, the organism extracts energy from the environment and uses it to maintain itself. This much also applies to species and ecosystems. As Lovelock points out, however, it is also true of flames, eddies in flowing streams (e.g., hurricanes), and such artifacts as refrigerators. Yet we all know that flames, eddies, and refrigerators are not living beings. In some way we can tell the difference.

There is an additional element. Even the simplest living beings have complex regulatory, that is, cybernetic, systems that maintain the being within an acceptable range of states of being. In the face of widely varying environmental conditions, its temperature, states of internal organs, biochemical states, and so on, are maintained in a harmoniously balanced fashion. This is not to say that a status quo is maintained. Rocks keep a status quo, while living beings change. What a living being has is a constancy in change. The center of homeostasis is not a specific condition of the entity but a whole range around which its life processes oscillate. Neither is it anything static. Acorns grow to be oaks and any other living system also changes over time, with change not necessarily representing a deterioration of the self-identity of the living system. It maintains a workable balance whereby its overall life processes are carried on with a functional degree of coordination. When the living being is no longer able to do that, it dies. The maintaining of an adequate balance has been given the name *homeostasis*.[1] At least part of the story,

1 See Lovelock (1979, 56 and subsequently). It has been suggested that

then, is that living beings maintain homeostasis. Things that are not living do not maintain homeostasis to anywhere near so high a degree. A flame, for instance, is a process that goes on when the environmental conditions are right, but which does little or nothing to reverse a tendency toward instability. It is an ordered system, but it does not act so as to maintain the order. Refrigerators are somewhat better that way, but only somewhat. A refrigerator, given a source of energy and a thermostat, maintains a roughly constant temperature. That, though, is about all it can do. To be sure, we can add an automatic defroster and a few other gimmicks, but we cannot even begin to approach the degree of complexity of homeostasis attained by even one-celled organisms. Earlier, in connection with species, I appealed to Sayre's characterization of living systems (1976, 91):

> The typifying mark of a living system . . . appears to be its persistent state of low entropy, sustained by metabolic processes for accumulating energy, and maintained in equilibrium with its environment by homeostatic feedback processes.

This characterization captures important aspects of what it is to be alive, and serves to separate living individuals from refrigerators, computers, and other nonliving things. It appears to be consistent with our everyday perception of life, and in spite of the terminology it supplies a distinction that we can easily make in practice when it comes to individual entities. Moreover, it goes in the right direction in that it characterizes life in terms of systems, in terms of processes rather than in terms of things. Life processes take place only in things, certainly, but it is what is *happening* that is critical. Right after death a once-living being will normally be highly similar to what was there just before death, only with the

instead of the terms *homeostatic* and *homeostasis* we use the terms *homeorrhetic* and *homeorrhesis*, since the former incorrectly suggest something static whereas the latter correctly suggest a dynamic process. This suggestion was made by Dorion Sagan and Lynn Margulis (1983). In spite of the misleading etymology, I shall continue to use the terms homeostatic and homeostasis on the grounds that those terms are by far the most frequently employed.

vital processes ceased. Yet a living entity can live, as the same living entity, through a great divergence of matter and form – as with the egg–caterpillar–butterfly sequence. Living entities are best understood as ongoing processes of a certain sort. Sayre's characterization is a fine start, though, as he recognized, it will require some fine tuning.

We might well ask for further elaboration about what sort of homeostatic processes are characteristic of living systems. Certainly the homeostatic processes of living systems are much more complex than those of nonliving systems. Is it only a matter of degree of complexity? Complexity has a lot to do with it, but I maintain that the complexity of homeostasis in a living system is an expression of an organic unity and self-identity on which the homeostatic feedback processes center. By saying that a living system has organic unity, I mean that its character is an integrated expression of the character of its subsidiary systems. By saying that a living system has self-identity, I mean that what it is and what serves to maintain it is determined by its own nature. These factors are fundamental and, subject to further elaboration, will be of critical importance as we make further inquiries about which things can be deemed to be living entities.

A zoo meets Sayre's given characterization of a living system. So too do species and ecosystems, though this may not be as apparent as in the case of individual organisms. Lovelock maintained that the biosphere as a whole has to be considered as a living entity, and it also meets Sayre's characterization. As well the characterization is met by a school of fish and by a committee. Should we accept these things as being living beings? Let us start with the committee. Is it itself a living system, or is it but a collection of individual living systems? The committee meets the characterization because its individual members do, and moreover, it may maintain its activities through some sort of feedback processes – as when it recommends further activities for it to undertake. As something of a Durkheimian social entity, it may well generate its own momentum and something like interests. Moreover, normally the committee would broadly be defined by the processes it performs. Is it alive? While it meets Sayre's characterization, I would say that it is not a living entity in its own right, in that the orderly activity it manifests as a committee is not the orderly activity that allows it to meet the characterization. What the committee does as a *committee* has very little, if anything, to do with sustaining order (low entropy) through an energy flow. For that matter, it could become totally dysfunctional and inactive as a committee, while yet meeting the characterization on the strength of its living members. The closest it could come as a committee to being a living system would be when it replaced a deceased member by recruiting a new member.

At this point, let us raise the question of individual organisms – for example, an animal. Is an animal a committee, as it were, of cells? Only so to speak. Certainly the cells of the animal (plus some other stuff that cannot properly be said to be cells) fit and work together to be the animal, with the life processes of the whole animal being compounded out of those of its individual cells. Plus, the whole animal has an identity and interests in its own right. To make this claim is not to invoke the hoary claim that the whole is greater than the sum of its parts – whatever that might mean. It is to make the claim that things can and often do fit together to do things and have properties that they cannot do/have individually. I remain agnostic on the question of whether all wholes can be analytically reduced to their parts (if only because no one seems to be able to explain clearly and convincingly in all cases what a successful job of analytic reduction would amount to, or what it would be to resist such reduction). Functional electrical outlets, cords, and toasters taken together do things and have properties they do not do/have individually. Toasters on their own do not make toast. Just as obviously, animals do things and have properties that their individual cells do not. These are compounded out of the properties and processes of the individual cells, though they are not those of individual cells multiplied by some large number. They form a complex unity, with its own self-identity, from the life processes of the cells. The animal is a living system, which meets Sayre's characterization, as the unity of its subsidiary living systems.

The committee as well as the animal does things and has properties that its individual members do not. With the committee, though, things start to be different. Members of a committee may do and be all sorts of things that are irrelevant to their membership on the committee. They may be members of unrelated committees, go bowling Thursday nights, eat tofu regularly, or have arthritis. So long as their function on the committee is not affected, these other things are beside the point. It is different with cells and animals. The cells have their own identity, and interests, as living systems, but as well, *all* of their life processes are part of the life process of the animal as a whole, with its own identity and interests. They may not manifest themselves on the conscious level, if the animal even has a conscious level, but animals, humans included, are not just consciousnesses. Our minds have unconscious depths, and we are more than our minds. (Indeed, were I to get a perfect bionic ear, and so to experience the world in quite the same way, my identity as a living system would still be somewhat different.) If not a gap, there is at least a discontinuity between what a person is as a living system and a committee of which they are a member, a discontinuity that is not there between the cells (organs, etc.) of an animal and that animal as a whole. The animal, unlike the committee, is an organic unity in that its life process is the integrated unity of its subsidiary life processes.

Moreover, the nature of each life process is to be the integration of its subsidiary life processes. It is maintained in health through the health and effective integration of those subsidiary life processes. The whole organism, then, has a center, or rather a central range, of homeostasis arising from its subsidiary life processes and their mode of integration. The identity of the parts and the way in which those life processes interact thus determine, within a certain range, the identity of the whole. What it is and does springs from within. Its identity is thus *self*-identity, arising from, literally, every fiber of its being. A committee does not have this sort of identity. The same four people could be a steering committee, a book-swapping club, or a bridge team. Neither, it should be noted, does something like a car have a self-identity. In contrast, the organic unity of the life processes of a living plant or animal impel it to be one sort of a thing and not another. Certain things, such as adequate nutrition and general environment, serve to maintain or enhance the self-identity of a living system, whereas other things detract from it. Cancer in a worm causes its self-identity to deteriorate – and, I believe, is thereby contrary to its interests – even though a human may identify the worm only as fish bait and consider its cancer to be irrelevant.

Sayre's characterization, I conclude, should be augmented so as to demand that living systems be only those with organic unity and self-identity forming their center of homeostasis. The question we must now pursue is that of whether there are living systems – having organic unity and their own self-identity (and interests) in their own right – that span more than one individual organism. If there are such, we must inquire concerning their moral status. In referring to such living systems or entities, I might add, I shall use the term *holistic entity* in preference to *collective entity*, as the latter incorrectly suggests that such entities are collections. Making such a presupposition would be to beg a vital question and quite to misconstrue the nature of certain entities apt to have moral significance.

HOLISTIC ENTITIES – SPECIES

We have already noted that it is incorrect to construe a species as a collection of individual organisms. A species is a type of ongoing process, the embodiment in organisms, progressively over time, of a genetic lineage. It was further argued that *Homo sapiens*, as distinguished from individual human beings, has morally significant interests. It is only on such a basis that we can properly account for the moral status of humanity. Indeed, it is only on such a basis, if at all, that we can accord direct moral significance to the preservation of any species. However, that species are subject to morally significant injury and, more broadly, that they have morally significant interests is possible only if having morally significant interests does not require sentience or any other feature that species lack. Further consideration led me to conclude that *all* wellbeing interests are morally significant, and that any entity that has sufficient self-identity for things to go better or worse for it (in its own right) thereby has wellbeing interests. Accordingly, I concluded species are among those entities having morally significant interests.

Becoming extinct is obviously bad for a species, whereas continuing in equilibrium with its environment is good for it. Survival and equilibrium with its environment facilitate its wellbeing. Like a wave moving over the water, a species is an ongoing process that is sequentially embodied in different bits of matter. Unlike a wave, however, a species has a cohesive self-identity that defines what is good for it. Some things contribute to the coherence, unity, and viability of a species, and some things detract. Unlike a wave, a species, when healthy, is a process that proceeds in a way serving to maintain its coherence, unity, and viability. As a species flows through the generations, it maintains a form of homeostasis that serves to facilitate its wellbeing needs, and which also in part serves to define itself and its needs. Geographical dispersion, optimal genetic diversity, optimal reproductive rates, and so forth often serve as centers of homeostasis around which the state of affairs of a species fluctuates. For instance, some species, such as the lion, will lower its reproductive rate during times of scarcity and increase it during times of abundance, which in either case serves to maintain the viability of the species, or at least that of the subpopulation (J. Stevenson-Hamilton 1954). No doubt individual lions tend to preserve their genetic fitness by, through some mechanism, altering their reproductive rates – concentrating or dispersing their genetic resources. By lowering their reproductive rate, as conditions dictate, they would tend to maximize the number of their *living* descendants. Through those individuals the species as a whole maintains its wellbeing. As well, the genetic diversity maintained by a species, and its various activities, serve to define the species and what is good for it. A species may even change and evolve, developing different requirements and striking a new balance with its environment, arriving at a new self-identity.

Although lions serve the wellbeing of their species together with their own genetic interests by varying their reproductive rate, it is not always true that the interests of the species are served by the satisfaction of individual genetic interests. In some cases, the welfare of the species is even undermined by things that serve the genetic interests of the individual. In such extreme cases, one would have to say that the species was unhealthy, being in a condition unfavorable to its wellbeing. An example is the Argus pheasant, whose males have very large secondary wing feathers.[2] These make it difficult for the male to fly properly or to escape predators, and so are quite dysfunctional – save for reproductive purposes. Large and attractive feathers are the primary consideration in the female's selection of a mate. Having long feathers is in the genetic interests of the male, since otherwise he would have no descendants. Mating with a large-feathered male is in the genetic interests of the female, for if she mated with a male with shorter feathers, her male descendants inheriting the trait would have less reproductive success. It would be an advantage for the female to mate with the male that had the largest wing feathers around. By the same token, if a male were blessed with exceptionally large secondary wing feathers, that would be even better for him, if he lived long enough to mate. The species thereby evolves in the direction of ever larger display feathers, all the while being nudged toward extinction by its more effective competitors. In an even more extreme case, the Irish deer was, arguably, driven to extinction by sexual selection favoring huge and otherwise dysfunctional antlers (Stephen Jay Gould 1974). Seven-foot

2   Mentioned by Konrad Lorenz (1967 [1963], 32).

antlers tend to get in the way. Yet, with deer and pheasant alike, reproductive probabilities dictate that it is advantageous for the individual to have attributes and follow mating strategies that are disadvantageous for the species as a whole. So, advantage for the individual does not always yield a functional homeostasis for the species. Yet species have an interest in maintaining their wellbeing and in not evolving in a way that undermines it. It follows that the interests of the species are not the aggregated interests of the individual species members.

It is still true that the interests of a species often, though not always, coincide with those of its individual species members. In any case, the interests of a species are affected only through those individuals that embody the species at a given time. Individual and species interests are further intertwined with those of other entities, such as ecosystems. The interests of ecosystems and of any other holistic entities are affected only by what happens to their individual organisms. Again, the various interests may or may not coincide. Optional reproductive levels may, for instance, be in the interests of individual, species, and ecosystem alike. In other cases, interests may diverge. Of course, we must first ask whether ecosystems and other holistic entities really do have wellbeing interests to be considered.

SOME OTHER HOLISTIC ENTITIES

Various holistic entities might, more or less plausibly, be suggested as having wellbeing needs and therefore having interests. Before I get to ecosystems themselves, it would be useful to discuss certain other holistic entities. I have already rejected zoos as having wellbeing, on the grounds that they lack sufficient organic unity and self-identity. However, by the same criterion, we might make a case that colonies of social insects, such as bees, ants, or termites, have wellbeing interests. It seems quite evident to me that a hive of bees has organic unity and self-identity, and that it can flourish or suffer. Certainly I would not want to destroy a wild hive for no good reason. One can make a similar and even stronger case that associations of certain more primitive beings have wellbeing interests as wholes.

Consider a colony of hydrozoans of the order Siphonophora. They look rather like the true jellyfish, scyphozoans, but siphonophoran colonies are composed of a great number of individuals (E. O. Wilson 1975, 383–7). *Nanomia cara* provides a good example. One individual takes the form of a gas-filled float, while other individuals join together in structures that ingest and distribute nutrients. These form tentacles hanging below the float. Yet other individuals serve to propel the colony by expelling tiny jets of water. Still other individuals form protective layers. Then, there are the sexual medusoids. These individuals carry the burden of the colony's reproductive function, freeing their genetically identical but physiologically very different partners to carry on with their own tasks. In fact, each colony arises from a single zygote, which, through a complex process, gives rise to a large number of individuals. Here it becomes difficult to distinguish colonies from individual organisms. Why is a siphonophoran colony a colony, and not one individual organism? For one thing, each colony member has a separate nervous system. In part, each zooid (as colony members are called) behaves independently, and in part each one is heavily influenced by other colony members. When ingesting prey, for instance, the zooids that share that task cooperate, but with separate movement and separate nervous activity. Another reason for believing siphonophorans to be colonial is phylogenetic: Their evolutionary antecedents were also colonial, though with a lesser degree of organic unity. The evolutionary trend here seems to be toward higher degrees of organic unity. It is evidently the case that the evolutionary line of hydrozoans, through progressively higher levels of integration of individuals into the colony, comes to what are highly integrated units. Although earlier hydrozoans are associations of individuals, more advanced siphonophoran hydrozoans are virtually organisms in their own right. Here we have quite an unusual evolutionary path. Whereas most other evolutionary lines of animals developed organs from mesoderm, the higher siphonophorans developed complex metazoan (multicellular) bodies by developing organs from individual organisms. In these strange beings we certainly have holistic entities that have their own self-identity and wellbeing needs.

Speculatively, and I stress *speculatively*, we might go considerably further. It has been suggested (Margulis 1971) that the chloroplasts that perform photosynthesis in plants originated as cells of primitive algae, separate living beings that became included within the cells of the ancestors of modern plants. If so, all green plants derive from a symbiotic partnership of very different organisms. There is some evidence for this in the fact that the genetic material of the chloroplast is significantly different from that of the rest of the plant cell, and seems to be transmitted separately. Even more remarkably, something similar seems to be the case with mitochondria, which are small bodies included within the cells of humans and all other animals (Margulis 1971). They are present in all of our cells, including those brain cells with which we think. These mitochondria are absolutely vital to us, in that they release the energy, stored in molecular bonds, that we require in order to live. It has been argued that our mitochondria originated as bacteria that formed a highly successful symbiotic partnership with our ancestral cells. Again, the genetic material of the mitochondria is quite different from the rest of our genetic material, and is transmitted separately. So, perhaps we all sprang from a symbiotic union. Now, if we were to make the claim, which I am not prepared to make, that all supposedly individual plants and animals are actually symbiotic partnerships of numerous entities, then it would certainly follow that some holistic entities do have their own self-identity and wellbeing interests. Even if we reject all claims about plants or animals being symbiotic associations, but still accept the claims about the origins of chloroplasts or mitochondria, then we must still accept the point that different entities can join together to form entities with self-identity and wellbeing interests. There are many unanswered questions here, and I would anticipate that research concerning the nature and origins of chloroplasts and mitochondria will continue to receive considerable attention.

I have already suggested lichens as holistic entities that have wellbeing interests. To the naked eye a lichen seems like an individual plant, but it is actually a symbiotic partnership of radically different organisms – fungi and green algae – that carry out quite separate yet complementary functions (for a discussion, see Hale 1974). The algae perform photosynthesis, while the fungi provide moisture, protection, and mineral nutrients. In reproduction, some lichens send forth bundles (soredia) of algal cells and fungal cells joined together, whereas in other cases fungal spores go forth on their own to seek new algal partners. The lichen's associated symbiotic organisms have their own separate identities, to an extent, and certainly to a greater extent than do the siphonophoran zooids. Still, throughout its existence, a lichen functions as an integrated unity. Certainly it, as a lichen, has an interest in the appropriate environmental conditions, and in the continued effective functioning of the symbiosis. The lichen has self-identity and wellbeing interests as a whole in its own right.

It is worth noting that within a holistic entity with its own wellbeing interests, there may be not only certain individual interests, but even conflicting interests. A beehive is clearly a holistic entity, a very highly integrated one. It has its own wellbeing interests, with the interests of the individual being almost totally subordinated to those of the whole. Yet even within this paradigmatic symbol of the totalitarian society, there arise conflicts of interest (Wilson 1975, chap. 20, "The Social Insects"). During the swarming season, the queen bee attempts to kill new (and rival) queens before they emerge from their cells, and the workers attempt to prevent her from doing so. Again, a worker sometimes attempts to deposit an unfertilized egg, which would result in a drone (male). The queen attempts to prevent such eggs from developing, since it is in her interests for her own drone offspring to do the reproducing. Later in the year, when the drones have no utility to the hive, they are ejected and left to perish so as not to be a burden over the winter. The latter is an instance of the interests of the hive overriding those of the drones. They do not leave voluntarily; they get thrown out. In the case of the competition over the laying of drone eggs, the competition is between the slightly different genetic interests of queen and worker, with the viability of the hive not being at stake. In the case of the workers preventing the old queen from killing the new queens, the workers protect their own interests together with those of the hive. Again there are those lichens that reproduce only by sending out fungal spores to find new algal partners. The algal cells are unable to reproduce themselves beyond their particular lichen entity. There, although the fungus and the alga cooperate on most matters, deriving mutual benefit and forming a holistic entity, the reproductive interests of the fungus have evidently crowded out those of the algae (and perhaps we could say that cancer is a matter of cells developing reproductive interests that are too idiosyncratic). It does seem to be the case, then, that holistic entities may have interests and yet encompass entities that have their own interests. These interests can be separate, varying from individual to individual or from species to species, and may even conflict from time to time. Perhaps ecosystems are holistic entities that have interests and span other entities with their own interests.

Before going on to discuss ecosystems, I shall include a few brief and incomplete remarks about the moral importance of entities of the sort just discussed. I claim that siphonophores, lichens, and various other holistic entities have wellbeing interests and therefore some level of moral significance, though in most cases I would not think it to be a very high level of significance. Most such entities are short-lived, and many have a comparatively low level of wellbeing interest. A few siphonophores more or less are not really all that important. I would take the interests of a species in survival to be much more important, inasmuch as a species has a life that can continue indefinitely. Extinction is more of a loss to such an entity than is death to a being that is soon to die anyway. Moreover, species, embodied genetic lineages, are much more complex organic entities than are the particular beings that embody them. Generally, we may conclude that the vital interests of a species take priority over those of its individuals. Certainly species of any sort are morally more important than individual lichens, siphonophores, or beehives. Yet another reason, an important one, why species are so important morally is that they contribute vitally to the wellbeing of their ecosystem. My intention now is to argue that ecosystems do have wellbeing interests, and that these interests are not merely the aggregated interests of those beings within the system. I shall then go on to discuss some of the ethical implications of these conclusions.

ECO-INTERESTS – AND FOREST FIRES

A piece of proverbial wisdom that is actually somewhat true is that there is such a thing as the balance of nature – though we must not take that to mean anything exact or unchanging. Ecosystems display quite a high level of homeostasis. That they do so is virtually a truism, in that they maintain themselves through time in the midst of quite a lot happening. Nor is it a matter of different things remaining more or less stable in parallel. Barry Commoner's "first law of ecology," that "everything is connected to everything else" (1972, 33), is particularly true of ecosystems. Not only do they maintain themselves, they do so with a very high degree of interconnection. Just as we may think of an individual organism as an ongoing life process, manifested in a continually changing combination of material elements, and a species as an ongoing process progressively embodied in different individuals, so may we think of an ecosystem as an ongoing process taking place through a complex system of interrelationships between organisms, and between organisms and their nonliving environment. The organisms change, and the interrelationships may vary somewhat, but there is a continuity to the ecosystem, and a center of homeostasis around which the states of the ecosystem fluctuate, which defines its self-identity. Normally, an ecosystem maintains its stability through an intricately complex feedback system. One example of that is the forage–deer–mountain lion balance, which remains roughly constant through continuous oscillation. However, an ecosystem can suffer stress and be impaired. It can be degraded to lower levels of stability and interconnected complexity. It can have its self-identity ruptured. In short, an ecosystem has wellbeing interests – and therefore has moral significance.

No more than in the case of species or individual organisms are the interests of an ecosystem the aggregated interests of its components, and, as in those cases, the various interests might sometimes be in conflict. It may even be in the interests of an ecosystem for a particular species (or sometimes for particular individuals) to die off, allowing the ecosystem to develop in accordance with its inherent nature. It is often the case that a particular species is a useful component of a given ecosystem only during certain stages of the ecosystem's life cycle. In such a case, the interests of the ecosystem are still the interests of a whole life process that integrally incorporates the problematic component. In some of the valleys of California's Sierra Nevada, for instance, ecosystems often contain a high proportion of junipers, which, in the natural progression, eventually make way for the more slowly growing oaks.[3] Junipers grow rapidly and, being full of sap, are very combustible. Under natural conditions, fires caused by lightening periodically burn out the juniper, preventing it from crowding out the oaks and other plants. After a fire, not only the oaks but the smaller plants and grasses have the opportunity to flourish, and there is an attendant increase in the populations of animals, birds, and insects. If the fires do not come, the juniper, together with a few other species, largely takes over, leading to an ecosystem of reduced diversity and stability. The integrity of the complex whole and

3   This material is based on public presentations at Yosemite National Park, California, and on my discussions with the staff there.

its diverse living unity is compromised in favor of an impoverished uniformity.

This is not to say that the juniper is only a weed, one that ought to be exterminated. The juniper has its role in the life of an ecosystem. There should always be a few around so that they may (re)establish themselves in that or a neighboring ecosystem if the conditions should ever become appropriate. When, for instance, there is a total burnout, completely devastating an area, the rapidly growing junipers are very useful in restoring the biotic community and maintaining it until the more slowly growing trees and the other beings of the mature ecosystem again hold sway. Most fires, though, do not devastate an area. They are generally benign. They burn through quickly, removing such things as juniper, and providing growing room for the annuals and other rapidly growing small plants. On the larger scale, they clear the way for the more slowly growing fire-resistant trees. Such trees usually sustain relatively little damage. Minor fires do not burn deeply enough to kill the living soil. When minor fires do not occur from time to time, there is a buildup of undergrowth and debris, and an overgrowth of highly flammable trees such as juniper. Then any fire will be a major one, killing everything including the soil. At certain stages, then, the juniper is helpful to the ecosystem and at others harmful to it. The ecosystem, it would be fair to say, is a life process having a self-identity distinct from that of its component entities, and which may call for juniper at some times and not at others, just as the life process of an oak calls for acorns at some times and not at others.

Homo sapiens, as so often happens, interferes to make a mess of things. When we are not making a mess of things from bad intentions, we too often make a mess of things from good intentions. When I was a boy, it was a well-known fact that forest fires were bad. Whatever our attitude toward good and bad might have been, everyone knew that forest fires were bad. The message was preached at us in school and over the media. If it was not the direct content of the message, it was a presupposition. It was drummed into us in the Boy Scouts, and Smokey Bear told us that only we could prevent forest fires. Display posters depicted animal orphans beside burned-out stumps. Forest fires were downright evil. We could no more doubt that than we could doubt that the earth went around the sun – though in both cases we were largely relying on the testimony of experts. No doubt this moral fact led some of the antisocial among us to throw around a few matches. For the most part, we were influenced to be careful not to cause fires accidentally. That was generally to the good, since the frequency of fires that benefit an ecosystem is that which occurs naturally. Ecosystems evolve that way. However, public policy was to extinguish or contain *all* fires, including those of natural origin. As a result, flammable material would accumulate to the point that a very large and very intense fire would utterly destroy an area. Where that did not happen, as in heavily protected Yosemite Valley, the resulting imbalance of species led to a weakened and impoverished ecosystem, with fewer animals, birds, and other species, less complexity and diversity, less stability and less integrity of being.

We cannot give proper recognition to the role of fires in ecosystems if we think only in terms of the welfare of individuals. In general, we can neither understand ecosystems properly nor act properly toward them if we think only in terms of individuals. Consider: Although a fire may contribute to the wellbeing of an ecosystem, it clearly does not enhance the wellbeing of each and every individual or species in the ecosystem. Being burned to death is bad for any plant or animal. Still, other individuals gain from improved habitat and decreased competition. Many of the beneficiaries do not yet exist, being future members of increased populations resulting from the fire. For all those affected among individuals that now exist, it would be virtually impossible to weigh up the profits and losses. It may be that the losers outnumber the winners and that their losses outweigh the gains of the winners, but that is only conjecture. It is very nearly irrelevant. It is not entirely irrelevant, since individuals do count, but normally the effects on the species involved and the ecosystem as a whole are weightier and less ambiguous. Species such as the oak, and the animal and small plant species – indeed, most species – largely benefit from periodic small fires in terms of securing and maintaining a viable position in a flourishing ecosystem. (Whether the juniper species suffers is not something I can say for certain. Perhaps it is injured by being periodically decimated, or perhaps it is benefited by the long-term wellbeing of ecosystems that have a role for juniper. Would an undisturbed ecosystem dominated by juniper be viable in the very long run?) As well as species the ecosystem as a whole flourishes, benefiting in terms of stability and the organic unity of complex interconnection. It flourishes as an ongoing life system. In Yosemite and other areas, I am pleased to note, attempts are now being made to right past wrongs through a program of controlled burning. While I have used fires as my example, we can make similar points concerning adding or eliminating species, or other things that would affect the life process of an ecosystem. We must consider the whole not merely as a collection, but as a whole with its very own interests. Only then can we develop an adequate environmental policy.

Developing a morally adequate environmental policy will not be easy. No one has developed a really convincing account of how we are to measure interest satisfaction and of how we are to balance distribution of benefits against maximization. This is true even on a purely anthropocentric basis, yet the problem is even more complex if we recognize the moral standing of nonhuman individuals, species, and ecosystems. If vastly different beings have vastly different interests, in differing ways to varying degrees, it will be no easy matter, if possible at all, to assign priorities. There arise a great host of issues. To start with, we certainly need a more detailed account of the interests of species and ecosystems. Then there are the more directly moral questions. What consideration is due to a rainforest, for instance, and under what circumstances might its interests be infringed? Some answers are better than other answers, but no general theory is adequate. Even when interests are commensurable, it is no easy matter to settle conflicts of interest, and it may just be that some interests, some benefits and injuries, are not properly commensurable at all. So, what are we to do? How are we humans to pursue a moral career in the natural world?

ARE WE TO POLICE THE BIOSPHERE?

It has sometimes been suggested – not always in jest – that admitting nonhumans to the moral community requires us to see to it that animals act toward one another properly. This raises issues of *reductio ad absurdum*: Are we to protect animals from predators – thereby condemning lions to an agonizing death by starvation? And so on. If we admit species and ecosystems into consideration, the problem seems even worse. How do we adjudicate conflicting claims? Do junipers have claims for protection against fires, or oaks for protection against junipers? Must we protect a swamp from a river changing its course due to natural causes? Could even Solomon give justice in such difficult cases? There are serious questions about whether we would have the knowledge to be able to intervene effectively, and whether we would be materially able to supervise the natural world. We cannot do everything, and too often, when we have tried to do right, we have done wrong. We try to protect the deer by eradicating the predators. In addition to questions about whether we can intervene effectively in the natural world to pursue moral ends, there is the question of whether we ought to intervene, even if we could do so effectively. Perhaps, it is suggested, the whole idea of admitting nonhumans into the moral sphere is absurd or incoherent, and ought to be abandoned.

It could just be that some things are none of our business. Moral philosophers sometimes seem to suggest that we must formulate a policy for every conceivable situation, a prescription for every ill, with minding our own business not being prominent among their recommendations. Arguably, though, there are some things in which we are not called upon to intermeddle. It may be that the internal affairs of independent ecosystems are among them. There are various reasons why this may be so. Just as in purely human affairs it is all too easy for us to think that we know what we are doing and that we are acting for the best, when actually we are making things worse. We may not know all of the relevant details. If nothing else, we may not know how our answers would work for those with different lives and different values. The problem is all the worse when we try to go beyond the human world, with which we are relatively familiar. Those who killed mountain lions and suppressed natural fires thought they were acting for the best. Even if we could, in our wisdom, produce a greater balance of good by interfering, it may possibly be that some parties to a conflict have a right not to be subject to even our benevolent interference. Children have some rights to misused autonomy. Perhaps this is sometimes true of nonhumans as well. For our part, we might have a right not to be our brother's keeper on a full-time basis. Particularly if we tried to oversee the natural world, having to horn in here, there, and everywhere would be an impossible drain on our time and energy. Sorting things out occasionally might be a supererogatory self-sacrifice on our part, which we are not obliged to make. It could be that ecosystems and other nonhuman entities have rights (of whatever strength) to noninterference, but not to interference. More controversially, it might conceivably be that it is not right – possibly even wrong – for us to interfere even if we infringed no rights and even if we could intercede with good result. Morality may just not call on us to do so (and may call on us not to do so).

Whether we are required to be do-gooders every time we could manage to do some good, the fact remains that it would only rarely be possible for us to improve the workings of a natural system, whatever wisdom we had. Even if we could, only rarely would we know enough. It is not our job, and it is utterly silly to think that the rest of the world needs us to run its affairs. For the greatest part, the very best thing we can do for a wild animal, a species, or an ecosystem, is to leave it alone. Moreover, it should be obvious that predators are not obliged to leave alone animals that we ought to leave alone. Predators, both species and individuals, have a different self-identity and relate differently to their prey and to their ecosystems. It is ourselves we ought to watch. It is not for us to emulate lions, nor to forbid them to get their meat from God.

ARE WE TO POLICE OURSELVES?

Although we are not morally obliged to police the biosphere, everything we do nevertheless affects the biosphere. If we chop a tree for firewood, if we clear a field for plowing, if we merely gather nuts from under a tree, we can never avoid affecting our environment in some way, and any course of action is bound to be injurious to some entity. Virtually anything *any* being does affects the ecosystem and somehow injures the interests of some other being. If we gather nuts from under the tree, that is fewer for the squirrels or other nut-eating animals. If they gather the nuts, that is fewer for the decay organisms in the soil. If the nuts are not gathered at all, this conflicts with the interests of the tree in having its seeds carried to new locations. So, at what moral conclusions should we humans arrive?

One conclusion that might, but should not, be drawn is that we are morally at liberty to treat the environment in whatever way most suits our own convenience. There are various superficially attractive arguments favoring such a result. One line of thought is that it would be inconsistent and even hypocritical to condemn some injurious acts while condoning others. Since everything we might do would be injurious to some morally significant entity, we might as well do as we please. That is bad reasoning. The mere fact that no matter what we do we must harm the interests of some entities does not mean that our choices are morally indifferent. On the human level, the fact that public policies characteristically benefit some humans and injure others does not make a choice between policies morally indifferent. The logic is no better when applied to actions affecting nonhumans. Some cost–benefit balances are better than others, some distributions are better than others, and infringing or respecting rights may or may not make a difference to a case. That any of our acts affecting the environment will have some injurious effects does not free our choices from moral assessment.

This may not seem entirely satisfactory, however. Why is it that we humans, alone, ought to restrain our impact on other creatures and ecosystems? Lions are not condemned for killing other animals, nor are they to be restrained from doing so. Lions are doing what is natural for them, and taking part in natural processes. But so are we. Over thousands and millions of years we humans have evolved as exploiters of our environment, it may be argued, and what we do is natural for us. It may be that we sometimes exploit our environment clumsily, thereby creating problems for ourselves, but why ought we to be condemned for doing in the way natural to us what every species does in its own way? We are by no means unique in altering our environment, nor even in doing so to the point of causing extinctions. If corals are not condemned for building reefs, nor beavers for constructing dams, and if we do not think harshly of lichens for eroding rock, why should humans be condemned for altering their environment? Any species alters its environment just by being there. As for extinction, most of the species that once lived on this planet are now extinct – having been driven to extinction by more efficient competitors. The greatest part of that happened before there were any humans to affect the issue. Lion or dove, if every species owes its very existence to the forced extinction of other species in the evolutionary struggle, why should only humans be condemned for causing extinctions when it suits their convenience? If nature is red in tooth and claw, being intrinsically a web of exploitation, then, so it may be argued, there is no reason why we ought not to act accordingly in our dealings with the natural world.

Against this sort of argument it will not do simply to point out that we are reflective moral agents, whereas lions are not. We cannot just rest on the claim that lions do not know any better, whereas we humans can work out valid moral principles and act on them. Not only does this make having awareness and rationality seem like a losing proposition, it really does not go to the central issues. Even if, miraculously, lions and other predators were transformed into rational, aware moral agents, they would be under no obligation either to become vegetarians or to starve in recognition of the interests of plants. The wellbeing of lions counts for something too. Apart from that, we have only to note that ecosystems deprived of their predators do not function nearly so well. The contribution of the lions would be sorely missed. Moreover, the sacrifice of the lions would be futile. The only way to abolish injury, exploitation, and so on, would be to abolish life. I take that to be a *reductio ad absurdum*.

A better answer is that lions, left to their own devices, live in a reasonable balance with healthy ecosystems, whereas humans tend to get far out of balance with the rest of the world. The argument that we have a right to do what comes naturally is unsound, insofar as our agriculture, our industries, and, in general, our human ways of life – in contrast to that of the lion – are quite disruptive of the wellbeing of the biosphere. The point I am making here is not the familiar prudential one that events in the biosphere are apt to rebound against us if we do not mend our ways. That is important, but the relevant point here concerns the morality of our effects on other entities. We act wrongly toward the biosphere if we severely disrupt it, even if it is in our nature to do so. Being natural does not imply being good, or even being morally acceptable. It is the wellbeing of morally significant entities that is the key factor, not the indiscriminate indulgence of our natural tendencies.

Cancer is a natural phenomenon. The malignant tumor arises through natural processes in the organism afflicted, and it develops in accordance with its own nature, yet it is clearly in conflict with the interests of the encompassing organism. In our unchecked drive toward proliferation, in our appropriation of all resources for our own benefit, and in our

increasing incompatibility with the viability of the life processes around us, we humans in great measure resemble a
cancer attacking the biosphere. Neither cancers nor we are
any the less injurious for being natural. What we can say for
humanity is that, unlike a cancer, it is possible in principle
for us to get on in a benign way.

The conclusion so far is that we cannot defend our exploitation of the rest of the world on the grounds that it is
in accordance with our nature. We cannot justify such exploitation on any grounds, since it disrupts the balance of
life processes in the biosphere. However, we cannot leap
from there to the opposite claim that any way of treating the
nonhuman world would be morally in order, so long as it
were not disruptive of the balance of nature. That we should
maintain a balance with the processes of the biosphere is a
necessary condition for the moral adequacy of our policy
toward nonhuman entities – not to mention being more conducive to our own long-term survival – but it is not sufficient.
For one thing, there are still individuals whose interests demand our respect. The abuse of battery chickens, pale-veal
calves, and draize-tested laboratory animals would not be
justified by any overall ecostability. There is yet another and
quite different reason why it is not morally sufficient just to
have a policy toward nonhuman entities that maintains a
balance with the biosphere. There are balances of different
sorts. It might be, and evidently is, possible to strike a degraded balance with nature wherein an ecosystem of richness
and thriving complexity is converted into one with considerably less complexity, diversity, and integrity. The resultant
ecosystem might maintain a wellbeing of some sort, though
a wellbeing of lower order. For instance, we may convert
natural forests into monocultures producing one kind of tim-
ber on a sustained yield basis. We may drown Lake Pedder,
and seventeen species in the process. We may eradicate predators and take over the role ourselves. Nature being resilient,
a stable ecosystem might eventually result. Even so, we have
infringed the interests of the ecosystem by causing it to be
degraded. An environmental policy that countenances the

systematic degradation of ecosystems is not morally adequate, and it remains morally inadequate even if the ecosystems do not suffer total collapse.

The best reason for rejecting the argument that natural precedent, taking that of lions as our paradigm case, excuses human treatment of the biosphere is not just that lions are in balance with the biosphere, but that they are in quite a good balance with it. Lions enhance the quality of their ecosystems, whereas humans, at least in recent times, have tended not to. It is we who ought to mend our ways. To be sure, it is true that nonhuman entities of various sorts tend to modify their environment, exploit their environment, and sometimes cause extinctions. However, on the whole, the evolutionary trend has been in the direction of greater balance, complexity, diversity, and interconnection – those things that enrich the character of ecosystems and other living things. Extinction, for the most part, did not result in fewer species, nor did use and even modification of the environment generally entail its degradation. Human abuse of the environment cannot be defended on the grounds that it is the common currency of the natural world. It is not.

If environmental degradation were central to natural process, it would be hard to conceive how evolution could have taken place, but even if it were that would not excuse human immorality. It should by now be clear that I do not define the good in terms of tendencies in evolution, or anything of the sort. So far as I am able to define it at all, I define it in terms of wellbeing and the satisfaction of wellbeing interests. Different entities of different sorts have different wellbeing – defined in terms of their own self-identity. Whether or not the entity actually achieves a condition of full wellbeing, its configuration of wellbeing interests is the configuration of that which is significant in that entity. Some wellbeing configurations are better than others, in terms of having greater complexity, diversity, balance, organic unity or integrity, and so on. Mill had something when he said that it was better to be a dissatisfied Socrates than a satisfied pig. This applies

to holistic entities as well as to individuals, and some ecosystems are better than others in those terms. Changes to
an ecosystem may enhance it, degrade it, or, perhaps, be
no more than change. Generally, the tendency of evolution seems to have been in the direction of producing better
types of wellbeing configuration in ecosystems, species,
and individuals. That is only a contingent truth, so far
as I know, and it might conceivably be that evolution will
some day go into decline. If ever it did so, however, any
attempt on our part to intercede would likely only make
matters worse.

Granted that we cannot avoid affecting nonhuman entities,
and that we ought to conduct ourselves properly in our dealings with them, an obligation that we cannot avoid by bringing *ad hominem* (as it were) charges against nature, there is
still the question of just what it is that we ought or ought
not to do. As I have already stated, I can neither propose
nor accept any comprehensive theory of how we may determine what is right or wrong in the generality of cases.
Still, we have not arrived at an impasse. After all, we do not
do things in the generality, but in more manageable units.
We do not necessarily need precise measures and complete
theories in order to cope with specific questions adequately.
This is not always required in practical affairs – nor even in
theoretical physics – and it is by no means a universal requirement for dealing with particular moral questions. We
do not need to have an exact measure of the value of rights
of an ecosystem or of a species in order to recognize that a
road or a dam is, or is not, likely to be too disruptive, or that
battery chickens lead unjustifiably miserable lives. The key
thing is to recognize that the interests of all beings that have
interests do count morally, be they human or nonhuman,
sentient or insentient, individual organisms or holistic entities; to arrive at a conception of their interests adequate for
practical purposes; and to develop an attitude of moral respect for them and their interests. Doing so may not yield
perfect solutions – does anything in practice ever yield perfect

solutions? – but it can carry us a very long way. In the final chapter I shall further discuss the adequacy of this conception of respect for interests as a general foundation of ethics, applying to humans and nonhumans, and how it can lead to effective practical moral action.

Chapter 7

Deep and shallow

In Tao the only motion is returning.

Tao Té Ching

There is more to be said on a variety of topics having to do
with interests, and with those beings of various sorts that
have interests. To start with, there is much yet to be discussed
in connection with my attempt to find a common foundation
for the ethics of our dealings with both holistic and individ-
ualistic entities. Then there is the vitally important matter of
the implications for our actual practice in dealing with nonhuman entities of various sorts. Overall, I suggest that the
important thing in our dealings with the rest of the world is
not a specific set of moral rules but a wider understanding
and a decent attitude. By having a wider moral awareness
and sense of values, I argue, we can better do justice to the
world around us, in practical terms, and we can better do
justice to ourselves.

ON RECONCILING HUMAN, HUMANE, AND
HOLISTIC ETHICS

I have been attempting to do something many people have
claimed is impossible in principle. Specifically, I have attempted to develop a coherent ethical scheme to serve as a
common foundation for the ethics of our dealings with other
humans, with nonhuman individuals, and with ecosystems
and other environmental wholes. This leads me to deny that

there is such a thing as peculiarly *environmental* ethics. As I see it, there is just *ethics,* based on respect for interests.[1] We may be faced with varying situations, which may or may not involve particularly environmental applications, and we may have to deal with entities of many different sorts, but there is a common foundation in respect for interests. Not everyone would agree that there is a common foundation.

In his "Animal Liberation: A Triangular Affair," J. Baird Callicott maintains that concern for humans, for sentient nonhumans, and for ecosystems defines three distinct corners of a moral triangle. As I interpret Callicott, he implicitly suggests that the humane apex of the triangle might be compatible with the humanistic apex, insofar as both are concerned with the interests of sentient beings. However, he strongly maintains that these two apexes of the moral triangle are truly irreconcilable with the remaining apex. In arguing to that effect, Callicott deploys what I would identify as the two major arguments against compatibility that have been given in the literature. One line of reasoning is that an ethic that calls for humane treatment of sentient beings would have to be radically different from an ethic that calls upon us to respect the integrity of insentient ecosystems. The second line of reasoning goes even further. It maintains that ethical systems calling for respect for the inter-

1 I am not claiming that our old ethical systems are adequate. They are not. What we need, though, is an ethic of respect for interests – which encompasses but is not restricted to environmental matters. To be sure, there are particularly environmental applications of ethics, and we might consider that there is a special branch of applied ethics, environmental ethics, that is concerned with those applications. Whether there is such a thing as environmental ethics is then a verbal issue, it becoming a real issue only if it is maintained that we need an environmental ethic with essentially different values or principles. For a different view, see Richard Routley, "Is there a Need for a New, an Environmental Ethic?" *Proceedings, 15th World Congress of Philosophy* 1 (1973): 205–10. See also, under his subsequent name, Richard Sylvan, *A Critique of Deep Ecology,* Discussion Papers in Environmental Philosophy 12, (Canberra: Australian National University, 1985). I agree with him that we need a new ethic, though not that we need a particularly environmental one. At this point I would like to acknowledge that I owe him a greater debt than the footnotes would indicate.

ests of environmental wholes are necessarily *inconsistent* with ethical systems calling for respect for the interests of individual organisms, because wholes and individuals have inconsistent interests. Not only would we need quite different systems for wholes and individuals, then, for the further claim is made that the systems would be incompatible in principle.

I believe that the polarities here are not nearly as absolute as Callicott concluded they are, that we can reconcile ethics centering on the interests of individuals, human and non-human, with the, or at least with a, land ethic. As I claim to have given the core, though not the articulated detail, of an ethical system that can accommodate the seemingly incompatible demands, it would be useful for me to review and respond to the irreconcilability arguments in more detail. I shall address myself particularly to the arguments as presented in Callicott's influential article, though I shall also discuss related points made by John Rodman, Arne Naess, and others. My aim is not to discuss varying arguments in detail for their own sake, but to try to shed further light on what is required of an adequate ethic. I claim that an ethic based on consideration of wellbeing interests can be adequate to the various demands made on an ethical theory. Instead of looking at three different ethical corners, we should look for one thing of which they are corners.

A GAP THAT IS NOT THERE

A first step in reconciling differences is to cease to defend the indefensible. Hedonistic ethics and preference ethics have to be abandoned if we are to have any hope of reconciling the demands of humane and humanistic ethics with those of a land ethic. (Indeed, they ought to be abandoned in any case.) If pleasure or preference satisfaction constitute the intrinsic good, then the wellbeing of insentient beings, species, and ecosystems could count for nothing in their own right. Even if we are extending our moral vision somewhat beyond the human moral arena, we are still tied to parochial human values when we adopt a pleasure or preference ethic. Callicott remarks that (1980, 318–19):

> The fundamental principle of humane moralism, as we see, is Benthamic. Good is equivalent to pleasure and, more pertinently, evil is equivalent to pain. The presently booming controversy between moral humanists and humane moralists appears, when all the learned dust has settled, to be essentially internecine; at least, the lines of battle are drawn along familiar watersheds of the conceptual terrain. A classical ethical theory, Bentham's, has been refitted and pressed into service to meet relatively new and unprecedented ethically relevant situations. . . . The issues have an apparent newness about them; moreover they are socially and politically *avant garde*. But there is no serious challenge to established first principles. Hence, without having to undertake any creative ethical reflection or exploration. . . . The familiar historical positions have simply been retrenched, applied, and exercised.

The point is quite the same if we move from a hedonism to a preference ethic. In a similar vein, John Rodman remarks that (1977, 91, 95):

> If it would seem arbitrary . . . to find one species claiming a monopoly of intrinsic value by virtue of its allegedly exclusive possession of reason, free will, soul, or some other occult quality, would it not seem almost as arbitrary to find that same species claiming a monopoly of intrinsic value for itself and those species most resembling it (e.g. in type of nervous system and behavior) by virtue of their common and allegedly exclusive possession of sentience?

> Why do our "new ethics" seem so old? . . . Because the attempt to produce a "new ethics" by the process of "extension" perpetuates the basic assumptions of the conventional modern paradigm, however much it fiddles with the boundaries.

Neither hedonism nor any ethic founded on the unique significance of preference satisfaction can do justice to the moral significance of insentient beings, species, or ecosystems. That does not create any unbridgeable gaps between areas of moral concern, however, since neither hedonism nor preference ethics can do justice to anything. Pleasure and preference satisfaction are morally significant only to the extent that these things answer to our wellbeing interests. Granted, insofar as we have preferences and experience pleasures and pains, we have wellbeing interests in consequence, but these do not exhaust our wellbeing interests and they are morally significant only as part of a being's whole wellbeing package. It may be that beings that can conceptualize preferences have different wellbeing interests from those that cannot, that sentient beings have different wellbeing interests from those that are insentient, and that holistic beings have different wellbeing interests from those that are atomistic. Indeed, I think that these things are true, and that, moreover, my interests are different from yours. Even so, the interests we have are, in each and every case, expressions of our wellbeing needs as whole living organisms.

Callicott makes an ancillary point that I believe is quite valid, and well worth noting in this connection. When we concentrate our moral thinking on pleasure and pain, we not only cut ourselves off from the natural world as a whole, we also cut ourselves off from our own nature as a whole. Pleasure and pain are truly significant only in terms of our wider context. As he puts it (1980, 332–4)

> Pleasure appears to be, for the most part (unfortunately it is not always so) a reward accompanying those activities which contribute to organic maintenance . . . or those which contribute to the continuation of the species. . . . The doctrine that life is the happier the freer it is from pain and that the happiest life conceivable is one in which there is continuous pleasure uninterrupted by pain is biologically preposterous. A living mammal which experienced no pain would be one which had a lethal dysfunction of the nervous system. The idea that pain is evil and ought to be minimized or eliminated is as primitive a notion as that of a tyrant who puts to death messengers bearing bad news on the supposition that thus his well-being and security is improved. [He adds a note that] I hereby declare in all soberness that I see nothing wrong with pain. [He goes on to claim that] The hidden agenda of the humane ethic

is the imposition of the anti-natural prophylactic ethos of comfort and soft pleasure on an even wider scale.

Actually, I do see disadvantages in pain, but certainly it is quite correct that pleasure and pain count only in terms of our whole being and its overall wellbeing. The same point could properly be made with regard to preference satisfaction, our preferences being important to the extent that they constitute or reflect our wellbeing needs. Once we turn our attention to what really counts about ourselves, we are more apt to recognize the significance of wellbeing when it comes to others of diverse sorts, and to take a coherent approach to the moral field as a whole.

There is a further hurdle that must be cleared. I have argued that humane and humanistic ethics can be founded on considerations of wellbeing and that a land ethic can be taken to be concerned with the wellbeing interests of environmental wholes. There is still the possibility, which must be considered, that the interests of holistic entities and those of individual beings might be so radically opposed that we cannot deal with them within the confines of a moral system that is coherent and consistent.

HOLISTIC ETHICS AND ATOMISTIC ETHICS

There are clear divergences between the *prima facie* demands of a humane ethic and those of a land ethic. We have noted that Regan, and others who concentrate on the welfare of individuals, would in extremus, countenance the destruction of species in preference to an injury to sentient beings that, on the individual level, would be a greater evil. In contrast, a land ethic would put the premium on the preservation of species, as conducive to the wellbeing of the biotic community, even at the expense of individual beings. Indeed, advocates of land ethics often seem to disregard the moral status of individual animals, even when the wellbeing of the biotic community is not at all at stake. This has seemed quite shockingly wrong to many who put the moral focus on the welfare of individuals. Not only did Leopold, for instance, partake of a carnivorous diet, he waxed quite lyrical about the joys of hunting, even while expounding our moral duties to the land community as a whole.

Leopold offered no moral justification for the killing of animals as such, and certainly he felt no moral anomaly in hunting. I doubt that it would have occurred to him that it needed to be justified. He no more than the wolf required an excuse for killing and eating deer. The moral question was whether the hunting was pursued in a manner consistent with the wellbeing of the biotic community. Indeed, Leopold saw considerable value in hunting and other activities that bring us into contact with wild things, one important benefit being that such experiences remind us of our dependency on and membership in the biotic community. (Accordingly, he castigated methods of hunting that separate hunter from nature through the interposition of gadgetry and artificial contrivance.) Moreover, hunting can be of value in developing a sense of sportsmanship and responsibility toward the biotic community (though it does not always have that effect). In several passages Leopold wrote beautifully of the hunting experience, conveying to me the impression that he took part in the activity as an expression of loving membership in the land community. Certainly there was loving appreciation of that which he hunted. Consider his description of the sky dance of the woodcock (1949, 32–4):

> He flies in low from some neighboring thicket, alights on the bare moss, and at once begins the overture: a series of queer throaty *peents* spaced about two seconds apart. . . . Suddenly the peenting ceases and the bird flutters skyward in a series of wide spirals, emitting a musical twitter. Up and up he goes, the spirals steeper and smaller, the twittering louder and louder, until the performer is only a speck in the sky. Then, without warning, he tumbles like a crippled plane, giving voice in a soft liquid warble that a March bluebird might envy. At a few feet from the ground he levels off and returns to his peenting ground, usually to the exact spot where the performance began, and there resumes his peenting.

The woodcock is a living refutation of the theory that the utility of a game bird is to serve as a target, or to pose gracefully on a slice of toast. No one would rather hunt woodcock in October than I, but since learning of the sky dance, I find myself calling one or two birds enough. I must be sure that, come April, there will be no dearth of dancers in the sunset sky.

Whether or not such love ought to be compatible with hunting, it is manifest that Leopold loved the woodcock.

Extending moral consideration beyond human concerns, then, does not automatically entail a disapproval of killing nonhumans, nor would everyone be shocked by the juxtaposition of approval of hunting with concern for the biotic community. Callicott remarks that the land ethic is not just an extrapolation from humanistic and humane ethics, but represents a difference in kind (1980, 319n):

> The land ethic is not part of this linear series of steps [from humanistic ethics to humane ethics to . . .] and hence may be represented as a point off the scale. The principle difference . . . is that the land ethic is collective or "holistic" while the others are distributive or "atomistic." Another relevant difference is that . . . the land ethic . . . abandons the "higher"/"lower" ontological and axiological schema, in favor of a functional system of value. The land ethic, in other words, is inclined to establish value distinctions not on the basis of higher and lower orders of being, but on the basis of the importance of organisms, minerals, and so on to the biotic community. Some bacteria, for example, may be of greater value to the health or economy of nature than dogs, and thus command more respect.

Here indeed, we have a gap that truly does seem to be unbridgeable. On the one side are humane and humanistic ethics, atomistic in nature, while on the other side is the holistic land ethic, unitarian in ontology and axiology. The biotic community is the one being with which the land ethic is concerned, and its welfare is the one value. I maintain that we can span the problematic chasm.

We are not forced to make a narrow choice between the interests of sentient beings on the one hand and the effective functioning of the biosphere on the other hand, with no body of coherent ethical theory between the two hands. The unifying moral principle is that of due respect for the wellbeing interests of every entity that has wellbeing interests. Neither are we restricted to morally considering the interests of only one class of entity – unless the relevant class is simply that of interest haver. Individuals have interests and ecosystems have interests, and there is no need to absorb the former into the latter, or to reduce the latter to the former. There is no forced choice between atomism and holism, parts and wholes. Everything that has wellbeing interests counts morally.

We must not let our ethics get bogged down by an ontological tunnel vision that sees only part of what there is. Consider: An animal is made up of a very large number of cells (plus various other stuff not properly described as cells, which I shall ignore). The animal is not just the collection of those individual cells, but it is not anything other than those cells. In saying this I am *not* buying into the formula, "the whole is greater than the sum of its parts." I do not even know what it means, since I do not know what "greater than" and "sum of" mean in such a context. I can accept that some wholes are *different* from the collection of their parts. How the parts are arranged and what they have to do with one another is critical. To again use the wave analogy, a wave is not just a certain amount of water, nor is it even that water arranged into a certain shape. There is nothing, or at least no thing, there in addition to the water, but if we just mention the water and not the wave we omit features of importance. If we think only of parts and not of wholes, we omit giving consideration to many wellbeing interests, and that leaves a hole in our morality.

We might think of an animal's life as a life process, going through different bits of matter, different cells, at different times. If we think only of the cells, we leave out important features, including the morally important feature of having wellbeing interests. In fact, if we took that approach to animals, or to ourselves, we would leave out just about everything which matters – including ourselves. If we take an extreme reductivist approach to the living world around us, seeing only individual living beings, we lose track of a lot of important things. The ongoing life processes of species and ecosystems form entities that are materially important to us and which have morally significant interests in their own right. Again, by losing sight of the part and seeing *only* the whole, we lose track of important things. Individuals undoubtedly are real and count morally. Losing sight of either the holistic side of things or the individual side of things is just as shortsighted morally as it is materially. Atomism or holism on its own, either one without the other, is not only incomplete, it is incoherent. We can understand neither the tree without the leaf, nor the leaf without the tree. The same goes for photosynthesis and leaf, for tree and ecosystem. Neither can we morally understand things in isolation. The wellbeing needs of an individual are a matter of its nature, and the nature and needs of a being cannot be understood except in context. We are what we are as individuals, but we also are what we are with respect to our social group, our species, and the biosphere, and this affects moral issues. Morally and ontologically, then, we must recognize different aspects of reality.

In all honesty, it must be admitted that a measure of responsibility for the perceived problem in reconciling the moral claims of holism and atomism must rest with none other than Aldo Leopold. When he writes that "a thing is right when it tends to preserve the integrity, stability and beauty of the biotic community. It is wrong when it tends otherwise" (1949, 224–5), he seems to be suggesting that the welfare of the biotic community is the one and only criterion of right and wrong. According to Regan (1983, 361): "The implications of this view include the clear prospect that the individual may be sacrificed for the greater biotic good, in the name of 'the integrity, stability and beauty of the biotic community.' " This is the view Regan went on to characterize and castigate as "environmental fascism." Indeed, if the welfare of the biotic community is the *sole* standard of right and

wrong, then if I beat my wife, cheat on my income tax, torture
kittens, ax-murder my neighbor, and burn down the local
schoolhouse, my actions are morally neutral so long as I do
not allow the sparks to start a bushfire. That is obviously
ridiculous. In fairness to Leopold, it should be pointed out
that the context indicates that he was talking about the morality of our dealings with the land community. I, not idio-
syncratically, interpret Leopold as saying that *when it comes
to dealing with the land community,* here is the way to tell right
from wrong. We need not interpret Leopold as claiming that
the land community is the one and only thing that has moral
significance. It is unnecessary, and I think uncharitable, to
attribute to Leopold that latter, less reasonable, position. In
any case, *we* certainly need not adopt such a position.[2]

It may very well be that, as Regan fears, the interests of
the biotic community will morally take priority over those of
an individual in some particular cases. That prospect does
not, of itself, horrify me. It is merely a consequence of the
biotic community having moral standing. A consequence of
recognizing that others have moral standing is that we must,
in some circumstances, defer to their interests. Even if we
do not accord them full moral standing, according them any
moral standing at all entails that there must be some conceivable cases wherein we ought to defer. It is quite absurd
to imagine that a being could have moral standing without
it being possible that this might some time morally require
us to give way. Because (to take an extreme example) I believe
that even amoebas have morally significant interests, I am
committed to the view that it is conceivable that some interest
of an amoeba (or some number of amoebas) might morally
take priority over some very minimal interest of mine – al-

2 Even were we unable to reconcile properly environmentalism with
humanistic or humane ethics, that, it should be obvious, is no reason
why we ought to neglect one or another area of moral application.
Although Callicott says that "environmental ethics locates ultimate
value in the 'biotic community' and assigns differential moral values
to the constitutive individuals relative to that standard" (1980, 337),
we must not conclude that environmental ethics requires this to be the
only standard relative to which individuals have moral value.

though nearly anything would tip the scales against the amoeba. I doubt that such a case would ever arise in practice, but I find no absurdity in thinking it theoretically possible. Much less do I think it absurd that the interests of the biotic community might morally take priority over even a major interest of an individual. Perhaps sometimes interests of the biotic community will outweigh interests of the individual, and sometimes the shoe will be on the other foot, as both the biotic community and the individual have moral standing. That the biotic community has moral standing does not mean that it must invariably take precedence. Although dumping soapy dishwater into a clear mountain stream stresses the biotic community, and is therefore wrong, it is not so important that I ought to commit murder to prevent some oaf from doing so.

DEEP OR SHALLOW?

Following Arne Naess, many writers distinguish between environmental philosophies that are shallow and those that are deep – shallow ones being those concerned solely with the welfare of human beings, or perhaps just some particular group of human beings. Less shallow, but certainly not deep, are those philosophies that broaden their scope to include concern for nonhuman organisms. These are said not to be deep because they still focus on discrete individuals, whereas deep philosophies are holistic. According to Naess (1973, 95) what he calls "Deep Ecology" entails

> rejection of the man-in-environment image in favor of the *relational, total-field image.* Organisms as knots in the bio-spherical net or field of intrinsic relationships. An intrinsic relation between two things A and B is such that the relation belongs to the definitions or basic constitutions of A and B, so that without the relation, A and B are no longer the same things. The total-field model dissolves not only the man-in-environment concept, but every compact thing-in-milieu concept – except when talking at a superficial or preliminary level of communication.

There is, then, nothing in isolation, no thing in itself.

The term *deep* and *shallow* have tended to become evaluative, as used by those who adopt a deep philosophy. Deep often seems to be used to suggest a deeper, more aware understanding, and deeper, more significant values, whereas shallow seems to suggest limited awareness and superficial values. Understandably, people are usually reluctant to admit that they have a shallow philosophy. Taken as referring to approaches concerned, respectively, with wholes and with individuals, these terms are not necessarily evaluative, nor need they be mutually exclusive in their application. Rather than choose between the two, I want an environmental philosophy that is both deep and shallow.

Naess proposes several points as applicable to both environmental philosophy and social philosophy, there being considerable analogy between the two fields. To start with, environmentally and socially, the individual is seen as a knot in a holistic fabric stitched together by intrinsic relations. Moreover, human societies are better or worse according to the extent to which they display diversity, complexity, autonomy, decentralization, symbiosis – the principle of "live and let live" – egalitarianism, and classlessness (1973, 95–8). Ecosystems, too, are healthy accordingly as they are diverse, complex, autonomous, decentralized, and symbiotic. As in a society, in an ecosystem each being has "the equal right to live and blossom," and no beings are in a privileged moral position over others. Naess paints a picture here that I find attractive in very many ways.

I yet feel some disquietude about these ideas. What is the position of individuals in all of this, individuals who, we are told, have identity only as knots in a holistic web? It is reassuring that no beings are to have a privileged moral position and that all have an equal right to live and blossom, but that does not answer all of my doubts. There are, of course, questions about what may be involved in rights, and in equal rights. However, my main worries concern the moral standing of the individual within the whole. Does the individual have interests *only* as a knot in the holistic fabric, with what is good for the whole therefore being good for the part according to its role within the encompassing environmental whole? I cannot find a passage where Naess specifically takes a position on that issue, and I would not want to attribute to him a position he does not hold.[3] Even so, the claim that the individual has its identity only in terms of the whole does lend itself to the interpretation that individuals have only a derivative moral identity and significance. Certainly there are those social philosophies that take a purely holistic stance, and one might adopt an environmental philosophy to match. I believe – of course – that it would be a mistake to adopt any such philosophy.

My position is that there is more than one level of interest, and that all interests are morally significant. The different levels are interdependent, to be sure, but are distinct and not interreducible. The interests of the whole are not the summed interests of the parts, nor are the interests of the part some proportional fraction of the interests of the whole. Individual interests will no doubt be heavily influenced by the nature of the species and its ecological role and evolutionary background, but individuals do not have morally significant interests merely as manifestations of their species or ecosystems. Although individuals have identity in terms of encompassing wholes, they also have their own self-identity. How much self-identity an individual has, as opposed to identity as a portion of a whole, will be a matter of cases, varying from one species to the next, and perhaps varying among individuals as well. I would think it clear, though, that more highly developed individuals will have greater self-identity. Accordingly, for instance, individual amoebas will have much less moral importance relative to their species than will individual humans relative to theirs.

Naess tells us (in the previous quotation) that "the total-field model dissolves not only the man-in-environment con-

3   Naess (1984) replies to a charge by Richard A. Watson (1983) that deep
    ecology is *anti*-anthropocentric. We count too. But, do we count as real
    parts of the web or, beyond that, because of what we are in ourselves?

cept, but every compact thing-in-milieu concept," and I believe that he is thoroughly correct if he means that (living)
beings are not atomic units that just happen to have certain
surroundings. Individuals have self-identity, but they also
have identity as components of greater wholes. Indeed, it is
part of the self-identity of a being that it does have its part
in a wider context. Yet, although the knots have to be understood in terms of the fabric, the fabric must be understood
in terms of its knots. It is quite incorrect to make the claim
that only the fabric as a whole has self-identity. Individuals
and wholes have distinct identities that are yet understand-
able in terms of one another. There is self-identity on the
individual level as well as on the holistic level, with the self-
identity on each level to be understood in terms of the other
levels. They have distinct moral identities and distinct interests that, while inherently interrelated, are yet not interreducible. Neither, therefore, is morality reducible. It is a matter of striking balances. We must not neglect the shallows of
concern for individuals in favor of the depths of holism – or
vice versa. As in the ocean, much – but by no means all –
that is of great importance occurs in the shallows. There are
morally significant interests on all levels, and all command
our respect. Our environmental philosophy must be *both*
deep and shallow.

Differing interests are not always compatible. Individuals
compete with individuals, ecosystems with ecosystems (as
when woodlands encroach upon grass), and the interests of
individuals may well compete with those of ecosystems (as
when an individual animal wards off hunger by taking part
in overgrazing). While there is symbiosis in nature, live and
let live, interaction for mutual benefit, there are also conflicts
of interest. Nature may not entirely be red in tooth and claw,
but certainly we cannot wish away the fact that, in many
forms, blood is shed. Fortunately, we are not called upon to
police the biosphere. Attempts to do so are normally futile,
and frequently counterproductive. This is not just because
we lack wisdom and power, but because introducing qualitative changes into ecosystems will generally result in less

satisfaction of interests. Not even in principle could we prevent all injuries. Only if the world were made sterile would there be no interests at all injured. Perhaps we shall sterilize it in the end. Certainly it is in our power to injure others and to change the world for the worse, and we can properly and profitably subject our own actions to moral assessment. Our actions have consequences for others, human and nonhuman, and we must conduct ourselves accordingly. We cannot prevent injuries even to ourselves, let alone throughout the biosphere, but we can strike and maintain balances. In this connection I shall say a few words about politics, said to be the art of compromise.

ON SHALLOW POLITICS

When it comes to politics and political theory, I am not favorably impressed with any of the popular alternatives. For one thing, politics of both the left and the right tend to be too preoccupied with Economic Man. We have being and interests that go well beyond those of hollow and fictitious Economic Man, and we live in a world of beings that are morally important. As well the left and the right have their own characteristic shortcomings. On the right we have individualism and laissez-faire economics – with their trickle-down theory of wealth and trickle-up theory of austerity. Insofar as there is any concern for the general good at all, it is hoped that somehow the aggregation of individual efforts toward individual goals will promote the general welfare. However, the "invisible hand" that is supposed to promote the general welfare through individual strivings does not work effectively even within the restricted sphere of economics – and there are more than economic interests to be considered. It is well known how our economic activities have disrupted our environment, as well as human life. There are holistic problems that require a holistic approach to solving. They need solving urgently, and cannot be solved on an atomistic basis. That, of course, is what the left keeps telling us.

245

Recently I have won considerable and unaccustomed approval from my Marxist colleagues for taking the line that a species, *Homo sapiens* in particular, is an entity in its own right, with interests in its own right, and for arguing that individuals, humans included, are by nature parts of broader wholes. However, I am by no means certain that I approve of their approval. Marxists, and others influenced by the Hegelian tradition, show a distressing tendency to see value only in terms of an encompassing whole, humanity, which is often tacitly equated with human society. I think that they are wrong on all of these points. To start with, it is wrong to equate human society with humanity. Moreover, I see no reason to accept human society as a morally significant entity in its own right. I see society as being morally significant only as it affects individuals, or as it affects humanity as a whole. Nor do I equate the moral sphere with the human sphere, as Marxists do. Moreover, I believe the Marxists et al. to be wrong in taking value to be found exclusively, or almost exclusively, on the level of the encompassing whole. In practice, this too often means that the individual is sacrificed for the good, or the supposed good, of the state.

We have morally significant interests as individuals, and our interests are more than Marxism takes them to be. According to Marxists, our consciousness is determined by our socioeconomic being, with working-class interests being of primary importance. In fact, though, we have individual interests as well as class interests. The sad thing is, when the importance of individual interests are minimized by the state, individuals too often get hurt. Moreover, not all interests have an economic base. Hence, Marx was wrong in thinking that conflict of interests could be abolished by reforming the economic base of society. For one thing, some people like power, and gravitate toward centers of power, even when power is not economically rewarding. Not recognizing this and not making provision for this, Marxist governments, with their holistic approach, concentrate too much power in too few hands, and tend to degenerate into grubby little totalitarianisms. In purely human terms, then, I find Marxism objectionable. As well, there are also nonhuman interests to be considered. Marxism cannot take them into account at all without changing its conception of value, and its conception of moral importance as well.

Left and right have their defects, and so does the middle, which tends to hope for the best while doing little or nothing. Yet there is much that demands to be done. Rather than advocating atomistic *or* holistic measures, or promoting a particular set of interests, we must develop a deep politics that takes a multilevel approach to multilevel problems in a multilevel world. As in an ecosystem, it is a matter of achieving a sustainable balance. We have individual interests and humanity has interests, all of which are important and must be kept in balance. As well, we must reach and maintain a balance with the rest of the world. We must do that for our own sakes, of course, and we ought to do that in recognition of the moral significance of the rest of the world. We must reach a balance that is not only a sustainable balance but a *just* balance. Again, I can offer no magic formula for getting from here to there. I can only point out that there are a great variety of differing interests of differing beings in a complex world, all of which deserves to be taken into account. We cannot solve the problem through the fool's expedient of pretending that part of the problem is not there. In a world that is morally significant on many levels, we need morally deep politics.

How then are we to proceed? Before we can proceed to do anything we need to have an awareness of the moral significance of interests and of the entities, human and nonhuman, that have interests. In this direction I have concentrated my efforts. Then, as moral beings, we can develop an attitude of respect for interests and a will to gather facts and take the practical steps to put that respect into practice. Although there is no sure and precise formula for doing so, recognition and respect for the interests of others can and do lead to practical action.

LEGAL STANDING FOR ECO-INTERESTS

These ideas about interests and moral considerability could serve as the foundation for workable and valuable legal innovations. In law it is possible to sue for appropriate redress for injury, and to sue for an enforceable injunction against injurious activity. Central, of course, is the question of whether one has been or could be injured by the activity in question. Equally central, though not as often noticed, is the question of whether one has standing before the law. One does if one is a person, and legal standing has also been extended to certain corporate "persons" such as clubs and companies. One does not have standing if one is a tree or other nonhuman entity. In his widely discussed *Should Trees Have Standing?* Christopher Stone argues that it would be legally practicable, and practically useful, to give legal standing to certain natural entities – which of course is not to say that they should have the same body of legal rights as do humans. Giving them legal standing would be particularly useful in cases where a governmental agency was charged with protecting such an entity but failed, either through error or because it was subject to undue influence.

Legal standing is not the same thing as moral standing, and the two are not always coextensive. In the past, certain courts have held that although no person may be deprived of liberty without due process of law, a slave was not a person within the meaning of the law. Moral progress can lead to legal progress, though, and we can rethink and improve the legal rules. In more recent times there have been debates about what ought to be the legal standing of certain corporate entities, and there have been numerous debates about fetuses. We may also raise the question of whether nonhuman entities of certain sorts morally ought to be entitled to legal standing of some sort. It is important to note that in order to have suit brought for protection or redress it is not necessary that one be able to bring suit in one's own person. One can have standing before the law even if it can only be exercised by others acting on one's behalf. Infants and incapacitated people, and corporations, for instance, may have suit brought for the protection of their interests by other people acting for them. This is done routinely by such as parents and corporate attorneys. The person who brings suit need not have a stake in the matter in his or her own right. However, although individuals and corporations may be protected in this way, it is not possible to bring suit on behalf of a tree, a species, an ecosystem, or any other nonhuman entity. Even so, such entities need not be entirely without protection. Laws can be passed concerning how we are to treat them. We may be legally prohibited from starting forest fires, polluting rivers, or defacing scenic attractions. This is not because forests, rivers, or scenic attractions are legally entitled to protection from injury. Rather, this is because humans find such prohibitions to be in their own interests. Too often, though, entities that morally ought to enjoy legal protection are not accorded that protection. Again, entities that supposedly have legal protection sometimes do not actually get the protection to which they are entitled. Such entities cannot, when that happens, petition the court for redress of grievances. Any initiative has to come from humans.

In the American case of *Sierra Club v. Morton* the Sierra Club sought to protect the Mineral King Valley in California's Sierra Nevada from a development project proposed by Walt Disney Enterprises, Inc. The project had been approved by the U.S. Forest Service, which was charged with the protection of the area, and the National Park Service had approved the widening of an access road through Sequoia National Park. The Sierra Club sought to argue that allowing the project to proceed contravened laws concerning national parks, forests, and game refuges. The U.S. Supreme Court, in a split decision, ruled that the Sierra Club did not have standing to bring legal action as it did not itself stand to suffer injury in the matter. Mineral King stood to be injured, but unlike individual humans, or human institutions such as the Sierra Club, the valley did not have standing before the law to seek protection of its interests. Had Mineral King standing in its own right, it would have been possible to bring suit on its behalf, claiming that its designated guardians, the U.S. Forest Service et al., had failed adequately to safeguard its interests. This would be parallel to a case wherein suit is brought on behalf of a child against its parent or other guardian. If convinced, the court may order the guardian to act differently, and may even appoint a new guardian. In his dissent to *Sierra Club v. Morton*, Mr. Justice Douglas cited Stone with approval (quoted in *Should Trees Have Standing?*, p. 73), maintaining that:

> The critical question of "standing" would be simplified and also put neatly in focus if we fashioned a federal rule that allowed environmental issues to be litigated before federal agencies or federal courts in the name of the inanimate object about to be dispoiled . . . [conferring standing] to sue for their own protection. . . . This suit would therefore more properly be labeled as *Mineral King v. Morton*.

Alternatively, as suggested by Justices Blackmun and Brennan, it might be possible to give concerned individuals and groups, such as the Sierra Club, standing to bring suit in certain cases even though their concern is not based on their directly having a stake in the matter and even though natural objects themselves are not given standing.

Concerning the problem of determining what is in the interests of a natural entity, Stone (1972, 24) remarked that:

> natural objects *can* communicate their wants (needs) to us, and in ways that are not terribly ambiguous. I am sure I can judge with more certainty and meaningfulness whether and when my lawn wants (needs) water, than the Attorney General can judge whether and when the United States wants (needs) to take an appeal from an adverse judgment by a lower court.

Certainly this is a point on which he had severely been criticized. As Mark Sagoff (1974, 222) posed the difficulty:

> Why wouldn't Mineral King want to host a ski resort, after doing nothing for a billion years? In another few millennia it

250

will be back to its original condition just the same. The Sequoia National Forest tells the developer that it wants a ski lift by a certain declivity of its hills and snowiness during the winter – immediately obvious to the sight – and that it needs a four lane highway by the appearance of certain valley passages and obvious scenic turnouts on the mountainsides.

One might also observe that the high cellulose content of rain forests proclaims to all the world a desire to be converted into Japanese wood chips, or that the shape of a river's gorge cries out for a hydroelectric development. And so on. There is an air of absurdity about all this. That valleys and forests should have such desires, or any desires, is fantasy. If interests sprang only from desires or preferences, then there could be no question of their having interests, no question of their interests being violated, and certainly none of their being represented in court. With the best will in the world, neither the Sierra Club nor anyone else can defend the interests of something that lacks interests to be defended. What I suggest, of course, is that interests do not spring only from preferences and desires, and that the ascription of interests to other entities need not be based on anthropomorphic fantasizing. The Mineral King Valley, or, more properly, the ecosystem that lives there, has interests that would be injured by a ski resort, even if the valley did revert to its previous condition after some number of years. The ecosystem would be protected by the valley's designation as a Wilderness Area. Its interests might well be represented or otherwise protected in law.

Stone, in the face of criticism, came to modify his stand, making the much less radical-seeming proposal that certain nonhuman entities be given *legal considerateness*. He gives the following "terse operational definition" for legal considerateness:[4]

4 Christopher Stone (1985, 24). In this later work, he gives a further discussion of the difficulties involved in giving natural entities legal standing of various sorts and in developing means and rationale for protecting their interests and adjudicating conflicts. A major difficulty he finds is in the intelligibility of the concept of interest and injury in

> Consider a lake. The lake is *considerate* within a legal system
> if the system's rules have as their immediate object to affect
> (as to preserve) some state of the lake, the law's operation
> turning upon proof that the lake is not in the state the law
> requires, without any further need to demonstrate anyone
> else's interests in or claims touching the lake.

Anything – tree, ecosystem, lake, or stone – can be legally
considerate. It need not have interests, as I understand interests or as anyone understands them. So long as it has
determinable states of some sort, the law can require that it
be maintained in some state. The law could also allow that
it be represented in court by a next friend seeking on its
behalf that it be maintained in the state specified by law. The
thing could even be said to have certain legal *rights*. Stone
is quite explicit in maintaining that interests are not a prerequisite for rights or legal considerateness (1987, 282). That,
however, is not the only way in which we could allow the
Sierra Club or other concerned parties to bring suit in cases
where they could not demonstrate that they stood to be injured in their own right. Perhaps we could frame the law so
that suit need not be brought on anyone's *behalf*. Suit might
be brought by any concerned party that can demonstrate a
prima facie case that the provisions of the law are not being
fulfilled. Such an approach would be consistent with the
thoughts expressed by Justices Blackmun and Brennan in
their own dissent to *Sierra Club v. Morton.*

I cannot offer a well-informed opinion as to what would
be the best way to reform the law so as to provide optimal
legal protection for eco-entities. Whether we give them legal
standing, though, or whether we try to protect them in some
other way, it could be very useful in practice to recognize
that they do have interests in their own right. To an extent,
the law already recognizes that certain nonhumans have interests. While animals do not have standing before the law,
in many places the law prohibits cruelty to animals under

the case of insentient beings. Naturally, I believe that the concept can
be made intelligible. See also Christopher Stone, *Earth and Other Ethics.*

certain circumstances. Sometimes there are prohibitions not just against specific acts, such as cock fighting, but against even unspecified acts that unnecessarily injure an animal. It is not a matter of maintaining the animals in a specific state but of protecting different animals in different circumstances from an unspecified variety of injury. If it could be shown that a person was causing intense mental anguish to a neighbor's dog by frequently yelling at it a particular phrase (e.g., "sic 'em!"), the Royal Society for the Prevention of Cruelty to Animals might be able to bring suit if the person persisted, even though there was no general prohibition against using that phrase. Such laws turn on at least a tacit recognition that the protected beings do have interests in their own right, implicitly defined in their own nature. It is important that protection be offered against injuries that the legislature cannot foresee in advance. This is certainly an important protection in the case of humans. We may seek injunction or redress in the case of injuries caused by actions that are unforeseen by law and not generally prohibited. Thus, a man might be ordered by the court to stay off Elm Street (where his estranged wife lives), though we can hardly have laws prohibiting people from being on Elm Street or even from being on streets where former marital partners live.

I suggest that there would be considerable practical benefit in a recognition that eco-entities have interests. Whether we call for legal standing or settle for legal considerateness, any legal code, to offer adequate protection for living entities, must do more than call for them to be preserved in some state. That might do for certain nonliving things, but living entities characteristically do not persist in particular states. They change and change is vital to them, yet they must be protected from certain changes. It would be helpful if we could recognize that certain changes are harmful *to* an entity – that it is harmed as harm is constituted in terms of that entity itself. This is so even though we cannot always foresee what possible changes might bear on the interests of an entity. Let us return to the example of Mineral King. As a geological formation, the Mineral King Valley does not have

253

interests. However, the ecosystem that lives there does, and so does that in Sequoia National Park, through which the access road would have run. Whatever fantasies we might spin about a valley demonstrating by its shape and climate that it desires a ski resort (or by its profit-generating potential that it desires to form a partnership with Mickey Mouse), the fact remains that such developments are harmful to the interests of the affected ecosystems. The law cannot foresee for ecosystems any more than it can for individual humans just what changes might harm it, or what possibilities might threaten it, so it cannot specify in advance just which states ought to be maintained or prohibited. Nevertheless, the law can specify that the vital interests of certain favored eco-entities are to have certain forms of protection, even if it has to be left to subsequent legal proceedings to determine what the entity's vital interests are or are not and whether they are at risk in a particular case. Thus, a hearing might be held to determine whether the Mineral King Ecosystem was protected by law and then, if it was, whether the proposed development threatened its vital interests in a manner contrary to its protected status. The court might determine that, in view of the facts and the protected status of the ecosystem, certain changes, such as a walking trail, were permissible whereas others, such as a resort, were not. By centering protection on interests rather than on specified states, the law could be given the flexibility to cope with the unforeseen and to utilize expanding knowledge of the protected entities. There would be these benefits whether the entity had legal standing or was accorded some other form of protection.

Were there legal recognition that species are not collections but entities with interests in their own right, this would offer additional ways of taking steps for their protection. Not only could individuals of a species be protected and particular things prevented, but steps could also be taken to protect the vital life processes of the species, even when (as in reproduction) the failure of a process does not endanger the individual, and even when we cannot foresee what particular things might affect the vital interests of the species. To be

254

sure, any given step we might take to protect a species might also be legislated for on the basis of some other rationale or on the basis of no stated rationale whatsoever. We might legislate in some way against disruptions to reproductive processes and we might ensure that species have sufficient amount and variety of habitat, and so on. We can legislate concerning any *particular* thing we can think of. Going beyond that, recognition that species are entities with interests gives us some flexibility in providing for expanded knowledge and unforeseen contingencies. In the light of expanded knowledge or in view of an arising contingency, and on the basis of such recognition, we might take legal steps to stop some new threat, at least until we can make a conscious decision whether we want that interest protected under those circumstances. Given the complexity of the living world and the speed at which things happen in the modern age, such a means for being aware of what we are or are not doing could have considerable value. Greater moral awareness in the past, together with more flexible law, might have prevented past extinctions and disruption of ecosystems.

SOONER OR LATER

Wherever we draw the moral lines, we must in some way arrive at an accommodation with the world around us. There are different ways in which we may do so, and we may do so sooner or later – though I think that time is more pressing than many would like to think – but our human interest in survival mandates that we must arrive at some accommodation. An awareness that entities other than individual human beings have morally significant interests, and some awareness of what their interests are, provide an additional reason, a moral one, for arriving at an accommodation sooner rather than later. This awareness will often be enough to allow us to reach morally adequate decisions.

To start with, there is the biosphere as a whole. Lovelock (1979, ix–x), as was touched on earlier, argues for the hypothesis . . . that the biosphere is a self-regulating entity with the capacity to keep our planet healthy by controlling the chemical and physical environment . . . [having] a composite identity with its own characteristic signature, as distinct from being the mere sum of its parts.

Lovelock presents convincing evidence for his view that the biosphere is a homeostatic organic unity. As I would put it, he presents the view that the biosphere is a life process with its own self-identity and wellbeing needs. He further tells us (1979, 12) that his hypothesis

is an alternative to that pessimistic view which sees nature as a primitive force to be subdued and conquered. It is also an alternative to that equally depressing picture of our planet as a demented spaceship, forever traveling, driverless and purposeless, around an inner circle of the sun.

Lovelock does not pursue the ethical implications, but it follows from the points I have been developing that the interests of the biosphere are morally significant.

The collapse of the biosphere would, morally, be a very bad thing – but of course it would be downright silly to propose *that* as the reason for not permitting the biosphere to collapse. If it collapses, we will not survive the collapse. Simple self-interest dictates that we keep it from collapsing. Moreover, as Lovelock suggested, we should not stress the biosphere too far as its homeostatic defenses might respond to eliminate the irritation by deleting the irritant, us, from the system. The biosphere would then survive while we would not. Even so, we can survive a partial degradation of the biosphere – which is very fortunate for us, as we have already degraded it. On purely prudential grounds, we must sooner or later reach a balance with the biosphere, limiting our numbers and limiting the demands we make on the biosphere, but even a degraded biosphere can support human life in large numbers. Until we are forced to do otherwise, we may wish to allow ourselves the luxury of postponing the day when we must face up to the necessity of changing our ways. Of course, if we are prudent, we will not push things right to the limit, but will allow ourselves an adequate margin of safety. Self-interest also indicates that we should allow ourselves the opportunity for optimal living conditions, and not just settle for hanging on with maximal numbers and minimal life-style. Even so, along the way we can allow ourselves to degrade or destroy various ecosystems, and to drive yet more species to extinction. So long as there is a strong enough life-support system to maintain human life, and so long as there are enough unique and beautiful things to satisfy human desires, there is no practical need for us to concern ourselves with the fate of minor ecosystems and species that are useless to us. We have already managed to dispense with many species, and with many complete but (in our own selfish terms) unimportant ecosystems, all without ill effects. Nobody *really* needs the snail darter. The fact is that a partially degraded biosphere can be quite comfortable.

Once we recognize that species, ecosystems, and the biosphere as a whole all have morally significant interests, the burden of responsibility for supplying justification for how we treat such entities is at least partially shifted. This can make a real difference when it comes to a certain type of "sooner-or-later" case. If the interests of species, ecosystems, and the biosphere did not count at all, then we would need to consult only our own convenience. It would be morally indifferent whether we struck the balance now or later. Given that their interests do count, though, we now have a moral reason for doing so sooner rather than later. Since degrading the biosphere, and injuring ecosystems and species, are in themselves morally bad, those who advocate that we continue to do so as long as possible must justify that course of action. It is all the harder to justify in that we must eventually strike a balance with nature, whatever our desires in the matter.

The exploitation of ecosystems on a nonrenewing basis provides examples of such sooner-or-later cases. Cases in point are the utilization of Tasmania's temperate-zone forests for the wood-chip industry, and the clearing of tropical rain forests for wood products or to provide additional (and often soon depleted) farmland for ever expanding populations. Sooner or later we must turn to sustained yield sylvaculture for wood products, and sooner or later we must strike a balance between population and existing farmland. There is a *prima facie* case that we ought to make these shifts before we have obliterated further ecosystems and eradicated their species. We may still cut wood, and we may reduce natural ecosystems in size – I will get back to these points – but we ought still to preserve ecosystems and their species as living entities, unless perhaps there is very convincing reason to the contrary. Those who would gain from destroying ecosystems and exterminating species may claim that what they or the economy/society as a whole would gain from their activities would outweigh the interests of the nonhumans involved. There is no precise way in which we may adjudicate the matter, but those who would exploit to the limits of possibility cannot rely on a presumption in favor of continuing to do what we are already doing. There can be no doubt that we must eventually stop. The question is not whether, but when. Moreover, if we continue on to the very end, we are not doing *only* what we were doing before. We are doing something more and worse. Chopping down trees is one thing. Chopping down a forest and killing an ecosystem is quite another, even though it is the act of chopping down trees that finally does the latter. Causing the deaths of individual organisms is one thing. Causing the extinction of a species is quite another. Utilizing the biosphere is one thing. Degrading it is quite another, even though the difference may be only cumulative. A society that is responsive to moral issues, and is aware that species, ecosystems, and the biosphere as a whole have moral significance, would require strong reasons before allowing such activities to continue to the bitter end.

It is not at all clear where the final line ought to be drawn. I do think it relevant that the last bit of human advantage, while real and significant, would normally be relatively short-lived, whereas the extinction of a species or an ecosystem, or the irreversible degradation of an ecosystem (or of the biosphere), would amount to a very long-term loss of interest satisfaction. Species and ecosystems, unlike individual humans, have quite long and seemingly indefinite life-spans, and so have a great deal to lose. Extinction, as the bumper sticker says, is forever. Even so, we cannot fix a precise system for determining priorities. Perhaps the long-term benefits to humans of a particular project might outweigh the interests of all nonhuman entities adversely affected. This is an area where reasonable people may reasonably differ, but I doubt whether very many reasonable people would (after due consideration) seriously maintain that all human interests must take precedence over all interests of nonhumans. If an entity has moral significance, then under some circumstances we would be obligated to respect its interests. We may not rate it very highly, but if we recognize it as having any moral status at all, this would follow. The major cases of injury to species, ecosystems, and the biosphere as a whole are usually sooner-or-later cases. There are limits that, like it or not, and regardless of our ethical stance, we must some day face up to in our dealings with the rest of the world. Were we to respect those limits now, we would therby cease to cause further stress to an already overstressed biosphere and to its subsidiary ecosystems and species, and that in itself would be going a long way toward allowing them to recover from the damage we have already caused. Some species are already so weakened that they may slide into extinction no matter what we now do, and some ecosystems are so crippled that they can never fully recover, but it is very nearly a truism to say that moving into a balance with the environment would put an end to the adding of further injury. Sooner or later, we will have to do that.

Moving into a balance with the environment is easier said than done. Although it is obvious to all who consider the matter that we will eventually have to do so as a matter of survival, and not only as a moral choice, it will certainly not be easy to do so, and the will to do so in advance of necessity will often be lacking. After all, although we (society, the human race) must sooner or later strike a balance with nature, individual humans may not have to in their lifetime, and they may profit from engaging in contrary activities. In order to protect the environment from further stress, we will undoubtedly have to resort to collective action of some sort, imposing collective restraints. We cannot rely on the self-restraint of individuals. This is true if we are to stop before the point of necessity, out of consideration for nonhuman entities, and it is just as true if we are only to maintain a viable environment for our own benefit. Individuals undoubtedly can and do act out of concern for the future prospects of humanity, and out of concern for the wellbeing of other entities, but many do not, and these are not matters that can entirely be entrusted to individual discretion. Effective action will require collective restraint, and collective support of restraint. Just where we, collectively, will draw the line cannot be foreseen, but I do believe that a moral awareness of nonhuman entities will lead us to impose restraints upon ourselves that are more considerate of nonhuman entities than would be required by purely practical necessity. It seems clear to me that a great many people are coming to accept the idea that nonhuman entities have moral significance, responding favorably when the idea is brought to their consciousness – a process in which television documentaries about the wonders of nature and the workings of ecosystems seem to have more impact than do philosophical writings. There also seems to me to be a growing support for environmental protection policies, support that is not entirely attributable to self-interest.

BETTER OR WORSE

Not all cases are of a sooner-or-later variety. There are other cases wherein we do, or might, threaten the interests of nonhuman entities, cases of a sort wherein we need never impose self-restraint. Where the moral lines ought to be drawn in such matters is a matter of cases, and the cases differ widely. Consider disease-causing and parasitic organisms. We have already caused the extinction, except *in vitro*, of the smallpox organism, and we may well eventually cause the extinction of other such organisms, overriding the interests of the species involved in order to improve the quality of human life. I applaud. If we can get rid of hookworm or typhoid, so much the better – though of course eliminating these pests would make it all the more necessary for us to institute our own measures for controlling our numbers. In such cases there are substantial long-term overall benefits to be gained. (Even so, there are limits. We ought not to pollute everything with DDT in order to attack malaria.) The case in favor of benefiting humans is much stronger when it comes to eradicating disease organisms and parasites than when there is only the short-term and often slight advantage of continuing somewhat longer with policies that will eventually have to be abandoned in any case. If we eradicate a disease, the benefit is considerable and, presumably, lasts as long as our own species. It certainly seems plausible that the human interest in health outweighs that of the smallpox organism in survival. Perhaps we are biased, but certainly it seems that humans are capable of a much higher level of wellbeing than is the smallpox organism. Apart from cost–benefit considerations, we might in such cases appeal, as a species, to a right of self-defense. Such a claim makes good sense in the case of smallpox, but is absurd in the case of the snail darter. While we could have built one dam less and spared the snail darter, it is impossible (except *in vitro*) to allow the smallpox organism a career of its own apart from humans. It is also relevant to the overall moral assessment that if we eliminate a species we usually weaken an ecosystem by doing so, whereas if we eradicate a disease afflicting humans, we do not necessarily weaken an ecosystem. (Of course, the result might be a human population explosion in some areas, causing havoc in ecosystems, but there are better ways of preventing that.)

I believe, then, that the eradication of disease-organisms is justified, though not without some degree of moral cost, and is in a different moral category from extinguishing (other) species, obliterating ecosystems, or degrading the biosphere at large. What makes the moral difference is not simply and solely that we must sooner or later desist from the latter activities, while we can go on exterminating those species that specialize in humans until we have gotten rid of the lot. Inevitability does not, of itself, imply any moral conclusion. (There is a limit to how tall we can build skyscrapers, but that is no reason to stop twenty stories short of the maximum safe limit.) What counts is the overall moral character of an act. It seems to me that on the whole, eradicating disease is quite a good thing to do.

There are some activities that, unlike the eradication of smallpox, are morally wrong even though there is no inevitability at all about our ceasing to engage in them. For instance we can continue to abuse individual animals until kingdom come and get away with it. That there is no inevitability about our ceasing to engage in such activities makes it no less morally urgent that we cease to abuse animals. Indeed, it puts us under a greater obligation to restrain ourselves. As with species, ecosystems, or the biosphere, an awareness that those entities are subject to injury can, and often does, lead us to be considerate of their interests. Some of us may not act for moral reasons, but if we do, we may well be considerate of the interests of others even though we may never be forced to do so and even though we do not have a fully articulated moral theory to support our response. We often do so. Children learn kindness before they learn moral theory. Even the rhesus monkey responded morally, though it could never have explained why. Those who, like Regan and Singer, can give an account of what moral consideration is due to others may give different and partially conflicting accounts. Many, like Kant, may give more consideration to animals and others than they can account for theoretically.

We can, in fact, act with moral consideration not only toward other humans and toward animals, but toward species, ecosystems, the biosphere, and toward anything else that may turn out to have interests. We can do this without having fully articulated theories, so long as we are considerate of the interests of the interest-having entity (acting out of concern for that entity). If we can work out moral theories that are more adequate and more comprehensive, so much the better, and so much the better for our moral agency. The better our principles, the better our philosophy, and the better we can act. The key to moral agency, though, is recognition of, and concern for, the interests of others. That we can act morally even in the absence of articulated principle is all to the good, since no one has ever articulated an adequate set of principles even for dealing with other humans. Much less do we have an adequate account of the proper rules of procedure when it comes to animals, plants, species, ecosystems, the biosphere, or whatever else might have interests. Even so, by arguing that interests, all interests, are morally significant, by giving a partial account of the nature of interests, and by arguing that not only sentient entities but also insentient entities of certain sorts have interests, as do various holistic entities, such as species and ecosystems, I have offered conclusions that can make a real difference, and a big difference, to the way we act in practice.

A BROADER VIEW

For convenience, I have sometimes treated species and ecosystems in a way that might suggest that they were discrete entities. I believe that this has not led the discussion astray thus far, but still, it may obscure important issues. I shall now try to clarify the matter, starting with some further remarks about species. As it happens, taxonomic biologists often have great difficulty in deciding just how many species there are in a given general classification, and just what their characteristics are. Isolated populations may have slight variations, overlapping populations may give rise to individuals with mixed ancestry, and particular characteristics may vary across populations with considerable independence from other characteristics. Different experts may give different answers about how many species there are in a general classification, and about what they are. The right answer, obviously, is that sometimes there is no right answer. There is the ongoing genetic lineage or, which I think is a better way to put it, the ongoing life process that is, over time, embodied in different individuals. Just how many species we decide that process is divided into is in considerable measure arbitrary. It is that ongoing life process itself that is important.

Consider the matter from another angle. Suppose that a species is one of several in its genus and, while distinguishably different, is yet very similar to the others. The extinction of such a species would be a loss to us and a violation of its own interests, yet I think that (everything else being equal, of course) its extinction would not be as bad as it would were it the sole species in its genus or, worse, in its taxonomic family. Then, the genus or family would be extinct. The loss of Australia's *Idiospermum australiense*, a strikingly unique flowering tree of an ancient kind, would be a loss of such a sort. Of course, the family would not be extinct *in addition* to the species, as the entities involved are not additive. Nor is the genus a collection of species. That is no more true than that the species is a collection of individuals. Rather, a genus can be considered as an entity with self-identity and interests in its own right, an ongoing life process – a process of which a species is one portion. As the horizontal distinction between different species is not at all absolute, so the vertical distinction between species and genera, and so forth, is also rather less than absolute. What is real, and what is important, is the ongoing life process itself. Both factually and morally, an atomistic approach is inadequate to handle such matters. Being a distinct life process is a matter of more and less, and so is having distinct moral status a matter of more and less. To the extent that the genus or family is more of a separate life process with separate self-identity than a particular one among a number of closely related species, to that extent it is morally more important than is the less distinct species. To that extent, its extinction would be more of a loss.

Just as a species is a portion (or, in some cases, all) of the life process that is its genus, so the genus is a portion of the family life process – and so on up the line. For example, our similarities to chimpanzees – similarities behavioral, structural, and in our blood chemistry, all stemming from similarities in our genetic structure – proclaim us to be collateral branches of the same ancient and continuing life process. This is so even though we and *Pan troglodytes* belong not only to different genera but to different families, being united only in the order *primates*. We may extend the point about more encompassing life processes on up to phyla, the plant and animal (or whatever) kingdoms, and the biosphere as a whole. None of those things is a collection, the biosphere no more so than is the species, and none of those things is an atomic entity that can be entirely distinguished. The line between species is frequently blurred, and there is really no line at all between species and the more encompassing life processes of genera, families, orders, . . . biosphere. There are differentiae, yes, but there are no lines, no totally separate entities with totally separate moral significance.

That goes for the biosphere as a whole, as well as for more restricted entities. The biosphere is not the sum of all living beings, nor yet is it a separate entity. It has interests that are not entirely separate, yet which are not the aggregated interests of the various living entities. And contrary to what some extreme holists might suggest, not just the interests of the biosphere are morally significant. Yet if we follow out the implications of taking species as morally significant entities, we certainly do come to the conclusion that the biosphere is a morally significant entity.

We also wind up with the biosphere if we start with ecosystems, for no ecosystem is complete in itself. There is an ecosystem in a tiny puddle of water in a rotting stump, and the stump itself is the site of a broader ecosystem. And then there is the forest wherein the stump rots. And so it goes. It is not just that we can keep drawing circles with ever greater radii. The circles, ecosystems, intersect and overlap in complex ways. The water that remains in the stump for a few weeks provides a nursery and nutrition for the mosquito larva that emerges as an adult to fly off to seek the blood of mammals elsewhere, or which fails to emerge and so provides nutrients for the microorganisms in the stump. Meanwhile, the stump provides haven and nutrients not only for the organisms of the water, but for the termites that affect the surrounding area. The stump may also provide termites for birds or other termite eaters, which go on to take part in yet other systems. The more we understand what is going on, the more we realize that there are no separate compartments within the biosphere. There is one web, which vibrates whenever a single strand is plucked.

A MATTER OF ATTITUDE

I have not advocated any particular set of moral rules we ought to follow, or even any very complete set of principles. What I do advocate is an attitude. It would be very good if we did have the right principles and rules, but even if we did have them, we would still need to have a good attitude toward the rest of the world. Without a comprehensive set of adequate rules and principles, having the right attitude is perhaps even more important. What we need is an attitude of respect and consideration for all entities that have interests. That includes ourselves, of course, but it also includes quite a lot else. With that respectful and considerate attitude, we need an awareness that we live in a world abounding with such entities. From the ecosystem down to the lowliest microorganism, from the biosphere, to endangered species, to our next door neighbor, we live in a world of beings that count. They are not just *objects*.

Part of our problem is our accustomed dualism between subject and object. If something is not a subject, it must be an object. And vice versa. If it is suggested that something is not just an object, then the suggestion must be that it is a subject. Our imagination may stretch to include animals as subjects – though even that is too much for some people. When it comes to trees, species, and ecosystems, taking them as subjects seems quite ridiculous. (Indeed, species and ecosystems may seem not even to be objects, but collections of objects.) Many cultures have avoided taking trees, forests, and other natural features as mere objects, and therefore morally neutral, by personifying them as nymphs, gods, or the like. Accordingly, Christianity and the Western tradition at large have long been deeply suspicious of any view that attributed intrinsic value to anything in the natural world. Such views seemed to reek of polytheism and superstition. Even Passmore, no religious dogmatist, dismissed such views as "nature mysticism," taking them to imply that nature is sacred.[5] Now, I do not think of my human neighbors as being sacred, yet I regard them as having intrinsic moral importance and morally significant interests. I also regard their dog and their tree as having intrinsic moral importance and morally significant interests, though they have very different interests and very different importance. I worship the dog and the tree no more than I worship the neighbors, but I regard none of them as being a mere object. From my point of view, a mere object is a being that lacks interests. A being that has interests is one that has enough self-identity and organic unity to have wellbeing needs, but to have interests, a being need not have those features to the point of being a person. That is the critical point here. Being a subject is often taken to imply being a person/human, or at least something that, like an animal, has consciousness. I prefer to take anything that is the subject of an interest to be a subject – or, at least, to be more than a mere object. We need not digress into the semantics of the words *subject* and *object*, however. The thing to be conscious of is that we live in a world abounding in entities, many of them nonhuman, and many of them holistic, that have morally significant interests.

Personifying things that are not persons is an error we ought to avoid. Yet error sometimes contains a touch of truth that we can too easily lose in seeking to avoid the error.

5 In his chapter "Removing the Rubbish" in *Man's Responsibility for Nature*, this figures prominently in that which he considers rubbish that ought to be removed.

Many of the views current among the American Indians had more than a small grain of truth.[6] It was widely held that the natural world was a community of which we were a part, not a world of mere objects. It was a world enfused with vitality and moral value. There were spirits in nature, all having their source in the Great Spirit implicit in nature. As Lame Deer put it (Erdoes 1972, p. 114):

> Nothing is so small and unimportant but it has a spirit given to it by Wakan Tanka . . . also a part of the Great Spirit. The gods are separate beings, but they are all united in Wakan Tanka. It is hard to understand – something like the Holy Trinity. You can't explain it except by going back to the "circles within circles" idea, the spirit splitting itself up into stones, trees, tiny insects even, making them all *wakan* by his ever-presence. And in turn all myriad of things which make up the universe flowing back to their source, united in one Grand-father Spirit.

When killing game, Indians would frequently pray to the spirit of the game animal – or of its species – giving the spirit their reverence and explaining their necessity. The natural world was seen as a continuing community to be lived in, not just a resource to be exploited. To be utilized, yes, but not exploited. In our wisdom we now know that there are no spirits in the rivers, no bear god, but have we come to a view that is really any better? It seems to me to be no more of a mistake to believe in a nature spirit that is not actually there than it is to disbelieve in moral significance that *is* there. The natural world is a community of living entities with moral significance, a community with which, for both practical and moral reasons, we must live in effective balance. That we live in a community of entities, human and nonhuman, that are morally significant, some of which are holistic in char-

6 Many sources might be cited. One I found very useful was J. Baird Callicott's "Traditional American Indian and Western European Attitudes toward Nature: An Overview." Well worth reading is John G. Neihardt's *Black Elk Speaks,* and also Richard Erdoes, *Lame Deer: Seeker of Visions.*

acter, is an insight worth retaining.[7] I would observe also that personifying species, ecosystems, and the like as spirits also avoids the error of understanding such entities as mere collections. As we are now starting to appreciate, quite apart from any moral considerations, truth requires that we understand such entities holistically. One cannot even begin to understand an ecosystem in nonholistic terms.

There are also some valuable lessons to be learned from Taoism. I do not advocate Taoist religious beliefs any more than I advocate that we believe in the existence of Pan or the bear god, nor do I advocate that we adopt Taoist metaphysics. Still, there are ideas and attitudes in Taoism from which we can well profit. Taoists see the world in terms of continuing intricately interconnected processes, continuously changing, with balance giving way to alteration giving way

7   While there are valuable lessons to be learned from the American Indians, I do not want to paint a picture that is too rosy. Certainly I make no claim that they were perfect conservationists with perfect attitudes toward the natural world. That would go well beyond the truth. Even within the same tribe they had a mixture of beliefs, practices, and attitudes. Some of their beliefs, practices, and attitudes were quite beneficial, and a few were quite disruptive to the environment. In many instances their value schemes and factual knowledge were quite unable to cope successfully with increased technology and the demands of the fur trade. Failures to cope sometimes led to environmental devastation. For a further discussion, see Tom Regan's "Environmental Ethics and the Ambiguity of the Native American's Relationship with Nature," in *All That Dwell Therein* (1982). Also, Paul and Anne Ehrlich take a negative view of the ethics of hunting peoples (1981, 113): "To assure a supply of game, one did not treat an animal population properly; one simply treated individual animals and their souls properly. Such a world view worked out fine for hunter and hunted – until some environmental change made the animals more vulnerable or some technological change made the hunter more deadly." Even so, although they may have been ignorant of the consequences of certain interactions within the biosphere, and of the consequences of some of their own actions, and while they may not have been aware of all the environmental entities with interests and moral significance, at least often they were acutely aware that they lived in a world of morally significant entities. Without such awareness, all the factual knowledge in the world would not give us a morally adequate way of dealing with the world. With such an awareness, we can learn to broaden our understanding of the moral world and come to terms with it.

to renewed balance. The world is a constant flux, though by no means a meaningless, valueless chaos. "In Tao the only motion is returning."[8] The processes of the world are not linear but cyclic, constantly returning. Return is never to *exactly* the same thing of course – no two summers are quite the same – but similar patterns continuously recur. As importantly, all of our actions are connected with all other things, and all of our actions return to affect us – just as ecology teaches us. Central to Taoism, as to most of Chinese philosophy, are the ideals of harmony and balance. We cannot overpower the world we live in. Instead of trying to, we must learn to live in harmonious balance with, and within, the eternal cycle of the world. We cannot despoil nature and leave the despoliation behind us, as if history were linear. Our history returns to us as our future. Yet there is a way to deal with the world.

According to Chuang Tzu (*Chuang Tzu*, bk. 19, pt. 2, sect. 12, para. 9):

> Confucius was looking at the cataract near the gorge of Lü, which fell a height of 240 cubits, and the spray of which floated a distance of forty lî, (producing a turbulence) in which no tortoise, gavial, fish, or turtle could play. He saw, however, an old man swimming about in it, as if he had sustained some great calamity, and wished to end his life. Confucius made his disciples hasten along the stream to rescue the man; and by the time they had gone several hundred paces, he was walking along singing, with his hair dishevelled, and enjoying himself at the foot of the embankment. Confucius followed and asked him, saying, "I thought you were a sprite; but, when I look closely at you, I see that you are a man. Let me ask if you have any particular way of treading the water." The man said, "No, I have no particular way. . . . I enter and go

8 *Tao Té Ching*, chap. 40. For discussions of Taoism and environmental ethics, see Russell Goodman, "Taoism and Ecology," and Po-Keung Ip, "Taoism and the Foundations of Environmental Ethics." Also, *Environmental Ethics* 8 (1986), no. 4, and *Philosophy East and West* 37 (1987), no. 2, were both devoted in their entirety to considerations of Asian philosophy and environmental ethics and have several articles concerning Taoism in that connection.

down with the water in the very center of its whirl, and come up again with it when it whirls the other way. I follow the way of the water, and do nothing contrary to it of myself; – this is how I tread it."

The old man did not try to force his way in the stream, nor did he just passively float along like a piece of wood. He maneuvered so as to make use of the natural movement in his environment to get where he wanted to go. This illustrates the Taoist principle of *wu wei* – doing by not doing. That requires much more than mere not doing. What we must not do is depart from the natural rhythms and harmonies and balances of the world. Rather, we act in accordance with the nature of things. Such action does not go against the grain of things and causes it no disruption. While such action does not, in that sense, do anything, it does what there is to be done. "*Tao* never does; yet through it all things are done" (*Tao Té Ching*, 37).

This is good practical advice for dealing with a complex and powerful natural world. It calls upon us to find a viable and continuing balance with our environment. If we followed this advice, it would lead us, for instance, to be more concerned with solar energy and to be less concerned with chemical solutions to agricultural problems. There is a very important moral dimension here as well. Indeed, there is no fact–value distinction in Taoist thinking, the world being understood as being a web of values as much as it is a web of facts – these being one and the same web. The way in which we ought to act toward all the rest of the world is with *wu wei*, the action that is actionless because it does not disrupt. That is the way for us to prosper, and that is the way for us to give other beings their due.

The *Tao* means the *way*. The Taoist, then, is the one who follows the true way. Moreover, since reality is a process, and everything within it is a subprocess, everything has its own way of being, its own *Tao*. With that *Tao*, indeed, an aspect of it, everything has its own *té*. The *té* is the force, power, or virtue of the *Tao*. Things go well for a being when it is able to freely exercise its own particular *té*, and thereby

271

follow its own *Tao*. As I would interpret this, a being's self-identity and wellbeing interests are aspects of its own particular life process, its own particular way of being alive. It follows that a being best serves its interests by living in accordance with its own self-identity. The policy of *wu wei*, then, applies to our own life as well as to our dealings with the external world. We do well by living a life appropriate to us, while others do well by living lives appropriate to them. The Taoists make this point with a story about how we cannot turn a duck into a crane, or vice versa. If, for instance, we try to stretch a duck into a crane, we get only a mutilated duck. It is no good as a crane, and it is no longer even any good as a duck. In living we must be careful not to mutilate ourselves, and we ought not to mutilate those beings that share the world with us.

I do not advocate that we adopt either Taoism or an American Indian world view, but there is much to be gained from those sources. Mostly, what is to be gained is a better attitude toward the world. While we need not personify things in the natural world, we ought never to think of living entities as being merely morally inert objects. Much less ought we to think of the world as a collection of objects. Rather, we ought to think of the world in terms of dynamic and highly integrated living processes that are to be valued in their own right for what they are in their own right. In getting along with the world, and with ourselves, we ought – morally and practically – to move in accordance with the flow of life, rather than try to move contrary to our own nature or that of the surrounding world. These are very general suggestions, obviously, rather than detailed prescriptions, but they lend themselves to a good and useful approach to dealing with particular cases.

RESPECTING THE BIOSPHERE

As Leopold points out, the trend of evolution has been to "elaborate and diversify the biota" (1949, 216). This, rather than any particular trend in the direction of producing *Homo sapiens*, has been the overall direction of evolution. Evolutionary processes seem to have gone pretty far in that direction, having produced an inconceivably intricate complex of interconnected, interacting, and overlapping life processes. Those life processes have – in a sense, *are* – an equally intricate complex of interconnected, interacting, overlapping interests. To be sure, the fabric of the biosphere is more richly woven in some places than in others, but everywhere it is rich enough for the interests to be morally significant. Of course we cannot just conclude, merely on the basis of evolutionary tendency, that encouraging elaborateness and diversity is the moral thing to do, for we have no reason to conclude that the trend of evolution is in a morally good direction. Still, these factors, together with organic unity, contribute to the moral importance of an interest. How, then, are we to act morally toward such a tangle of entities with tangled, overlapping, conflicting interests? Is it possible to do so at all? If we build a house, operate a farm, or just gather nuts and berries in the wild, any way we have of living will have an impact on the biosphere (though in modern economies, much of the impact will often be caused by others on our behalf). Everything we do, even if it is only to wash our hands, injures some interests. Can we look for guidance to Leopold's ethic, calling for us to "preserve the integrity, stability, and beauty of the biotic community" (1949, 224–5)? I certainly think we can find guidance there, at least with respect to holistic entities, though I do believe that his recommendations must be interpreted in terms of interest satisfaction. In interpreting them, we would do well to bear in mind the ideal of acting without acting.

Let us start with beauty, which is perhaps the most problematic part of Leopold's recommendation. Prizing beauty can easily be to take a human-centered point of view, valuing natural things for their instrumental value in producing pleasing aesthetic experiences. As Mark Sagoff points out, valuing nature for its beauty, like valuing a woman for her beauty, tends to trivialize the object, valuing it not for what it is in itself but for how it pleases us (1974, 211). I think we might largely avoid that result by analyzing beauty in terms of harmony, balance, complex unity, and other things being in the interests of the biosphere. Certainly there is beauty in the workings of the biosphere. Yet some natural things that are ecologically important – such as maggots or lice (or the snail darter?) – hardly seem beautiful. Still, if we acted to preserve those features of the biosphere that are (generally agreed to be) beautiful, taking those steps that were causally useful to preserve that beauty, we would be going a considerable way toward protecting the essential functions of the biosphere. Even so, we have to go further than that.

The stability criterion has a great deal to recommend it. Maintaining the overall stability of its life processes is clearly very important for the wellbeing of ecosystems and the biosphere, and too often we have sinned against them by disrupting their vital functions. Yet stability in itself cannot be the ultimate good. Apart from the extreme and obvious counterexample that the extermination of life on earth would lead to a condition of much greater stability, there is the fact that degraded ecosystems are sometimes more stable than they were in their richer but more precariously balanced original condition. But mere stability for the sake of stability is not at all what Leopold was advocating. What is important is maintaining the viability of the life processes within the biosphere, in all of their richness and diversity. That is the stability that is morally important, being a matter of the protection of vital interests. Diversity, a factor commonly mentioned in connection with stability, is very important and must be interpreted in much the same way. No more than stability is diversity an end in its own right. Otherwise, packing ecosystems with alien species would be the thing to do, so long as introductions outnumbered extinctions. But to do that to an ecosystem would be to undermine its coherence and self-identity. Rather, the thing to do is to respect that characteristic integrated diversity so essential to the wellbeing of the biosphere and its ecosystems, species, and so on. This interpretation would certainly be consistent with Leopold's writings.

Integrity, the other factor mentioned by Leopold, is the one of critical importance. We cannot avoid affecting the world around us, but the important thing is to avoid *injuring* it. That is, we ought to avoid violations of the vital interests of the land community, or the erosion of its self-identity. This, I suggest, would be a viable interpretation and elaboration of Leopold's views. What it comes to is that the morally right way to treat the biosphere is to protect the essential life processes of the biosphere in all of their richness and integrated coherent diversity. In so doing, we would thereby be respecting the wellbeing interests of the biosphere and of those holistic entities within the biosphere that have enough self-identity to have wellbeing interests. Ecosystems would be protected from degradation and species from extinction, and so on, but these are not things with which we ought to try to deal one item at a time. Our primary moral concern is not with artificially isolated entities, but with life processes that are often not discrete and often have overlapping interests. When it comes to the biosphere, our primary concern is with the whole flow of its ongoing life processes.

At this point, I think we can start to see the outline of some answers to our questions about whether we can farm, mine, build houses, and so forth without acting wrongly. It would seem to be *reductio ad absurdum* if we could act no other way than wrongly, but I do think it is possible for us to live and yet act rightly toward the things of the biosphere. Indeed, by living in balance with nature – and with ourselves – we would live better lives in our own right. Like the old man in the mountain stream, we must act without acting. Let us suppose that we were considering engaging in some activity that affected the biosphere. Perhaps we contemplate clearing some land for farming – an example that may serve for general purposes. To clear the land would be at least to reduce the native ecosystem in size, and would destroy it if we cleared totally. This, as we all know, has often happened. Even if it were not destroyed totally, an ecosystem may be qualitatively altered if it is reduced below a certain critical size, as certain species and other life processes require large

ranges in order to continue. Moreover, if an ecosystem becomes too restricted, even species that survive may lose a
significant portion of their genetic variability. That erodes
the richness of the self-identity of both species and ecosystem. We must also bear in mind that ecosystems overlap and
are related in intricate ways to other ecosystems. We might
merely reduce one ecosystem in size and thereby, quite un-
knowingly, completely upset a related ecosystem, as when
we fill mangrove swamps and so upset marine food chains.
The mangrove ecosystem seems the same, only smaller, with
the dramatic differences showing up offshore. All that being
acknowledged, though, I think we can still avoid the conclusion that we ought never to affect an ecosystem. To avoid
that totally would not be possible for us, and it would not
be required if it were.

We do not sin against the biosphere if we allow its life
processes to carry on, healthily and unendangered by our
interference. It is possible to farm, chop trees, build houses,
dig mines, and so forth without upsetting the life processes
of the ecosystems affected, though we might well reduce the
extent of the territory in which certain processes are carried
out. The interests of the environmental holistic entities involved are threatened only when there is danger that a life
process might be terminated, or that its self-identity might
be eroded due to qualitative changes springing from a severe
change of scale. We must take care that the impact of our
actions be not too massive or of the wrong sort. So long as
the life processes are not threatened, reduction in scale is not
of itself injurious. Chopping some trees is one thing, then,
but destroying a forest is something else. In our dealings
with the world, we should always stop short of entirely destroying or irreparably degrading any ecosystem, species, or
other such holistic entity. Our farms, cities, factories, mines,
and resorts ought always to coexist with, rather than disrupt
or displace, the morally significant entities of the biosphere.
If we maintain species, if we preserve viable remnants of
ecosystems of all types, and if, as good husbanders, we respect the integrity of even those living systems that we have

modified for our own benefit, we shall have done well. This is moral advice. As a general policy, following this advice also has considerable practical value. Although we can often get away with acting to the contrary, we have too often found to our cost that disrupting the biosphere can rebound against us in unexpected ways. In Tao the only motion is returning.

We can never be absolutely certain that our actions will not have catastrophic consequences, a point that applies with respect to the effects of our actions on other humans as well as on the biosphere; however, we can often be reasonably certain that they will not. The moral to draw is not that we should give up acting, but that we should monitor the effects of our actions closely, and that we should be particularly wary of things that are novel in the type or scale of their effects. There is much to be done. In doing, we should take good care to act in accordance with the flow of nature.

A MATTER OF DEGREE

We must recognize that it is not always possible to respect the interests of all holistic entities such as ecosystems. Trivially, one drop of water in the hollow of a leaf is an ecosystem in its own right, as is the decaying body of a dead mouse. We destroy thriving ecosystems whenever we lop a rotten tree branch or scrub the bathroom floor. We cannot avoid destroying such ecosystems from time to time, and there seems no plausible reason to think it a tragedy that this is so. These are only small components of more encompassing systems. Yet that goes for every living system, as nothing short of the biosphere is absolutely discrete. So, do even these very minor ecosystems count as having some slight degree of moral significance? A possible reason why they do not may be that none of their life processes are unique. The bacterial growth in the dead mouse and the life processes of the molds on the bathroom tiles are not separate processes unique in those mini-ecosystems, but are merely local manifestations of processes found many other places. Unlike material objects, processes do not have to be all in the same place. There is nothing going on in the dead mouse that is not going on many other places, and nothing that would be lost were that tiny ecosystem disrupted. This is in contrast to, let us say, a rain forest, where there is a very great deal to be lost. Even if, quite contrary to actual fact, the species and other life processes found there were all to be found elsewhere, the forest would still have its own separate self-identity in the coherent integrated unity of those life processes in their unique manifestation there. On the other hand, although the species and other life processes involved in the dead mouse have moral significance in their own right, their combination in the dead mouse has no very significant self-identity about which to be concerned.

I find this way of looking at things largely satisfactory, but only largely. Even in the tiny dead-mouse ecosystem, or in a drop of stagnant water, there is still *some* self-identity to have moral significance. Although the web of life covers the whole earth, every portion of the web has at least some self-identity with some degree of coherent integrated unity, giving that portion its own significance. Not only would each rotifer in the drop of water have some very minimal degree of moral significance, the whole drop-of-water ecosystem would have some minuscule moral significance, even though it is very like countless other stagnant drops. Once again we come to what is a matter of degree, with the bottom end of the scale being virtually negligible. At the lower end of the scale, instances of ecosystems degenerate into such relatively trivial cases as drops of water or rotting stumps, species into insignificant variations in genetic detail, and individual organisms into the simplest of microorganisms. Their moral significance is also a matter of degree, ranging to very much from not quite nothing.

The thing for us to do is to find our way in the world, while giving due respect to the widely disparate interests of other beings. This is not essentially different from what we ought to do concerning other humans. Other humans also have widely divergent interests, ranging from the insignificant to the monumental, and it is for us to make appropriate

278

moral responses. In morally dealing with others, human or nonhuman, we must estimate the importance of various interests of various entities (including ourselves). In so doing it would to appropriate to consider how highly developed an entity and its interests are, how vital an interest is to it, and what the alternatives are. Whether we are dealing with individual or holistic entities, it remains a matter of assessing interests and interest packages, which remains a matter of trying to estimate such things as level of complex unity and the role within it of a given interest. From there we must go on to work out the moral priorities.

There is no unambiguously right way to assign moral priorities, nor, with the best will in the world, is there any way at all in which we can avoid affecting and sometimes injuring the interests of other beings, individual or holistic. Yet we cannot take the lack of certitude and the inevitability of injury as an excuse for shedding a guilt-relieving tear and proceeding to do whatever suits our own inclinations. We can no more use that excuse with reference to nonhuman entities than we can with reference to humans. Everything we do, even if it is only eating and taking up space affects other humans, but that does not make it a matter of moral indifference how we treat others. Neither is it a matter of indifference how we treat the biosphere and the nonhuman entities within it.

VALUING THE NONLIVING ENVIRONMENT

There remains a very important problem to be considered, a problem, concerning the nonliving environment, that I have hitherto not discussed. Ecosystems and other life systems are not the only features of the natural world that seem to deserve our care and protection, or at least our noninterference. The Grand Canyon, Ayer's Rock, Victoria Falls, and various other natural features seem, at least to my intuitions, to be worthy of protection. But why? I cannot claim that we owe it directly to Ayer's Rock to respect its interests, since rocks of any size do not have interests. The General Sherman tree has interests to be respected, and so do our endangered rain forests, but Ayer's Rock can suffer no injury to its wellbeing, and neither can the Grand Canyon. To be sure, there are ecosystems at both of those places, and they and their organisms count morally, but there seems to be some *additional* factor that makes damaging such places grossly improper. If we could convert Ayer's Rock to road gravel, doing so without injuring the biotic community, then I would not have grounds for condemning such a project on the basis of respect for interests unless it could be condemned on the grounds of human interests. That we would be able to condemn such a project on the basis of human interests seems to me only partially satisfactory. Even were such projects in the overall interests of human beings, and made no difference to the biosphere, many of us would still sense that there was an element of vandalism in them, something that was wrong for reasons other than those of human self-interest. Is this a mere prejudice? I cannot offer a definitive answer to that problem, but I shall forward a suggestion I believe helps. Let us continue with Ayer's Rock as our example.

Ayer's Rock is a quite striking monolith that rises abruptly from the plains of central Australia. Its sandstone glows fiery red at sunrise and sunset, an impressive sight that draws tourists from distant places. The rock is remarkable not only for its beauty (at all hours) but for its scale, and for being in sharp contrast with its surroundings. The climb to the top is an enjoyable scramble, when the bush flies are not being too annoying, and the summit offers views over the plains and to the distant rounded knobs of the Olgas. Since the first Europeans came, Ayer's Rock has been a valued landmark and object of interest.

Actually, of course, Ayer's Rock has held an honored place in human thinking since long before European settlement. Since the Dreamtime, Uluru, as it is known to the Australian Aborigines, was revered. Certainly, Uluru was a good place to camp. Water was almost always available, and there was game in the somewhat less arid ecosystem around the Rock. Such places were of considerable utilitarian significance in the thinking of the first Australians. Yet there was more to it than that. The rock itself, the moods of light, the grottoes and fantastic shapes around its base, the very feel of it all conveyed the idea that this was a spiritual place. Modern non-Aboriginal tourists respond to these things as well, though they may not think in spiritual terms. For the Aborigines, it was a natural sacred site. They held ceremonies there, and added their art works to the base of the rock. To this day, Uluru is one of their spiritual treasures.

There are obviously excellent grounds for preserving Ayer's Rock for present and future generations of humans, both Aboriginal and non-Aboriginal. But what if no one cared? Better, let us suppose that only a tiny handful of people cared. What sound arguments could they use to persuade others that they ought to care? (This may seem farfetched in the case of Ayer's Rock, but certainly there are cases in which public opinion is much less firmly on the side of preservation.) We might even imagine a future generation so tied to an artificial environment that the overwhelming majority feels no interest in such places as Ayer's Rock. Possibly they consider the computer-designed abstract color patterns produced on their wall-sized high-resolution three-dimensional television screens to be infinitely preferable to any sunset, and perhaps they feel threatened by distant horizons. Maybe there is no longer reverence for the relics of human cultural history. And so forth. If a few still care, they are entitled to some consideration for their peculiar interests, but let us assume that the interests of the great majority are to the contrary. Why should they not proceed, if it best suited the overall interests of that generation, to grind the rock up for gravel?

One reaction we might have is that they should go ahead and grind it. Such people do not deserve Ayer's Rock. But why *should* they care? It might be argued that we should preserve it for future generations, but that is a doubtful argument since future generations might be trained to value other things. Again, we might try to persuade them by showing them Ayer's Rock and pointing out how beautiful it is —

but perhaps they do not respond. Could we then argue that there is a beauty, even a sublimity, manifested in Ayer's Rock that one ought to value, even if one does not value it, because it is objectively and intrinsically valuable in its own right? Such a claim cannot be conclusively refuted, but there is no substantial evidence in favor of it, either, and it is little apt to convince those who are not already so inclined. By a similar token, we could not prove to anyone that they ought to revere the relics of human cultural history present at Ayer's Rock. (We might imagine that any useful scientific information about the paintings would be perfectly preserved in color holograms and by other means – though few would be interested.) And so it would go for any other values that we might think this benighted generation ought to recognize.

It is time to start again. Instead of pointing to various things about Ayer's Rock as reasons why we should value it, perhaps we should consider possible reasons why *we* should value it. Perhaps there are some things that it is better for *us* that we value for their own sakes. Mark Sagoff offers us a suggestion:[9]

> These values we cherish as citizens express not just what we want collectively but what we think we are: We use them to reveal to ourselves and to others what we stand for and how we perceive ourselves as a nation. These values are not merely chosen; rather they constitute and identify we who chose. . . . Wilderness, rivers, estuaries, bays, forests, and farms have voices: They express our shared values and transmit them. They speak for us.

What we value, then, expresses what we are. Moreover, he suggests that we should not try to determine our collective values by cost–benefit analysis, because "we have values or commitments as citizens that often contradict the preferences

9 "Ethics and Economics in Environmental Law" (1984, 175). See also his "On Preserving the Natural Environment." For another useful effort to bridge the gap, see "Are Values in Nature Subjective or Objective?" by Holmes Rolston III. This essay, together with much other valuable material is reprinted in his *Philosophy Gone Wild*. Also of value is his *Environmental Ethics*.

or interests we would pursue as individuals'' (1984, 175). The values of a nation are not an aggregate of individual values. Furthermore, it is not necessarily the interests of natural entities that we ought to pursue in our environmental policy. For all we know, it might be in the interests of trees to be farmed in rows, rather than to take their chances in a wilderness. Rather, he recommends that we value wilderness as an affirmation of what we ourselves are. Sagoff does not consider the interests of ecosystems, which is an important omission. The interests of nonhuman individuals in general seem to be of no great importance to him. Even so, I believe that Sagoff's view has a grain of truth in it.

If we were to cease to value Ayer's Rock, we – particularly the Aborigines among us – would be losing contact with some of our human background. Of course it goes well beyond that. According to the idea under consideration, the Aborigines *did right* to value Uluru. Had they not, they would have been missing something important. Not only did it express some of their cultural ideals, but it helped to create and give coherent form to them. Although our responses may take different forms these days, we, most of us, still respond. There is something about such places to which we should respond.

It is well worth noting that there may be more reasons than one why we should value a magnificent living entity such as a rain forest: because we owe it to that entity, and because we owe it to ourselves. It is at least conceivable that we owe it to ourselves to be alive to the moral significance of other entities that have interests. It may be, then, that such an entity as a rain forest is entitled to moral respect, that we benefit in ourselves from respecting its moral significance, and that we benefit in ourselves from valuing it, even apart from its moral significance, for its manifesting certain qualities (such as beauty). These reasons are compatible, and may partially overlap, but they are distinct reasons. In general, I do find considerable intuitive plausibility in the notion that we cheapen and diminish ourselves if we do not respond to certain values. Moreover, given, as a starting point, that we do have certain values as a people or as individuals, valuing certain things for their own sakes does seem, as Sagoff suggests, a natural consequence and an appropriate symbol. Personal observation leads me to believe that this was a significant factor in the success of the campaign to stop the Gordon-below-Franklin dam project in Tasmania.

The dam would have drowned a large part of a unique ecosystem, it was unnecessary and grossly inefficient economically, and it would have flooded the beautiful canyon of the Franklin, Australia's last sizable wild river. Uniqueness, beauty, and waste were important issues. However, what I think really turned the tide for us was the plea to, as one of our songs put it, "let the Gordon and Franklin wild rivers run free." People can identify with a river. From frisky youth to sedate old age, a river can be said to be born, to move through its life in progressive stages, to encounter things along the way, and eventually to end its life in the great beyond. Likening the river to human life, we equally liken our life to the river. This is the stuff of metaphor, of course, but metaphor that we can all understand and find quite meaningful. Otherwise, this metaphor would not have been invoked so very frequently throughout history. Most of us fear to lose our freedom, and these days we are particularly wary of losing it to the blind machinations of bureaucracy. Similarly, many people feel that their lives are at least in danger of being cluttered up and distorted by the falsity and contrivance of modern civilization. As we would desire to live a free and natural life in accordance with our own nature, so might we desire to allow the river to follow its own career without interference, particularly a career so beautiful and exciting. I believe that this line of reasoning, whether or not articulated, was highly instrumental in saving "the last wild river."

On these grounds alone we did well to save the Franklin. It seems quite correct to me that valuing certain things for themselves is a natural and appropriate expression of having certain values. But is there any reason *why* we should have some particular values and not others? Sagoff does not tell us, though the suggestion seems strongly to be that this is no arbitrary matter. The idea comes naturally to mind that it might work out better *for us* to have certain values. According to Rodman (1977, 113), we have a *need* for wilderness, this being

> the need to experience a realm of reality beyond the manipulations of commodity production and technology, the need for a norm given "in the nature of things," the need for realities that function as symbols of otherness that can arouse a response from the suppressed potentialities of human nature.

Because of the inherent nature and potentialities of the human being, then, we need experiences and norms of certain sorts. Wilderness, accordingly, is a type of resource for us, one that serves not our material but our psychological needs. That seems to me to be quite clearly true, but it also seems to me that there is something more to it than that.

I want to go just a bit further than this. While we need to have experiences of certain sorts, and to find norms "out there," these things being wellbeing needs of ours, it may also be that we have wellbeing needs to have values of certain sorts "in here." The "paradox of hedonism," as it has been called, is that we get more pleasure by valuing some other things directly, rather than by concentrating solely on achieving maximal levels of pleasure. You get more fun out of music, for instance, if you get interested in the music itself and are not just concerned for the pleasure it might give you. We might extend the point, saying that our wellbeing interests are best served if we value things of *certain* sorts for their own sake, and not because of what they can do for us. This is not a need to value just anything for its own sake, nor is it a need to find just any norm "out there." There are any number of sorts of things we could value for their own sakes, and some people have found the most dreadful norms (war, cruelty, callous exploitation) in nature. I cannot offer any even semidefinitive account of just what specific values it is truly in our interests to have, or of why it is of benefit to us to have them.

One might assert, I believe truly, that we cheapen and lessen ourselves if we are indifferent to the welfare of those around us, or if we are not responsive to natural beauty or, once it is pointed out to us, the living integrity of an ecosystem, and so on. However, it is no more than *ad hominem*, and begging the question, to use that sort of assertion as the basis of an argument that we should have such values. Moreover, it is notoriously the case that people can be quite sensitive to some moral or aesthetic or "environmental" values, while being amazingly insensitive to others. (We have all heard about Nazi concentration camp officials who were devoted to classical music in their spare time.) Even so, observation suggests to me that people who are responsive to moral, aesthetic, and "environmental" values are more apt than others to have good (healthy, well-integrated) lives, and that the acquiring of such values tends to enrich people's lives. The Nazi officer, I think, would have had a life that was better *for him* had he learned to be more compassionate and, presumably, less rigid. It seems to me that having values of certain sorts helps us to coordinate and integrate our own priorities effectively, and to live a well-balanced and effective life. I believe, then, that there is a *prima facie* case that someone who can find something to value for its own sake in Ayer's Rock or in the Grand Canyon, or in a thriving natural ecosystem, is better off in terms of his or her own life than is someone who cannot. This is not to say that we should all like exactly the same things. There are many different ways in which we can order our priorities. Still, some choices are better for us than are others. (There is no special reason why someone should like my favorite brand of breakfast cereal, but if someone does not find something to value in Mozart or the Grand Canyon, there is something missing in that person.) I believe that if we, individually and as societies, learned to develop values genuinely conducive to our overall wellbeing, we would then treat the environment, and one another, and ourselves quite a lot better. I offer this only as a suggestion, and not as a well-argued and properly articulated conclusion. I am persuaded of what I have here sketched out, though I also believe that the questions involved are considerably more complex. My central conclusions are those that concern respect for the interests of those features of the world that, unlike Ayer's Rock, do have interests.

A MORALLY DEEP WORLD

The overall conclusion I have come to is that we live in a morally deep world. We are morally significant ourselves, and we live in a world of beings, on many different levels, that are morally significant. We do not all have the same moral significance, but if the rest of the world had absolutely no moral significance at all, then neither would we. It is not just our being rational or sentient, much less our being human, that gives us moral significance. Our interests are morally significant just because they are interests. Our wellbeing can suffer or flourish. We humans being what we are, rationality and sentience have a lot to do with our interests, yet we are beings with depth as well as rational and sentient surface. It is in those depths that our wellbeing interests have their roots. Even among humans, neither rationality nor sentience is a necessary condition for the moral significance of an interest. For us to recognize the moral standing of only those beings who are like us in being human, rational, or sentient would be arbitrary and morally unjustified.

The depth of moral significance extends at least to the depths of the living world. While individual organisms, be they humans or protozoans, have their own particular degree of moral importance, often a very high degree, it is not individual organisms alone that have moral standing. There is moral value on many different and diverse levels, levels that can be separated only artificially. Species, rain forests, ecosystems, the biosphere – all of these entities have morally significant interests to one degree or another. We live in a world of life, and all life processes, of whatever sort, define interests that count morally. It is respect for interests that is, at least, the core if not the whole of morality.

I can offer no magic formula for determining, in each instance, the morally best way to act toward those others of various sorts with whom or which we share the world. No one has ever developed an adequate and comprehensive formula for applying the principle of respect for interests to even the more restricted sphere of human affairs. In the living world at large, the tangle of conflicting and complementary interests is all the more dense. Whether we are dealing with our fellow humans, though, or whether we are not, the absence of an effective moral algorithm does not excuse us from our responsibility to give due consideration and respect, so far as we can do so, to the varied, and variably significant, interests of very different entities. The best we can do, which will carry us quite a long way, is to develop an awareness of other beings, and of their interests, together with an attitude of respect and consideration for their interests.

Individually, we live a life that is best, that is healthiest for us, when we live a life as an integrated organic whole, a life that is coherent yet richly diverse, continuing in effective balance with itself and with its environment. That is true for us, and it is true for other beings, whether they are individual organisms, or whether they are entities of other sorts. To live effectively, we must fulfill our own wellbeing needs, living in harmony and balance with ourselves, and with the world around us. Morally we ought, as best we can, to allow the living world, and the entities thereof, in their diversity, to thrive in richness, harmony, and balance. In all things we must ask whether our actions are conducive to, or at least compatible with, the fullness and wellbeing of life. Thereby we may better live deep and worthwhile lives in a deep and valuable world.

Bibliography

Adams, Douglas. *Life, The Universe and Everything.* New York: Pocket Books, 1982.

Aquinas, Thomas. *Summa Contra Gentiles.* Translated by the English Dominican Fathers. New York: Benziger Brothers, 1928.

Aristotle. *The Basic Works of Aristotle.* Edited by Richard McKeon. New York: Random House, 1941. All references will be according to standard pagination.

Attfield, Robin. *The Ethics of Environmental Concern.* Oxford: Blackwell, 1983.

Bacon, Francis. *De Interpretatione Naturae.*

Bentham, Jeremy. *An Introduction to the Principles of Morals and Legislation* in *The Works of Jeremy Bentham,* vol. 1. Edited by John Bowring. New York: Russell & Russell, Inc., 1962.

Bernier R. "The Species as an Individual: Facing Essentialism." *Systematic Zoology* 33 (1984): 460–9.

Borschmann, Gregg. *Greater Daintree: World Heritage Tropical Rainforest at Risk.* Hawthorn, Victoria, Australia: Australian Conservation Foundation, 1984.

Callicott, J. Baird. "Elements of an Environmental Ethic: Moral Considerability and the Biotic Community." *Environmental Ethics* 1 (1979): 71–81.

"Animal Liberation: A Triangular Affair." *Environmental Ethics* 2 (1980): 311–38.

"Hume's *Is/Ought* Dichotomy and the Relation of Ecology to Leopold's Land Ethic." *Environmental Ethics* 4 (1982): 163–74.

"Traditional American Indian and Western European Attitudes toward Nature: An Overview." *Environmental Ethics* 4 (1982): 293–318.

Callicott, J. Baird. ed. *Companion to a Sand County Almanac: Interpretive & Critical Essays.* Madison: University of Wisconsin Press, 1987.

Carson, Rachel. *Silent Spring.* Boston: Houghton Mifflin, 1962. Reprint, Harmondsworth: Penguin, 1965.

Cicero. *De Natura Deorum,* in *De Natura Deorum; Academica.* Translated by

H. Rackham. Cambridge, Mass.: Harvard University Press, 1957 and London: William Heineman, Ltd., 1957.

Commoner, Barry. *The Closing Circle.* London: Jonathan Cape, 1972.

Cranston, Maurice. "Bacon, Francis" in *The Encyclopedia of Philosophy.* Edited by Paul Edwards. London and New York: Macmillan, 1967, vol. I, 235–40.

Descartes, René. *Discourse on Method.* In *Philosophical Works of Descartes.* vol. 1. Rendered into English by E. S. Haldane and G. R. T. Ross. Cambridge: Cambridge University Press, 1911, 1931. Reprint, New York: Dover, 1955.

Principles of Philosophy. In *Philosophical Works of Descartes.* vol. 1. Rendered into English by E. S. Haldane and G. R. T. Ross. Cambridge: Cambridge University Press, 1911, 1931. Reprint, New York: Dover, 1955.

Ehrlich, Paul, and Anne Ehrlich. *Extinction.* New York: Random House, 1981.

Eldridge, N., and Stephen Jay Gould. "Punctuated Equilibria: An Alternative to Phyletic Gradualism." In *Models in Paleobiology,* edited by T. Schopf. San Francisco: Feeman, Cooper & Co., 1972: 82–115.

Unfinished Synthesis: Biological Hierarchies and Modern Evolutionary Thought. Oxford: Oxford University Press, 1985.

Erdoes, Richard. *Lame Deer: Seeker of Visions.* New York: Simon and Schuster, 1972.

Fichte, J. G. *Johann Gottlieb Fichte's Popular Works.* Compiled by W. Smith. London: Trübner & Co. 1873.

Flader, Susan L. *Thinking Like a Mountain: Aldo Leopold and the Evolution of an Ecological Attitude toward Deer, Wolves and Forests.* Columbia: University of Missouri Press, 1974.

Flew, Antony. *Evolutionary Ethics.* London: Macmillan, 1967.

Flowers, R. Wills. "Ethics and the Hypermodern Species." *Environmental Ethics* 8 (1986):185–8.

Frey, R. G. *Interests and Rights: The Case against Animals.* Oxford: Clarendon, 1980.

Rights, Killing, and Suffering. Oxford: Blackwell, 1983.

Gardiner, R. Allen, and Beatrice Gardiner. "Teaching Sign-Language to a Chimpanzee." *Science* 165 (1969): 664–72.

"Two-Way Communication with an Infant Chimpanzee." In *Behavior of Nonhuman Primates.* vol. 4. Edited by A. Schier, et al. New York: Academic Press, 1971.

Ghiselin, M. T. "A Radical Solution to the Species Problem." *Systematic Zoology* 23 (1974): 536–44.

"Can Aristotle Be Reconciled with Darwin?" *Systematic Zoology* 34 (1985): 457–9.

Goodman, Russell. "Taoism and Ecology." *Environmental Ethics* 2 (1982): 73–80.

Bibliography

Goodpaster, Kenneth E. "On Being Morally Considerable." *Journal of Philosophy* 75 (1978): 308–25.

"From Egoism to Environmentalism." In *Ethics and Problems of the 21st Century*. South Bend, Ind.: Notre Dame, 21–35.

Gould, Stephen Jay. "The Origin and Function of 'Bizarre' Structures." *Evolution* 4 (1974): 191–220.

Green, Roger. *Battle for the Franklin*. Melbourne: Fontana, 1983.

Hale, Mason E., Jr. *The Biology of Lichens*. London: Edward Arnold, 1974.

Hardin, Garrett. "The Tragedy of the Commons." *Science* 162 (1968): 1243–8.

Heffernan, James D. "The Land Ethic: A Critical Appraisal." *Environmental Ethics* 4 (1982): 235–47.

Hoff, Christina. "Human Lives and Animal Lives." Unpublished manuscript.

Hofstadter, R. *Social Darwinism in American Thought (1860–1915)*. Philadelphia: University of Pennsylvania Press, 1944.

Hölldobler, Bert. "Ways of the Ant", *National Geographic*, vol. 165, no. 6, (June, 1984): 778–813.

Hull, David L. "Are Species Really Individuals?" *Systematic Zoology* 25 (1976): 174–91.

"A Matter of Individuality." *Philosophy of Science* 45 (1978): 335–60.

"Kitts & Kitts & Caplan on Species." *Philosophy of Science* 48 (1981): 141–52.

Hume, David. *A Treatise of Human Nature*. New York: Doubleday, 1961.

Huxley, T. H. *Life and Letters*. Edited by Leonard Huxley. London: Macmillan, 1900.

Ip, Po-Keung. "Taoism and the Foundations of Environmental Ethics." *Environmental Ethics* 5 (1983): 335–43.

Johnson, Lawrence E. "Can Animals be Moral Agents." *Ethics and Animals* 4 (1983): 50–61.

"Do Animals Have an Interest in Life?" *Australasian Journal of Philosophy* 62 (1983): 172–84.

"Humanity, Holism, and Environmental Ethics." *Environmental Ethics* 5 (1983): 345–54.

Kant, Immanuel. "Idea for a Universal History with Cosmopolitan Purpose." Translated by H. B. Nisbet. In *Kant's Political Writings*, edited by H. Reiss. Cambridge: Cambridge University Press, 1970.

Fundamental Principles of the Metaphysic of Morals. Translated and edited by Lewis White Beck. New York: Bobbs-Merrill Company, Inc., 1959.

Kitts, D. B. "The Names of Species: A Reply to Hull." *Systematic Zoology* 33 (1984): 112–115.

Kohl, Larry. "Saving Pére David's Deer." *National Geographic*, vol. 162, no. 4 (October, 1982): 478–85.

Lecky, W. E. H. *History of European Morals: From Augustus to Charlemagne*, vol. 2. New York: Braziller, 1955.

Bibliography

Leopold, Aldo. *A Sand County Almanac.* New York: Oxford University Press, 1949.

Linden, Eugene. *Apes, Men and Language.* Harmondsworth: Penguin, 1974.

Lockwood, Michael. "Singer on Killing and the Preference for Life." *Inquiry* 22 (1979): 168–169. Includes quotations from Christina Hoff, "Human Lives and Animal Lives." Unpublished manuscript.

Lorenz, Konrad. *On Aggression.* London: Methuen, 1967. Translation of *Das Sogenannte Bose.* Vienna: Dr. G. Borotha-Schoeler Verlag, 1963.

Lovelock, J. E. *Gaia: A New Look at Life on Earth.* Oxford: Oxford University Press, 1979.

Margulis, Lynn. "Symbiosis and Evolution." *Scientific American*, vol. 225, no. 2 (August 1971): 48–57.

Midgley, Mary. "The Concept of Beastliness." In Regan and Singer, 1976.
Beast and Man. Brighton: Harvester 1979.
Evolution as a Religion. London: Methuen, 1985.

Naess, Arne. "The Shallow and The Deep, Long-Range Ecology Movement. A Summary." *Inquiry* 16 (1973): 95–100.
"A Defence of the Deep Ecology Movement." *Environmental Ethics* 6 (1984): 265–270.

Neihardt, John G. *Black Elk Speaks.* Lincoln: University of Nebraska Press, 1932.

Nietzsche, Friedrich. *Thus Spake Zarathustra.* vol. II of *The Complete Works of Friedrich Nietzsche,* edited by Oscar Levy. New York: Russell and Russell, 1964.

Norton, Bryon G. "Environmental Ethics and the Rights of Future Generations." *Environmental Ethics* 4 (1982): 319–37.

Norton, Byron G., ed. *The Preservation of Species.* Princeton: Princeton University Press, 1986.

Nozick, Robert. *Anarchy, State and Utopia.* New York: Basic Books, 1974.

Parfit, Derek. "Rights, Interests, and Possible People." In *Moral Problems in Medicine,* edited by Samuel Gorovitz et al. Englewood Cliffs, NJ: Prentice-Hall, 1976: 369–75.
"Future Generations: Further Problems." *Philosophy and Public Affairs* 11 (1982): 113–72.
Reasons and Persons. Oxford: Oxford University Press, 1984.

Passmore, John. *Man's Responsibility for Nature.* London: Duckworth, 1974. 2nd ed., with additional preface in response to criticism, 1980.
Passmore, John. "Attitudes to Nature." In *Nature and Conduct,* edited by R. S. Peters, Royal Institute of Philosophy Lectures, vol. 8. London: Macmillan, 1975.

Plato. *The Dialogues of Plato.* Translated and edited by B. Jowett. London: Macmillan, 1892. All references will be according to standard pagination.

Plutarch. *On the Eating of Flesh,* in *Plutarch's Moralia XII.* Translated by Harold Cherniss and William C. Helmbold. Cambridge, Massachusetts: Harvard University Press, 1961 and London: William Heineman, Ltd., 1961.

Porter, William Sydney (O. Henry). "The Theory and the Hound." In *Whirligigs*. New York: Doubleday, 1910.

Rachels, James. "Do Animals Have a Right to Liberty?" In Regan and Singer, 1976.

Rawls, John. *A Theory of Justice*. Oxford: Oxford University Press, 1972.

Regan, Tom. "McCloskey on Why Animals Cannot Have Rights." *Philosophical Quarterly* 26 (1976): 251–7.

All That Dwell Therein: Essays on Animal Rights and Environmental Ethics. Berkeley: University of California Press, 1982.

The Case for Animal Rights. Berkeley: University of California Press, 1983.

Regan, Tom, ed. *Earthbound: New Introductory Essays in Environmental Ethics*. New York: Random House, 1984.

Regan, Tom, and Peter Singer, eds. *Animal Rights and Human Obligation*. Englewood Cliffs, N.J.: Prentice-Hall, 1976.

Reynolds, Peter. *On the Evolution of Human Behavior*. Berkeley: University of California Press, 1981.

Rodman, John. "The Liberation of Nature." *Inquiry* 20 (1977): 83–131.

Rolston, Holmes, III. "Are Values in Nature Subjective or Objective?" *Environmental Ethics* 4 (1982): 125–51.

Philosophy Gone Wild. Buffalo: Prometheus, 1986.

Environmental Ethics. Philadelphia: Temple University Press, 1987.

Routley, Richard. "Is There a Need for a New, an Environmental Ethic?" *Proceedings, 15th World Congress of Philosophy* 1 (1973): 205–10. See also entry under Richard Sylvan.

Routley, Val. Review of *Man's Responsibility for Nature* by John Passmore. *Australasian Journal of Philosophy* 53 (1975): 171–85.

Russo, John P. *The Kaibab North Deer Herd – Its History, Problems, and Management*. State of Arizona Game and Fish Department, Wildlife Bulletin No. 7. Phoenix, Arizona (July, 1964).

Sagan, Dorion, and Lynn Margulis. "The Gaian Perspective of Ecology." *The Ecologist* 13 (1983): 161–4.

Sagoff, Mark. "On Preserving the Natural Environment." *The Yale Law Journal* 84 (1974): 205–67.

"Ethics and Economics in Environmental Law." In Regan, 1984: 147–78.

Sayre, Kenneth M. *Cybernetics and the Philosophy of Mind*. New York: Humanities Press, 1976.

Scanlon, T. M. "Preference and Urgency." *The Journal of Philosophy* 72 (1975): 655–69.

Schweitzer, Albert. *Civilization and Ethics*, part II of *The Philosophy of Civilization*. Translated by John Naish. London: A. and C. Black, 1923.

"The Ethics of Reverence for Life." *Christendom* (1936).

The Teaching of Reverence for Life. Translated by Richard Winston and Clara Winston. New York, 1965.

Bibliography

Reverence for Life. Translated by Reginald H. Fuller. New York: Harper and Row, 1969.

Singer, Peter. *Animal Liberation*. London: Jonathan Cape, 1976, and London: Granada, 1977. References are to the Granada edition.

"Killing Humans and Killing Animals." *Inquiry* 22 (1979): 145–56.

Practical Ethics. Cambridge: Cambridge University Press, 1979. Cited as 1979a in notes.

Spencer, Herbert. *Social Statics*. London: John Chapman, 1851.

Spinoza, Benedictus de. *Ethics*. Translated by A. Boyle. London: J. M. Dent & Sons, Ltd., 1910.

Stevenson-Hamilton, J. *Wildlife in South Africa*. London: Cassell, 1954.

Stone, Christopher D., "Should Trees Have Standing? Toward Legal Rights for Natural Objects." 45 *Southern California Law Review* (1972): 450–501. Republished as a book under that title, with foreword by Garrett Hardin and the Supreme Court opinions in the case of *Sierra Club v. Morton*. Los Altos, Calif.: William Kaufmann, 1974.

"*Should Trees Have Standing?* Revisited: How Far Will Law and Morals Reach? A Pluralist Perspective." 59 *Southern California Law Review* (1985):1–154.

"Legal Rights and Moral Pluralism." *Environmental Ethics* 5 (1987): 281–4.

Earth and Other Ethics: The Case for Moral Pluralism. New York: Harper and Row, 1987.

Sylvan, Richard. "A Critique of Deep Ecology." *Discussion Papers in Environmental Philosophy* 12. Canberra: Australian National University, 1985. See also entry under Richard Routley.

Taylor, Paul W. *Respect for Nature*. Princeton: Princeton University Press, 1986.

Waley, Arthur. *The Way and Its Power*. New York: Grove Press, 1958.

Walker, Stephen. *Animal Thought*. London: Routledge and Kegan Paul, 1983.

Watson, Richard A. "A Critique of Anti-Anthropocentric Biocentrism." *Environmental Ethics* 5 (1983): 245–56.

Wechkin, Stanley, Jules H. Masserman, and William Terris, Jr. "Shock to Conspecific as an Aversive Stimula." *Psychonomic Science* 1 (1964): 47–48.

Wilson, E. O. *Sociobiology: The New Synthesis*. Cambridge, Mass.: Belknap Press and Harvard University Press, 1975.

ANONYMOUS AND TRADITIONAL

Chuang Tzu. In, among many places, *The Texts of Taoism*. Translated by James Legge. Oxford: Oxford University Press, 1891.

Holy Bible. All references are to the King James version.

Katha Upanishad

Bibliography

Physiologus. Translated by James Carlill in *The Epic of the Beast*. London: Geo. Routledge & Sons., 1924.

Tao Té Ching. Translated, with introduction, by Arthur Waley in his *The Way and Its Power*. References are by chapter.

295

Index

ethics (*cont.*)
ethics; interests; Kant
difficulties with reconciling holistic and atomistic theories of, 231–41
is there a need for a new environmental ethic? 231
political ideologies, poverty of, 245–7
principle of respect for interests, 117–18, 185
right attitude of critical importance, 266–87
eudaimonia, 143
evolution, 36–40, 272–3
extinction
may be acceptable in some cases, 262–3
moral reasons against causing or allowing, 163–75, 215–16

Fichte, J. G., 35–36, 41
fire, role in certain ecosystems, 217–20
Franklin River, 284
Francis of Assisi, 21
Frey, R. G., 75–96, 119, 197

Galileo, 1, 51n
Ghislin, M. T., 153n
Goodpaster, Kenneth E., 141n, 144n

Hardin, Garrett, 150
hedonism. *See* pleasure
Hegel, G. W. F.
hegelianism, 34, 246
Henry, O. *See* Porter, William Sydney
holism, 148–83
interests of certain holistic entities morally significant, 158–83

interests of holistic entities as opposed to interests of component individuals, 162–3, 214–221
on reconciling holistic and atomistic ethics, 230–45
Hoff, Christina, 121
Hull, David, 153–4
Hume, David, 62
Huxley, T. H., 39
hydrozoans. *See* Siphonophora

Idiospermum australiense, 264
interests
of all species as morally significant, 162
determined by the nature of the living being whose interests they are, 119–33
of human species as morally significant, 158–62
of living beings as opposed to machines, 77–80, 145–6
nature of, 75–96, 97–147
not to be identified in terms of mental states, 98–102
not to be identified in terms of preferences/prudent desires, 102–15
of species as opposed to aggregated interests of species-members, 162–3, 209–11
to be identified in terms of wellbeing, 116–18
to be respected, 117–18, 185
of various other holistic entities as morally significant, 162–83
of wholes as opposed to those of component individuals, 209–11, 214–21
Irish deer, 210

juniper, 217–20, 221